Microsoft System Center 2012 Service Manager Cookbook

Learn how to configure and administer System Center 2012 Service Manager and solve specific problems and scenarios that arise

Samuel Erskine (MCT)

Anders Asp (MVP)

Andreas Baumgarten (MVP)

Steve Beaumont

Dieter Gasser

[PACKT] enterprise
PUBLISHING
professional expertise distilled

BIRMINGHAM - MUMBAI

Microsoft System Center 2012 Service Manager Cookbook

First published: October 2012

Production Reference: 1191012

Published by Packt Publishing Ltd.
Livery Place
35 Livery Street
Birmingham B3 2PB, UK.

ISBN 978-1-84968-694-5

www.packtpub.com

Cover Image by Jungfraubahnen Management AG (http://www.jungfrau.ch/)

Credits

Authors

Samuel Erskine (MCT)

Anders Asp (MVP)

Andreas Baumgarten (MVP)

Steve Beaumont

Dieter Gasser

Reviewers

Stefan Allansson

Steve Buchanan

Wayne Robinson

Acquisition Editor

Andrew Duckworth

Lead Technical Editor

Dayan Hyames

Technical Editors

Joyslita D'Souza

Pooja Pande

Project Coordinator

Abhishek Kori

Proofreaders

Elinor Perry-Smith

Lesley Harrison

Indexer

Tejal R. Soni

Graphics

Valentina D'silva

Aditi Gajjar

Production Coordinators

Prachali Bhiwandkar

Manu Joseph

Cover Work

Prachali Bhiwandkar

About the Authors

Samuel Erskine (MCT) has over 15 years' experience in a wide range of technologies and industries (public and private) including working for fortune 500 organizations. In 2009 he founded a consultancy practice organization in the United Kingdom focused on implementing Microsoft System Center systems management and IT Service management products. He merged the United Kingdom organization with Syliance IT Services in 2012 and became the third member of the Syliance global management team. He is a Computer Engineering graduate and holds various technology vendor/industry certifications. He is an active participant in the System Center community with a blog at `www.frameworktorealwork.com`.

> Thanks to Jungfraubahnen Management AG (`http://www.jungfrau.ch/`) for the Photo of "Top of Europe".

Anders Asp (MVP) started his IT career working with storage and backup solutions, but discovered Service Manager back in 2009 and has been working full time with the product ever since. He is currently working at a Swedish company named Lumagate as a Service Manager Specialist and Product Manager. He also teaches the official Service Manager course at the two largest training centers in Sweden and has presented at several large events.

He is very active on the official Service Manager forums at TechNet and regularly blogs about the product on his own blog at `www.scsm.se`. In April 2012, he was awarded with the Microsoft Most Valuable Professional (MVP) title in the "System Center Cloud and Datacenter Management" area.

Andreas Baumgarten (MVP), IT Architect with the German IT service provider H&D International Group, has worked as an IT pro for more than 20 years. Microsoft technologies have always accompanied him and he can also look back on 14 years of experience as a Microsoft Certified Trainer.

Since 2008, he has been responsible for the field of System Center technology consulting and ever since he took part in SCSM 2010 and 2012 and System Center Orchestrator 2012 Technology Adoption Program with H&D.

With his deep inside technology know-how and his broad experience across the System Center product family and IT management, he now designs and develops Private Cloud solutions for customers all over Germany.

In October 2012, he was awarded with the Microsoft Most Valuable Professional (MVP) title for "System Center Cloud and Datacenter Management".

Steve Beaumont has been working in IT since 1998, working his way through the ranks starting with low-end system building and support through to managing a crack team of enterprise class support specialists, and to now provide consultancy and designs for System Center 2012 and Private Cloud solutions.

With the release of Service Manager 2010, he ventured into the dark side of customization and released some solutions to the community via the TechNet Gallery helping to show how to extend the usage of the product.

He also runs his own blog (`http://systemscentre.blogspot.com`) covering the full range of System Center components and areas related to desktop design, deployment, and optimization.

Dieter Gasser is an IT Consultant and co-founder of the company Syliance IT Services, headquartered in Switzerland, and specializes in Service Manager delivery and customization.

He has been working in IT for more than 13 years and has had a strong focus on Microsoft technologies. He started his career as an application and database developer, and was later appointed IT Manager for an international manufacturing company.

In 2010 he entered the systems management and automation market. With his technical and managerial background, he has been focusing on Service Manager ever since. Together with his colleagues, he delivers datacenter management and automation solutions based on Microsoft System Center to customers all over Switzerland.

About the Reviewers

Stefan Allansson is a Service Manager Specialist and has worked as a Service Manager consultant at Lumagate since the Beta version of Service Manager 2010. He is also the co-writer at the blog `www.scsm.se` and is active on the official Service Manager forum, `http://social.technet.microsoft.com/Forums/en-US/category/servicemanager`.

Steve Buchanan is currently an Infrastructure Consultant. He has 12 years of hands-on experience in Information Technology and an integrated understanding of how information systems, networks, and people work together to achieve business objectives. As a Microsoft System Center Cloud and Datacenter Management MVP, he is among the highly select group of experts that represent the technology's best and brightest, who share a deep commitment to community and a willingness to help others. He has authored *Data Protection Manager 2010* and is an author of the upcoming *Data Protection Manager 2012* book with other System Center MVPs.

He holds the following certifications in A +, Linux +, MCP, MCSA, MCITP: Server Administrator, and MCTS: (Hyper-V, SharePoint 2007, SharePoint 2010, Exchange 2007, Vista).

His blog is located at `www.buchatech.com`.

He is the author of *Microsoft Data Protection Manager 2010*.

Wayne Robinson has worked professionally in IT for over seven years, starting out on a service desk at a local IT Consultancy, working his way up to deploying and managing thousands of devices; he has vast experience in Windows Server, Windows Client, and the Systems Center Suite. He spent most of his IT career at a local authority where he managed a wide range of devices through Configuration Manager, Service Manager, and Operations Manager. He now works as a Technical Architect for a firm based in York.

I would like to thank Steve Beaumont and Sam Erskine for the opportunity to work with them on such a great publication.

www.PacktPub.com

Support files, eBooks, discount offers and more

You might want to visit www.PacktPub.com for support files and downloads related to your book.

Did you know that Packt offers eBook versions of every book published, with PDF and ePub files available? You can upgrade to the eBook version at www.PacktPub.com and as a print book customer, you are entitled to a discount on the eBook copy. Get in touch with us at service@packtpub.com for more details.

At www.PacktPub.com, you can also read a collection of free technical articles, sign up for a range of free newsletters and receive exclusive discounts and offers on Packt books and eBooks.

http://PacktLib.PacktPub.com

Do you need instant solutions to your IT questions? PacktLib is Packt's online digital book library. Here, you can access, read and search across Packt's entire library of books.

Why Subscribe?

- ▸ Fully searchable across every book published by Packt
- ▸ Copy and paste, print and bookmark content
- ▸ On demand and accessible via web browser

Free Access for Packt account holders

If you have an account with Packt at www.PacktPub.com, you can use this to access PacktLib today and view nine entirely free books. Simply use your login credentials for immediate access.

Instant Updates on New Packt Books

Get notified! Find out when new books are published by following @PacktEnterprise on Twitter, or the *Packt Enterprise* Facebook page.

Table of Contents

Preface

System Center 2012 Service Manager builds on its predecessor System Center Service Manager 2010, by extending the ITIL© process features to include Service Request fulfillment, Release Management, and automated orchestration with significant enhancements in its reporting capabilities. The full set of additions and improvements can be found at the official Microsoft website for the product.

System Center 2012 Service Manager (SCSM) is a modular product made up of a series of submodular components. Installing the product is simple using the official product documentation and online community resources.

The post-installation phase requires you to plan and configure the product in a methodical sequence. The aim of the book is to address the challenges faced by many first-time users of SCSM post-installation, and also to share valuable insight from real-world implementations.

The book is written in the Packt style, which provides the reader with independent task-oriented steps to achieve specific SCSM objectives. The authors recommend that you read the first two chapters as a background for subsequent chapters, if you are new to SCSM and process-oriented software products. The book may be read in the order of interest, but where relevant, the authors refer to dependent recipes in other chapters.

What this book covers

Chapter 1, ITSM Frameworks and Processes, aims to provide a background to ITSM frameworks with a particular focus on the Information Technology Infrastructure Library (ITIL©) and Microsoft Operations Framework (MOF). The objective is to explain the relevant key areas of these frameworks and how they relate to Service Manager as a solution.

Chapter 2, Personalizing SCSM 2012 Administration, covers the initial process dependent critical settings and tasks a Service Manager administrator would need to configure after successfully installing the product.

Chapter 3, Configuring Service Level Agreements (SLAs), delves into the Service Level Agreement areas of Service Manager 2012 and provides you with recipes, which simplify the implementation of this complex topic.

Chapter 4, Building the Configuration Management Database (CMDB), shows Service Manager Administrators how to build the SCSM 2012 Configuration Management Database (CMDB). The recipes in this chapter include various options, from a manual approach, right through to automating the importing of information from external systems.

Chapter 5, Deploying Service Request Fulfillment, focuses on Service Requests in Service Manager 2012. These recipes will show the reader how to set up the underlying components and all the steps required to present Service Requests to end users as catalog items in the Self-Service Portal.

Chapter 6, Working with Incident and Problem Management, takes two core features of Service Manager, Incident and Problem Management, and provides recipes that will accelerate the reader's knowledge and implementation of these vital ITSM processes.

Chapter 7, Designing Change and Release Management, provides recipes for Change and Release Management in SCSM. A modular approach is provided to aid the readers understanding of the mechanics of this complex organization specific processes.

Chapter 8, Implementing Security Roles, simplifies one of the least understood areas of System Center 2012 Service Manager, the role-based security module.

Chapter 9, Reporting, provides the recipes required to expose the wealth of information stored within Service Manager using the supported reporting interfaces to the product.

Chapter 10, Extending SCSM with Advanced Personalization, contains the recipes to take a standard SCSM deployment to an organization-specific personal implementation, using supported Authoring and Development Tools. SCSM is an extendible product but requires expert knowledge of the product's internal mechanisms.

Chapter 11, Automating Service Manager 2012, takes Service Manager to the next level by providing you with recipes that introduce automation of the ITSM processes in scope of the product.

Appendix A, Community Extensions and Third-party Commercial SCSM Solutions, presents a brief summary of some of the most requested and useful extensions to SCSM as solutions from trusted Microsoft Partners. SCSM, similar to most Microsoft products, has an extended solutions partner community.

Appendix B, Useful Websites and Community Resources, is the SCSM administrator's directory of online resources.

What you need for this book

In order to complete all the recipes in this book you will need a minimum of three servers configured with System Center 2012 Service Manager RTM.

Server 1: System Center 2012 Service Manager management server hosting the CMDB and workflow role.

Server 2: System Center 2012 Service Manager management server hosting the data warehouse role.

Server 3: System Center 2012 Service Manager management server hosting the SharePoint based self-service portal.

The required software and deployment guides of System Center 2012 Service Manager can be found at the official Microsoft website available at `http://technet.microsoft.com/en-us/library/hh495575.aspx`.

The authors recommend using the online Microsoft resource due to the frequency of updates to the product's supported requirements.

Who this book is for

The target audience of this book is SCSM administrators and process owners responsible for implementing the ITSM processes in scope of the product. The recipes in this book range from beginner level to expert level SCSM administration knowledge. The ultimate goal is to provide the reader with knowledge to enhance their existing skills, and more importantly to share real-world experience from seasoned technology implementers.

Conventions

In this book, you will find a number of styles of text that distinguish between different kinds of information. Here are some examples of these styles, and an explanation of their meaning.

Code words in text are shown as follows: "One generic form is bound to the `System.Entity` class, which ultimately all the classes inherit from."

A block of code is set as follows:

```
<Component Alias="Custodian">
  <Seed>
    <Class Type="System.Domain.User">
      <Property ID="Domain"/>
      <Property ID="UserName"/>
    </Class>
  </Seed>
</Component>
```

Any command-line input or output is written as follows:

```
Import-Module 'C:\Program Files\Microsoft System Center 2012\Service
Manager\Powershell\System.Center.Service.Manager.psd1'


$RootPath = C:\Service Manager MP Backup\

$Date = Get-Date

$Path = $RootPath + $Date.ToString(yyyy-MM-dd)
```

New terms and **important words** are shown in bold. Words that you see on the screen, in menus or dialog boxes for example, appear in the text like this: "When the import process is finished, click on **OK**."

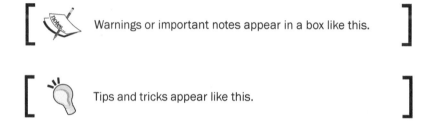

> Warnings or important notes appear in a box like this.

> Tips and tricks appear like this.

Reader feedback

Feedback from our readers is always welcome. Let us know what you think about this book—what you liked or may have disliked. Reader feedback is important for us to develop titles that you really get the most out of.

To send us general feedback, simply send an e-mail to feedback@packtpub.com, and mention the book title via the subject of your message.

If there is a topic that you have expertise in and you are interested in either writing or contributing to a book, see our author guide on www.packtpub.com/authors.

Customer support

Now that you are the proud owner of a Packt book, we have a number of things to help you to get the most from your purchase.

Downloading the example code

You can download the example code files for all Packt books you have purchased from your account at `http://www.PacktPub.com`. If you purchased this book elsewhere, you can visit `http://www.PacktPub.com/support` and register to have the files e-mailed directly to you.

Errata

Although we have taken every care to ensure the accuracy of our content, mistakes do happen. If you find a mistake in one of our books—maybe a mistake in the text or the code—we would be grateful if you would report this to us. By doing so, you can save other readers from frustration and help us improve subsequent versions of this book. If you find any errata, please report them by visiting `http://www.packtpub.com/support`, selecting your book, clicking on the **errata submission form** link, and entering the details of your errata. Once your errata are verified, your submission will be accepted and the errata will be uploaded on our website, or added to any list of existing errata, under the Errata section of that title. Any existing errata can be viewed by selecting your title from `http://www.packtpub.com/support`.

Piracy

Piracy of copyright material on the Internet is an ongoing problem across all media. At Packt, we take the protection of our copyright and licenses very seriously. If you come across any illegal copies of our works, in any form, on the Internet, please provide us with the location address or website name immediately so that we can pursue a remedy.

Please contact us at `copyright@packtpub.com` with a link to the suspected pirated material.

We appreciate your help in protecting our authors, and our ability to bring you valuable content.

Questions

You can contact us at `questions@packtpub.com` if you are having a problem with any aspect of the book, and we will do our best to address it.

1

ITSM Frameworks and Processes

This chapter provides a background into the creation of processes aligned with ITIL© and MOF (Microsoft Operations Framework) principles, and explains some of the key areas and how they relate to Service Manager; specifically we will cover the following areas:

- ▸ Understanding ITSM frameworks
- ▸ ITIL© processes
- ▸ Creating an Asset Management process
- ▸ Creating a Configuration Management System (CMS) process
- ▸ Creating a Service Request Fulfillment process
- ▸ Creating an Incident and Problem Management process
- ▸ Creating a Change and Release Management process
- ▸ Creating an IT Service Desk process
- ▸ Service Level Management process

Introduction

System Center 2012 Service Manager (SCSM) is built on the principles of the Information Technology Infrastructure Library (ITIL©) and the operational principles of the Microsoft Operations Framework (MOF). This chapter discusses the operational execution of these principles in real world implementations.

There are various books and online resources available to you on ITIL© and MOF. The authors recommend you review and research the principles of ITIL© and MOF in the areas in scope of your SCSM implementation.

The goal of creating processes regardless of the framework, is to move your organization or teams from using individual flexible approaches, to using an agreed uniform policy-driven best practice approach to meet your objectives. This approach is usually described as process maturity.

ITIL© is commonly described as an industry recognized process framework. MOF is the Microsoft standard for the execution of the processes typically using (but not limited to) Microsoft products.

Understanding ITSM frameworks

This recipe provides a summary analysis of the ITSM frameworks in general and what they mean to each organization.

Getting ready

A general understanding of the objectives of standards and frameworks is required for this recipe.

How to do it...

Plan to invest in one or more of the following:

- Buy this book
- Research the subject of frameworks using your preferred method of learning
- Attend an accredited training course in the subject
- Adopt and adapt frameworks to your specific organization needs, strategies, and capabilities

How it works...

IT Service Management is a broad term used to describe a process-focused approach to IT management. The goal for most organizations is to implement a service-focused approach to deliver IT dependent services to the end customer.

The industry standard approach for achieving the ITSM objective is to use best-in-class standards as a guide. Examples of common industry frameworks include, but are not limited to, the following:

- Information Technology Infrastructure Library (ITIL©)
- Microsoft Operations Framework (MOF)
- Core Practice

Frameworks are guides and can be compared to the rules of a game (for example, Soccer). In a game, the rules provide a consistent approach but do not limit the individual or team strategy. Another critical factor is individual creativity, which is championed and often leads to a strategic advantage.

ITSM frameworks work best for organizations when the adoption is personalized to the organizations specific strategies and internal capabilities.

ITIL© processes

This recipe provides a summary discussion of the current ITIL© V3 processes.

Getting ready

The authors recommend that you read the *Understanding ITSM frameworks* recipe.

How to do it...

Plan to do one or more of the following:

▸ Attend one or more ITIL© training courses in the recommended order

▸ Invest in the ITIL© official book(s) and complementary books

▸ Use the vast free resources on the Internet

▸ Implement and improve your organizational ITSM processes using the ITIL© knowledge as a guide

▸ Review and update your processes in line with organization strategies and capabilities

How it works...

ITIL© processes take a repeatable cyclic approach to organization IT Service Management underpinned by continual service improvements. The ITIL© goals are aimed at ensuring that the organization:

▸ Plans for services

▸ Catalogue and track IT services

▸ Introduces new services with minimal risks

▸ Manages and operates active services consistently

▸ Performs maintenance and updates to existing services with minimum risk and maximum value to the business

▸ Continually monitors and improves the services delivered to the business

The official phases of ITIL© are as follows:

- ▶ Service Strategy
- ▶ Service Design
- ▶ Service Transition
- ▶ Service Operation
- ▶ Continual Service Improvement

SCSM is a technology capability enabler of a subset of the ITIL© processes. It is important to follow the principle of: People, Processes, and Products. SCSM is the product that complements your organizations agreed processes and needs people to implement, manage, and continually improve the overall IT service strategy.

ITIL© implementation is not mandatory for SCSM deployment, but an understanding of ITIL© is recommended.

See also

- ▶ *Appendix B, Useful Websites and Community Resources* provides a list of useful websites for ITIL© and is highly recommended by the authors

Creating an Asset Management process

This recipe will provide steps for creating a sample Asset Management process.

Getting ready

For this recipe the authors recommend you read up on the difference between asset inventory and asset management as an organizational process.

How to do it...

Asset Management is a life cycle process, which tracks an IT asset with its associated financial data from when the asset is requested to when the asset is retired as shown in the following figure:

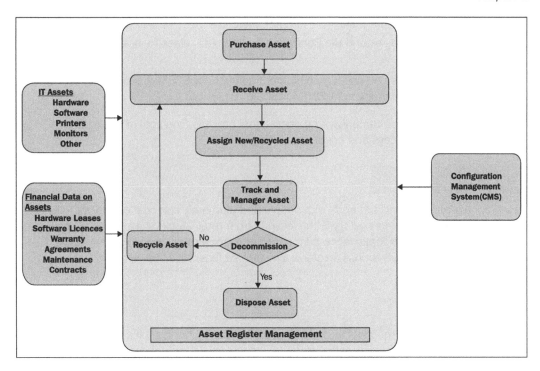

An example of the steps for creating an Asset management process is as follows:

1. Agree and document the organization's asset management policy.

2. Document the operational process to support the asset management policy.

3. Create and assign people roles to manage the process. At a minimum you should plan to include the following:

   ❑ Hardware Asset Managers

   ❑ Hardware Asset Inventory agents

   ❑ Software Asset Managers

   ❑ Software Asset Inventory agents

4. Identify and agree on an asset register management system. An asset register in its basic form is a manual process. It should capture the following:

   ❑ IT Asset type

   ❑ Financial information

   ❑ Align the IT asset to its financial data

   ❑ Input to a configuration Management system (CMS)

   ❑ Continually aligned to the CMS

5. Implement Asset Management in SCSM using one of the following methods:

❑ Manually extend the Configuration Items (CI) class to include financial data for assets

❑ Purchase an asset management solution for SCSM (for example, Provance IT Asset Management Pack for SCSM)

6. Continually review the policy and operational process. The goal of this step is to improve the process and ensure compliance.

How it works...

Asset Management begins and ends with people and ultimately can cost or add value to a business. A non-IT related analogy is the lessons from retail stock takes, which typically happen annually. The stocktake is the best opportunity for a retail shop to get the most accurate figure for its profit or loss on stock. Two forms of lost revenues are:

▸ Damaged goods

▸ Missing goods

IT asset management is the stocktake required for all your technological assets, and its resultant analysis for intelligent decision making to provide factual compliance measurements. The IT equivalent of the stock take process is referred to as audits for software and hardware. SCSM with partner extensions or in-house authoring provides 80 percent of the Asset Management for the organization. People and process critically account for the high value 20 percent.

There's more...

There are various tools (products) labeled as Asset Management tools. The true Asset Management tools should have the capability of tracking assets from order to decommission.

Asset Management is an end-to-end process, and the tools are enablers of successful implementation. The successful Asset Management organization programs recognize the full life cycle management of assets.

See also

▸ See the *Using the SCSM Authoring Tool* and *Extending Service Manager classes* recipes in *Chapter 10, Extending SCSM with Advanced Personalization* for advanced recipes on management pack authoring

Creating a Configuration Management System (CMS) process

This recipe provides steps for creating a Configuration Management System process.

Getting ready

This recipe is focused on a Configuration Management System process using SCSM. The CMS process differs from a Configuration Management Database (CMDB). A CMS combines one or more CMDBs. SCSM implements a CMS within its CMDB by merging data from multiple CMDBs including the following:

- Active directory (AD)
- System Center Configuration Manager (ConfigMgr)
- System Center Operations Manager (OpsMgr)

This recipe is focused on how you create a CMS process with SCSM using AD, ConfigMgr, and OpsMgr.

How to do it...

An example of the steps for creating CMS process is as follows:

1. Plan to agree and document the organization configuration management policy.
2. Document the operational process to support the configuration management policy.
3. Create and assign people roles to manage the process.
4. Install and configure the CMDB systems in scope (in this example, AD, ConfigMgr, and OpsMgr).
5. Add the AD capable assets to the AD CMDB.
6. Discover the AD joined assets with ConfigMgr and deploy the ConfigMgr agent.
7. Discover the AD joined assets with OpsMgr and deploy the OpsMgr agent.
8. Configure the AD connector for SCSM and synchronize the data from AD with SCSM.
9. Configure the ConfigMgr connector and synchronize the data from ConfigMgr with SCSM.
10. Configure the OpsMgr connector and synchronize the the data from OpsMgr with SCSM.

11. The CMS example structure is shown in the following figure:

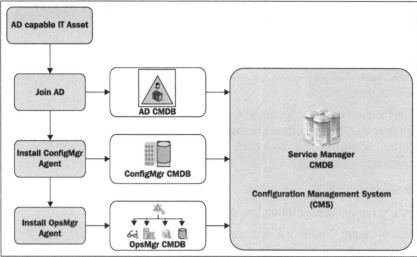

How it works...

SCSM addresses the technology requirements of a CMS process by providing a simplified and consistent framework for connecting multiple CMDBs. In the example the three CMDBs provide information, which SCSM merges to provide a single view of the asset. Using a database server as our asset example:

▸ AD provides the computer details and information registered in the AD CMDB

▸ ConfigMgr provides information on the hardware and software of the asset (for example, 64-bit operating system with Microsoft SQL Server 2008)

▸ OpsMgr provides information on what databases are installed on the computer

SCSM presents a consolidated view of this information to the analyst and is dynamically refreshed by the owner of the data.

SCSM builds the ITIL© process on its CMDB, which is a dynamic CMS. The CMS approach ensures that the data accuracy and management is performed at the source (AD, ConfigMgr, OpsMgr, or other supported connector). This approach removes the risk of data inconsistency typical of other systems where the IT Service Management (ITSM) tool does not automatically synchronize with CMDBs in scope.

See also

▸ The *Importing active directory configuration items* recipe in *Chapter 4, Building the Configuration Management Database (CMDB)*

▸ The *Importing configuration manager configuration items* recipe in *Chapter 4, Building the Configuration Management Database (CMDB)*

▸ The *Importing Operations Manager configuration items* recipe in *Chapter 4, Building the Configuration Management Database (CMDB)*

Creating a Service Request Fulfillment process

This recipe provides guidance on creating an organization Service Request Fulfillment process.

Getting ready

Service Request Fulfillment is typically a process put in place to support a proactive approach to providing services to customers.

How to do it...

An example of the steps for creating a Service Request Fulfillment process is as follows:

1. Agree and document the organization Service Request Fulfillment policy.
2. Document the operational process to support the Service Request Fulfillment policy.
3. Create and assign people roles to manage the process.
4. Create a service catalog of the organization services available to the end customers.
5. Sort the services by categories. An example of two category types are:
   - Approval required services
   - Non approval required services (standard services)
6. Agree and establish the organization supported channels for requesting services. Examples of channels include the following:
   - Phone calls into the service desk
   - E-mail
   - Self-service Web Portal
7. Publish the list of services and provide guidance on how to order services, including approval processes and costs.
8. Provide training and guidance to the support teams responsible for service request fulfillment.

9. Plan to review the process and improve the service based on customer feedback and technological advances.

    An example of a Service Request Fulfillment process structure is shown in the following figure:

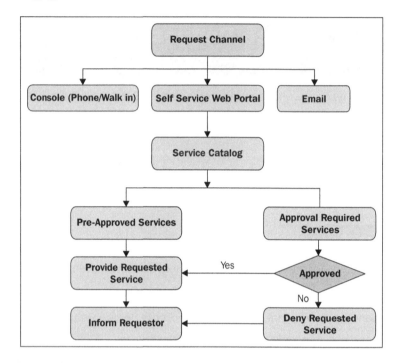

How it works...

A Service Request Fulfillment process aims to address the proactive goals of ITSM. Some of the common objectives when establishing this process are to:

▶ Provide predictable services at a known cost.

▶ Engage customers by using predictable published channels of service delivery.

▶ Improve the change management processes. A repeatable change request with a low risk known outcome may qualify for a published service request with a simpler approval process.

▶ Provide visibility and proactive management of services in the service catalog.

Service requests are typically requests for services that do not require change management, but may or may not require approval. As an example, we can have a process for requesting access to a special printer or a request for premium software.

Creating an Incident and Problem Management process

This recipe discusses creating an Incident and Problem Management process.

Getting ready

In Incident Management we focus on restoring a service to its known mode of operation before an unplanned interruption. Problem Management requires you to focus on understanding the actual cause of the interruption with the goal of providing a permanent resolution.

The ITIL© framework books and online resources discuss best practice for Incident and Problem Management processes. You must plan to review and understand Incident and Problem Management principles as a prerequisite to creating the processes.

How to do it...

An example of the steps for creating an Incident and Problem Management process is as follows.

Incident Management

Here are the example steps specific to an Incident Management process:

1. Agree and document the organization incident management policy.
2. Document the operational process to support the incident management policy. This should include but not be limited to:
   - Support hours
   - Classification categories
   - Escalation procedures
3. Create and assign people roles to manage the process. For example:
   - Service Desk analysts
   - Desktop support
   - Infrastructure analyst
   - Service Desk managers
4. We typically have two channels for incident management:
   - Service Desk team-created incidents using the SCSM console.

Sample process steps from incident creation to priority allocation are shown in the following figure:

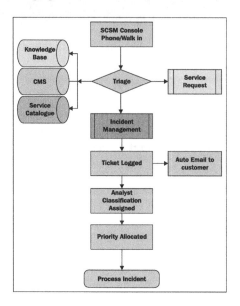

❑ Automated or end user self-service created incidents (end user web portal, e-mail, or automatic system event driven).

Sample process steps from incident creation to priority allocation are shown in the following screenshot:

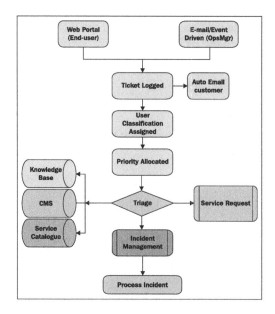

5. The difference between the two typical channels is how the incident is initially categorized (triage). The next step "Process Incident" involves the creation of a process flow to match how the incident management team manage the incident based on your policies and procedures. An example is shown in the following figure:

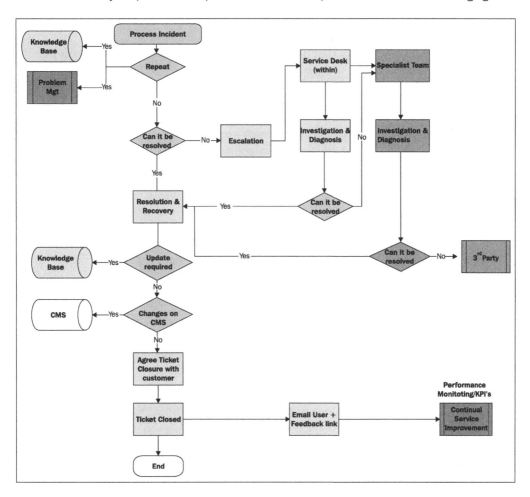

6. Monitor and report on the performance of the incident management process. The aim is to improve the process and also identify incidents which require Problem Management.

Problem Management

Here are the example steps specific to a Problem Management process:

1. Agree and document the organization Problem Management policy.
2. Document the operational process to support the Problem Management policy.

3. Create and assign people roles to manage the process. For example:

   ❑ Problem analysts

   ❑ Problem managers

4. Review the Incident Management process with the aim of identifying instances of the following type:

   ❑ Repeated issues over a defined period (for example, monthly, quarterly, or annually)

   ❑ Incidents with known workarounds (typically implies there is an opportunity for root cause investigation)

5. Perform detailed investigation on incidents escalated to Problem management using internal experts or third-party external support.

6. Create a change request for problems with known permanent fixes.

How it works...

Incident Management is about getting services that people rely on back to an agreed operational state as soon as possible. An example of Incident Management is a customer who is unable to access their documents:

1. On investigation we find that the issue is with the laptop assigned to the customer.

2. We issue the customer with a loan laptop and confirm access to their document.

The previous steps will resolve the incident but we still have a problem. What is wrong with the customer's laptop?

The answer to the question is Problem Management. We use Problem Management to identify the true (root) cause of the issue. Continuing with our scenario from Incident Management:

1. The desktop engineering team identify the issue as a network hardware device failure in the laptop.

2. The team also identify that this issue has been happening to a number of laptops over the last quarter.

3. The team also identify through asset management that we purchase a set of laptops from a vendor and all the issues relate to this set.

4. We escalate to the vendor and get a driver fix.

5. A change request is raised to proactively apply the fix to all laptops from the set.

The fix applied to all laptops in scope resolves the issue on the original laptop. We can close the problem and also change the original status of the incident to *close*. A final best practice will be to create a knowledge article about this known issue and its corresponding fix.

The previous examples illustrate how Incident Management and Problem Management work in practice.

Creating a Change and Release Management process

This recipe discusses creating a Change and Release Management process for an organization.

Getting ready

In Change Management we focus on enhancing existing services, service components, or introducing new services and components without an unplanned interruption to existing services. Release Management focuses on when the changes are implemented and manages planned interruption to services.

The ITIL© framework online resources delve much deeper into the best practices for the Change and Release Management processes. You must plan to review and understand Change and Release Management principles as a prerequisite to creating the processes.

How to do it...

An example of the steps for creating a Change and Release Management process is as follows:

1. Agree and document the organization Change and Release Management policy with the aim of identifying the following :

   ❏ Change types and categories

   ❏ Change type priorities

   ❏ Policy owner

2. Create and continually update a service map for all services and applications in scope of Change and Release Management. Examples include but are not limited to the following types of services: infrastructure services, messaging, and collaboration services. A best practice industry approach is the RACI model:

   ❏ **Responsible (R)**: Who is responsible for the service or service component?

   ❏ **Accountable (A)**: Who is accountable for the service? This is typically the assigned business unit application owner.

   ❏ **Consulted (C)**: Who is consulted about the service operations? Typically support team acting as the subject matter experts.

   ❏ **Informed (I)**: Who is informed about service availability?

3. Document the operational process to support the Change and Release Management policy. The operational procedures should include the following:

   ❑ Technical approvers and management approvers

   ❑ Plan for proxy approvers to cover expected or non-expected absence of main approvers

   ❑ Maintenance schedules (approved change implementation windows)

   ❑ Release process structure:

      By Change stage

      By Change Type

      By Maintenance window

4. Create and assign people roles to manage the process. For example:

   ❑ Change managers

   ❑ Release managers

   ❑ Change implementers (this would be a logical role as implementers will vary based on the change type and related service)

5. Review the Change and Release Management process with the aim of identifying instances of the following type:

   ❑ Candidates for Service Request fulfillment (changes that have been successfully validated as low risk and low impact based on an agreed number of successful implementation results).

   ❑ Changes requiring re-classification. For example, a minor change that results in a major outage due to an identified dependency service.

   ❑ Release window adjustment due to a business process schedule change. For example, a financial audit application used during peak accounting periods may require a special release window.

6. The Change and Release Management process once established typically have the following operational states:

   ❑ Initiate

   ❑ Approve

      ▸ Technical (validation from a technical perspective)

      ▸ Management (validation from a cost and business risk perspective)

   ❑ Implement and Release

      ▸ Implementation steps and owners (who does it and how)

      ▸ Release schedule alignment (when it gets done)

❑   Post implementation review. For example:

  ▸   Successful in the time allocated

  ▸   Successful but overrun time allocated

  ▸   Failed

❑   Resubmissions

The following figure provides an example of the process from the change initiation stage:

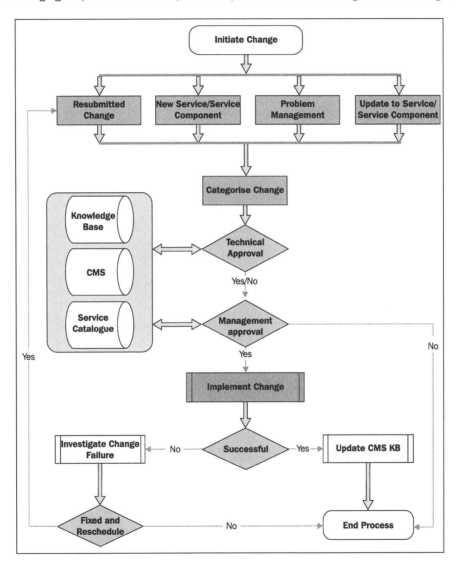

How it works...

In Change Management we use Release Management principles to coordinate multiple changes in cases where these changes may impact on each other. We focus on the following areas when creating and implementing Change Management:

- ▸ Organization culture
    - ❑ Successful Change Management creation requires complete buy in from the whole organization
    - ❑ Exceptions and breaches of Change Management are opportunities to educate and refine the process as appropriate
    - ❑ Change Management is a journey not a destination (expect changing conditions and adapt as appropriate)

- ▸ Categorization and classification
    - ❑ What type of change, and how it impacts existing services?
    - ❑ How important is the change?

- ▸ Approvals
    - ❑ Who has the authority to approve?
    - ❑ Who has the best knowledge on the impact and risk to the existing services?
    - ❑ Cost justification

- ▸ Post implementation analysis
    - ❑ Unplanned impact of changes
    - ❑ Configuration management updates and service catalogue maintenance
    - ❑ Lessons learnt (Knowledge management)

There's more...

Release Management can be:

- ▸ **Simple**:
    - ❑ Manage the forward change schedule
    - ❑ Multiple changes that affect the same service component requires coordination
    - ❑ Multiple changes grouped and released during the same maintenance window

▶ **Complex**:

> ❏ Extension of application life cycle management
>
> ❏ New software developed in house
>
> ❏ Patch Management is a candidate for Release Management

Release Management is a discipline with broad and wide coverage. Best practice for creating the process is; you should plan to assign a release management expert. The process should also have a supported agreed organizational policy.

Creating an IT Service Desk process

This section provides an example of what is typically required to create a Service Desk process.

Getting ready

Service Desks are organization specific but share a common goal. The goal of most Service Desks is to be the central point of contact for customers in the following areas:

▶ Request for services

▶ Unplanned outages or interruptions to services

▶ Feedback channels for improvement to existing services

▶ Coordination and tracking of active requests and incidents

A prerequisite for creating a Service Desk process is to define what role it would play in the overall ITSM strategy.

Service Desks principles are defined in the ITIL© Service Operations books. Plan to review the industry best practice before creating an organization specific version.

How to do it...

There are three main types of service desks

▶ **Local Service Desk**: Service desk in each customer geographic location, independently managing support services

▶ **Central Service Desk**: One service desk that supports all geographic locations and offers a consolidated picture of issues and requests across the organization

▶ **Virtual service Desk**: Use technology to manage either of the first two types from any location

The successful service desk process is based on communication and coordination. Here are some categories of tools you must plan to implement to support the process:

- ▶ Integrated Service Management and Operations Management systems (For example, the Microsoft System Center Management product)
- ▶ Advanced telephony systems (For example, auto-routing, hunt groups, Computer Telephony Integration (CTI), Voice Over Internet Protocol (VOIP))
- ▶ Interactive Voice Response (IVR) systems
- ▶ Electronic communication (Voice, video, mobile, intranet, Internet, and e-mail systems)
- ▶ Knowledge, search, and diagnostic tools
- ▶ Automated operations and Network Management tools

Here are the common functions the service desk should aim to perform:

- ▶ Receive calls and act as the first-line customer liaison
- ▶ Record and track incidents and complaints
- ▶ Keep customers informed on request status and progress
- ▶ Make an initial assessment of requests, attempt to resolve them, or escalate as appropriate
- ▶ Manage the request and issues life cycle, including closure and verification
- ▶ Communicate planned changes and disruption to services
- ▶ Coordinate hierarchical and functional escalations
- ▶ Highlight customer and service desk personnel training opportunities
- ▶ Monitor and track Service Level Agreements (SLA) and Operational Level Agreements (OLA)
- ▶ Report on customer trends and service desk performance

How it works...

The service desk process, once established, should deliver the following:

- ▶ Act to lower the total cost IT ownership
- ▶ Support the integration and management of the service portfolio and catalogue
- ▶ Make efficient use of resources and technology
- ▶ Optimize investments and the management of business support services

A service desk should aim to provide a unified and simplified experience to the customers it serves.

Service Level Management process

Service Level Management (SLM) is the foundation and underpinning element of ITSM. This recipe looks at the common input components of SLM and the deliverables of the process. SLM typically can be applied internally, externally, or both. The external application of SLM can be complex as it typically requires legal contracts with external providers outside an organization. In this recipe our focus will be on the internal execution of SLM.

Getting ready

SLM is a vital organization function. The goal of SLM is to ensure that the customers' expectations are met in line with formal published agreements. We must be able to consistently capture the inputs, and accurately report on the adherence or non-compliance to the agreed SLM objectives. We must have organization buy-in and a full understanding of SLM through official ITIL© material, or appropriate training in the SLM discipline.

How to do it...

SLM is the key to all processes and functions in ITIL©. The common area in SLM is Service Level Agreements (SLA). We will use Incident Management and Service Request Fulfillment as our functions in how to do it:

1. Agree and publish Service Level Agreements for Incident Management response times and resolution times. The following table provides an example of the SLM inputs for five categories (priority) of incidents based on urgency and impact. The second table provides an example of the SLM inputs for the service request fulfillment.

Incident Priority	Target First Response	Target Resolution Time
1	30 minutes	4 hours
2	2 hours	8 hours
3	8 hours	24 hours
4	16 hours	80 hours
5	24 hours	160 hours
Service Request Priority	Target First Response	Target Implementation
1	8 hours	16 hours
2	16 hours	24 hours
3	24 hours	72 hours

2. Install and configure an appropriate ITSM tool with SLM implementation capabilities (for example, System Center Service Manager).

3. Configure the tool with the details of the organization SLM requirements.

4. Capture the SLM metrics. Examples of some incident metrics are:

    ❑ Number of SLA breaches

    ❑ Average time to resolve incidents

    ❑ Number of incidents per week/month/quarter

5. Monitor the operational adherence to the SLM metric.

6. Report and adjust the appropriate execution of the processes to ensure adherence is in line with the agreed SLM objectives.

How it works...

Service Level Management is what we use to ensure that IT capabilities are aligned with customer expectations of the services provided by IT. The successful implementation of SLM involves creating agreements between the supplier of services (IT and supporting third parties), and the consumer of the services (business customers). A driver for successful SLM is when an organization commits to compliance with industry recognized standards. The following standards are typical drivers:

▸ ISO 9001

▸ ISO 27001

▸ ITIL© Certification

The overall goal is to ensure services are delivered at the right cost to the expectations of the service consumers. SLM is at its most effective when we create credible agreements, report proactively on performance of the service, and accurately capture the service consumer's feedback (for example, using customer satisfaction surveys).

2
Personalizing SCSM 2012 Administration

In this chapter, we will provide recipes for the initial configuration tasks an SCSM administrator should perform following a successful installation of the environment. We will cover the following areas and topics:

- Configuring how long to keep your SCSM data
- Configuring the Incident Management global settings
- Configuring the Service Requests, Activity, Release, Knowledge, and Change Management global settings
- Configuring the behavior of child incidents when resolving, reactivating, and closing the parent Incident
- Configuring Priority and Urgency for your SLA targets
- Configuring global e-mail notification infrastructure settings
- Creating Management Packs in the Authoring tool to save your SCSM personalization
- Creating formatted e-mail notification templates
- Creating a basic queue

Introduction

The Microsoft System Center Service Manager (SCSM) console is where you will configure and manage typical settings and activities associated with the ITIL© processes implemented by the product. This chapter will provide steps for the global settings and some basic activities you may want to perform, before delving into the configuration and management of the supported product processes.

The settings addressed by this chapter have a significant impact on the behavior of Work Items and Configuration Items. In some cases, there is no retrospective application of the settings to existing items. The authors recommend you review and apply the settings in this chapter as a first step in the full configuration of your environment, post installation of the product.

Configuring how long to keep your SCSM data

This recipe provides the steps required to configure how long SCSM retains the data presented in the console. We will also provide steps on how long to retain data for historical use.

Getting ready

You need to ensure you have successfully installed the SCSM product, are a user in SCSM Administrators role, and have the SCSM console open.

How to do it...

1. Navigate to **Service Manager Console | Administration | Settings | Data Retention Settings** and click on **Properties** under **Tasks**, as shown in the following screenshot:

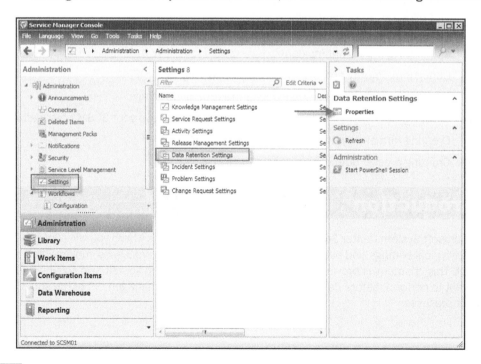

2. Select **Work Items | Review** and adjust retention times (in days) to reflect how long the items should be kept in the SCSM ServiceManager database:

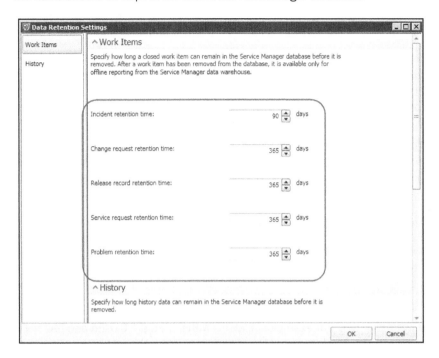

3. Select **History | Review** and adjust the history retention times (in days) to reflect how long the history of items should be kept in the SCSM ServiceManager database:

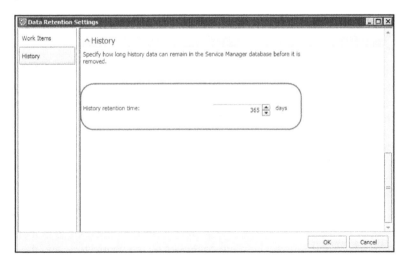

4. Click on **OK** to confirm the data retention settings.

How it works...

Service Manager by default has grooming settings in place to keep the performance of the product at its most desired state. There are two types of data in SCSM:

- ▶ **Configuration Items**: These are typically the console objects you see in the Configuration Items node and are of the class type `configuration item`. The Configuration Items are typically introduced and maintained by the connectors (for example, the Active Directory connector imports the users, computers, and printer Configuration Items).

- ▶ **Work Items**: These are typically the objects you see in the Work Items node of the console and are of the class type `work item`. These objects are associated with their respective process class (for example, the incident management Work Items class for all incidents).

The retention settings are related to the Work Items class. The Work Items class, for example incidents, cannot be deleted from the console. An automated deletion process using the data retention settings you specify is responsible for removing the Work Items data from the SCSM database. The automated process for deleting items is known as grooming. It is important to note that the criterion uses the following formula to groom (delete) the respective Work Items data:

Delete the work item type (for example, incident) with a status = Closed and has not been modified in x days (where x is the number of days you set for the respective Work Items type).

You must plan to have a data warehouse configuration with the following desired objectives of typical "best practice" organizations:

- ▶ **Improve the performance and efficiency of the console**: The old work items in the working database (the database name is `ServiceManager` by default) slows down the console and provides a negative experience for the service management team.

- ▶ **Historical retention and reporting**: You need to install and configure a data warehouse in order to have reporting capabilities. The data warehouse is optimized for reporting and is the recommended option for retaining the old Work or Configuration Items information.

A data warehouse combined with optimal data retention settings will provide your environment with the desired objectives.

There's more...

This recipe focused on the Work Items grooming and provided instructions to that effect. Configuration Items are also groomed but are controlled by the connectors, and the delete actions are manually performed by an SCSM administrator with the relevant role in the console.

Additionally grooming has an internal schedule. The schedule control requires you to export and edit the internal management packs. The default schedule is midnight every day and it is run on the server that is assigned the workflow role. (This is typically the first management server unless you manually move the role.)

Configuration Items data grooming using the console

The Configuration Items displayed in the console can be manually deleted. The console user needs to be either an Advanced Operator, or an Administrator role user to perform a delete action. For example, you can delete a user in the console by selecting the **Delete** task in the console, as shown in the following screenshot:

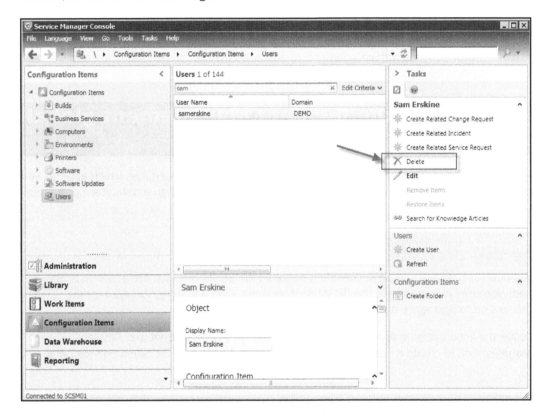

The delete action marks the Configuration Items in scope for automated grooming and does not perform an immediate removal from the database. The Configuration Items will not show in the Configuration Items space and will be marked with a status of *pending delete* in the database. The deleted item will be placed in the **Deleted items** node and can be restored by an Administrator, if the action is performed before the internal grooming process runs. Note that if the Configuration Items is from an active connector then it would be re-imported into the database and displayed the next time the connector is synchronized. You must delete the object from the source (for example, Active Directory) if it is a Configuration Items from a connector.

The history setting determines how long Configuration Items are kept in the **Deleted items** node outside of the normal connector behavior.

See also

Modifying grooming settings is performed in the respective management pack responsible for the grooming process. This type of modification is typically performed in the authoring tool or an XML editor.

> ▸ See the *Using the SCSM Authoring Tool* and *Extending Service Manager classes* recipes in *Chapter 10, Extending SCSM with Advanced Personalization* for advanced recipes on management pack authoring

> ▸ *Appendix B, Useful Websites and Community Resources*, provides a list of useful websites with comprehensive advanced instructions on authoring and configuring SCSM

Configuring the Incident Management global settings

This recipe will provide the steps required to configure the general settings, which apply to all incident class Work Items. We will also provide steps on how to assign a default support group for new incidents.

Getting ready

You need to ensure you have successfully installed the SCSM product, are a user in SCSM Administrators role, and have the SCSM console open. Plan a naming standard for the process prefix and agree a size limitation for attachments.

Follow the list creation instructions in *Chapter 6, Working with Incident and Problem Management*, to create a new list item for the *Incident Tier Queue* list called *Service Desk*.

How to do it...

1. Navigate to **Service Manager Console | Administration | Settings | Incident Settings** and click on **Properties** under **Tasks**, as shown in the following screenshot:

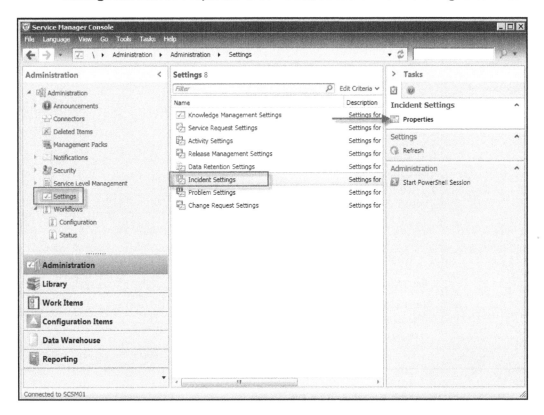

2. Click on **General** and configure the following settings to your organization's standard:

   ❑ **Prefix: IM**

   ❑ **Maximum number of attached files: 10** (default setting)

   ❑ **Maximum size (KB): 2048** (default setting)

> ❏ **Default support group: Service Desk** (a custom Incident Tier queue list item)

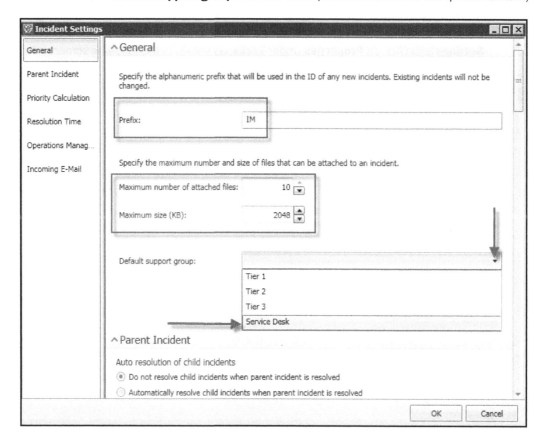

3. Review the settings and click on **OK**.

How it works...

The global settings we have configured will apply to all incidents you create. Prefix is the first part of the incident reference number. It is automatically generated and is always higher than the last incident number in the database. The attachment settings apply to how many files you, or a user using the self-service portal, can attach to the incident. The attachment size is used to specify the maximum size of a file that can be attached. The final setting, **Default support group** is the logical group to whom the incident is assigned.

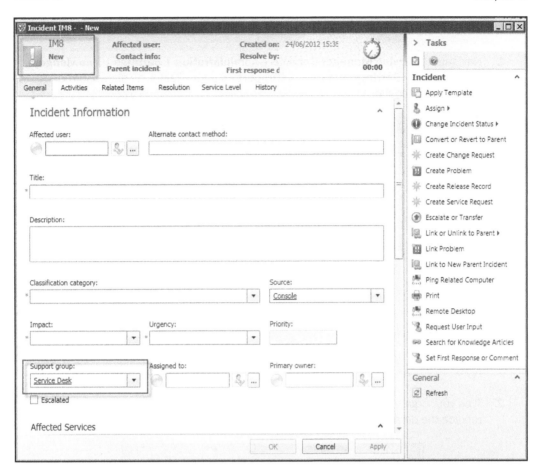

Configuring the Service Requests, Activity, Release, Knowledge, and Change Management global settings

This recipe will provide the steps required to configure the general settings, which apply to all Service Requests, all Activity class types, Release, Knowledge, and Change Management class Work Items.

Getting ready

You must ensure you have successfully installed the SCSM product, are a user in SCSM Administrators role, and have the SCSM console open. Plan a naming standard for the process prefix and agree a size limitation for attachments.

How to do it...

1. Navigate to **Service Manager Console | Administration | Settings | Knowledge Management Settings** and click on **Properties** under **Tasks**, as shown in the following screenshot:

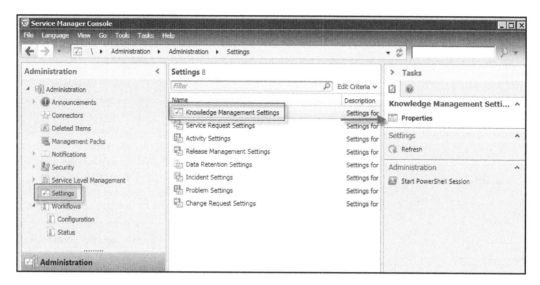

2. Type your organization's agreed prefix under **Knowledge article prefix:** (for example, replace the default **KA** with **KB**). Click on **OK** to commit your change.

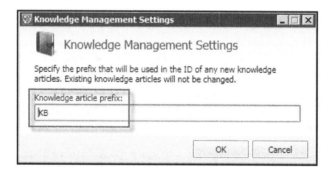

3. Repeat step 1 and this time select **Service Request Settings**. Type in the agreed prefix and the organization's agreed standard for service request attachments. Click on **OK** to commit your change.

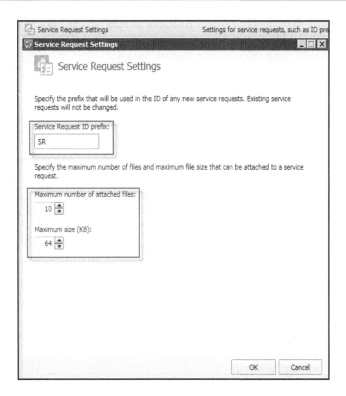

4. Repeat step 1 and this time select **Activity Settings**. Type in the agreed relevant **Activity prefix**. Click on **OK** to commit your change.

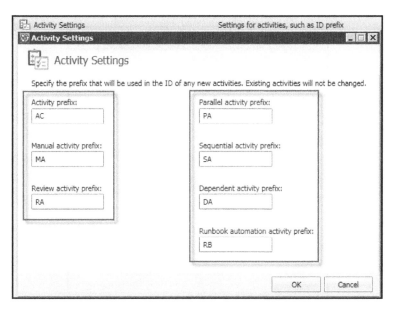

5. Repeat step 1 and this time select **Release Management Settings**. Type in the agreed prefix and the organization's agreed standard for Release Management attachments. Click on **OK** to commit your change.

6. Repeat step 1 and this time select **Change Management Settings**. Type in the agreed prefix and the organization's agreed standard for Change Management attachments. Click on **OK** to commit your change.

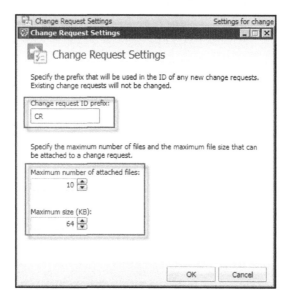

How it works...

This recipe has two components that you must decide on before applying them to the settings:

▸ Prefix settings

▸ File attachment settings, including the size per file

Working with Prefix settings

SCSM by default has the prefix configured. You have the option to change the default settings to one relevant to your organization. The authors recommend you to document changes to these settings and perform any changes before you go into production use. The prefix will also have an impact in reports and query based settings.

File attachment settings

The default file settings in SCSM may not meet your organization's requirements. You have the option to increase the size and the number of files you can attach to Service Requests, Change, and Release Management records. You can view the file attachments by selecting the related items tab of the relevant supported process.

Configuring the behavior of child incidents when resolving, reactivating, and closing the parent Incident

SCSM supports parent child relationships for the incident class. This recipe provides the steps required for the automatic configuration of child incidents, when there is a change to the parent incident.

Getting ready

You must ensure you have successfully installed the SCSM product, are a user in the SCSM Administrators role, and have the SCSM console open.

How to do it...

There are three options you can configure for the Parent Incident settings, as follows:

▸ Auto resolution of child incidents

▸ Auto reactivation of child incidents

▸ Status of child incidents when linked to a parent

These three options are discussed in the next section.

1. Navigate to **Service Manager Console | Administration | Settings | Incident Settings** an click on **Properties** under **Tasks**.

2. Select the **Parent Incident** tab on the left and set the following:

   ❑ **Auto resolution of child incidents**

   ❑ **Auto reactivation of child incidents**

   ❑ **Status of active child incidents when linked to a parent**

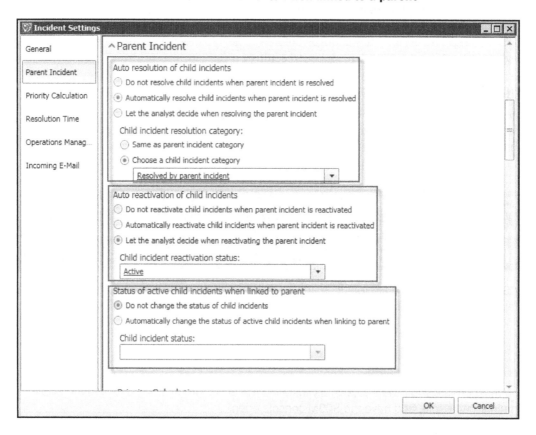

3. Click on **OK** to confirm the **Parent Incident** settings.

How it works...

The Parent Incident settings provide you with a means to standardize by using three options. The explanation of how these three options work is as follows.

Auto resolution of child incidents

This option should be set to reflect the agreed Incident Management process. The options you select have an impact on the SLA you set for incidents and the resulting reports. In the example settings, we set the option to **Automatically resolve child incidents when parent incident is resolved** and set the **Child incident resolution category** value to **Resolved by parent incident**.

The result of the example setting is a reduction of manual activity and the ability to report accurately on linked incidents. Selecting any of the other two options will require a manual action to the child incidents and may be prone to human errors.

Auto reactivation of child incidents

This action is the opposite of the auto resolution setting. Child incidents linked with the parent can either be automatically reactivated, manually activated, or controlled by the SCSM analyst. In the example, we show a setting where the action is to allow the analysts decide.

The approach gives the analysts control over the number of child incidents to reactivate. The configuration every organization selects should be aligned with the policies and procedures agreed for Incident Management.

Status of child incidents when linked with a parent

The final option provides us with an ability to change the child status when we link it to a parent incident. SCSM automatically displays the parent incident as a link in the child incident form. Parent incident forms have an additional tab for child incidents. In the example, this is set to **Do not change the status of child incidents**. Due to the automatic behavior, you should plan to use a status change only if your internal processes require you to do so, or you have a need to report on the status.

Configuring Priority and Urgency for your SLA targets

In this recipe we will provide the steps to configure the Priority and Urgency settings in SCSM. The example we will use for the configuration is an organization with Priority 1 to 5 Service Level Agreements (SLA).

Getting ready

The input required for this task is a table with the values for calculating the matrix.

The following table is an example of a five priority matrix:

		Impact		
		Low	**Medium**	**High**
	Low	5	4	3
Urgency	**Medium**	4	3	2
	High	3	2	1

You must ensure you have successfully installed the SCSM product, are a user in the SCSM Administrators role, and have the SCSM console open.

How to do it...

1. Let's navigate to **Service Manager Console | Administration | Settings | Incident Settings** and click on **Properties** under **Tasks**.

2. Select the **Priority Calculation** tab on the left and fill the settings in using the **Priority Calculation** matrix table:

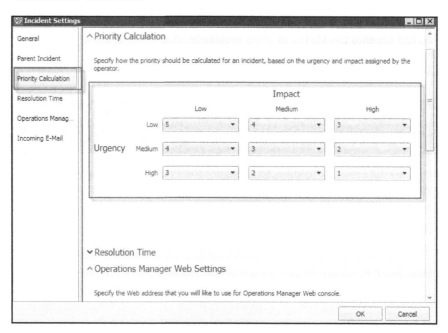

3. Click on **OK** to confirm the priority calculation settings.

How it works...

The priority that is assigned to an incident is determined using the priority calculation table. There are two mandatory selections when you create an incident, as follows:

- ▶ **Impact**: What is the effect of on incident on the business service? The values available in a default installation are low, medium, or high. The selected value will depend on the organization process. The value can be modified to change the priority.

- ▶ **Urgency**: How soon do we need to bring the service back on line? The values available in a default installation are low, medium, and high.

Using the example table, we can determine that an incident with a low impact and low urgency will be set to priority **5**.

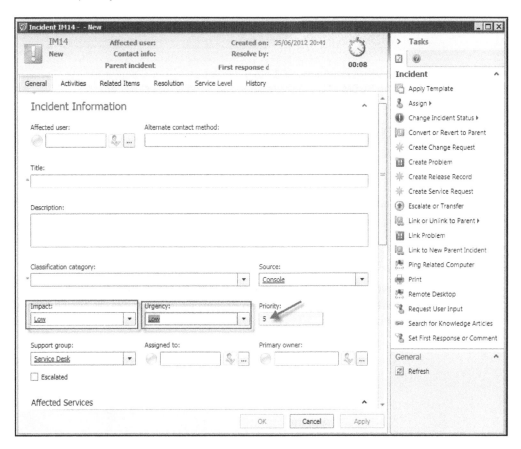

See also

▶ See the *Creating Incident Management SLAs* recipe in *Chapter 3, Configuring Service Level Agreements (SLAs)*, which covers the SLA configuration using the priority settings as a dependence configuration

Configuring global e-mail notification infrastructure settings

Service Manager has numerous notification capabilities. The e-mail notification capabilities require you to configure global infrastructure settings. This recipe provides the steps to complete the infrastructure settings the e-mail capable functionality depends on.

Getting ready

Ensure you have Service Manager supported SMTP server and have configured your infrastructure to allow the SCSM Management server to send e-mails. Record the following details:

▶ Fully Qualified Domain Name (FQDN) of the SMTP server

▶ The return e-mail address for notifications

▶ The configured allowed port for SMTP communication

You must also ensure that you are in the SCSM Administrators role and have the SCSM console open.

How to do it...

1. Navigate to **Service Manager Console | Administration | Notification | Channels | Email Notification Channel** and click on **Properties** under **Tasks**, as shown in the following screenshot:

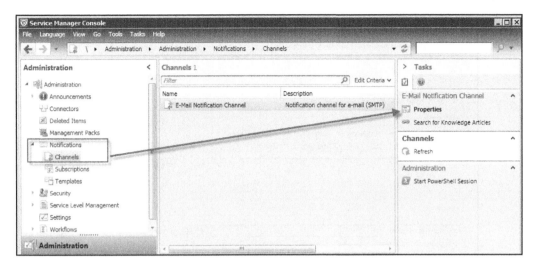

2. Tick **Enable e-mail notification**. Click on **Add...**:

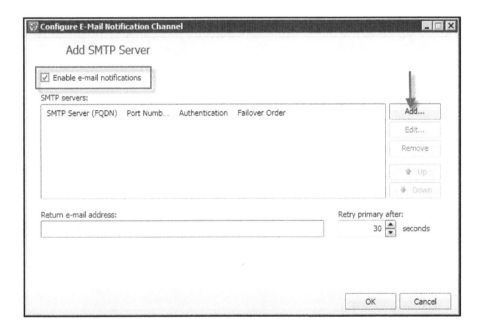

3. Type in the FQDN of the SMTP server, accept or change the default port, accept or change the default authentication, and then click on **OK**.

4. Type in the **Return e-mail address**. Review the settings and click on **OK** to confirm.

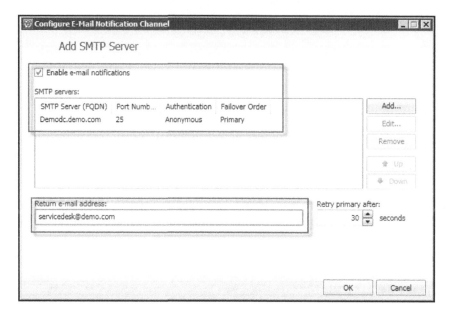

How it works...

The SMTP server configuration enables the e-mail notification function. When you configure the e-mail notification either through a workflow setting or subscription, the SMTP server(s) is/are used to route the e-mail to the targeted recipient.

Creating Management Packs in the Authoring tool to save your SCSM personalization

This recipe provides the steps required to create a management pack in the SCSM Authoring tool. It also provides steps to import the management pack into the SCSM console.

Getting ready

You must successfully install the SCSM Authoring tool. You must either create an operating system folder or use an existing filesystem location to store the management pack.

Launch the SCSM Authoring tool console.

Launch the SCSM Console as a user in the SCSM Administrators role.

How to do it...

1. Launch the Authoring tool console and click on the new file icon to create a new Management pack:

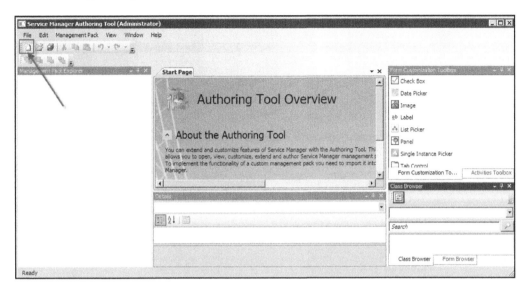

2. Navigate to your management pack file storage location. In the file name field, change the name to match your naming convention (note no spaces are allowed, use period (.) to separate words). Click on **Save**:

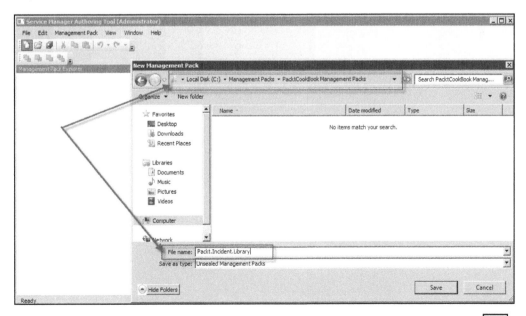

3. Select the newly-created management pack (left-hand pane). In the middle pane click on the following fields and perform the actions described:

   ❑ **Description**: Type a friendly description for the management pack

   ❑ **Management Pack Name**: You can replace (.) with spaces

   Save the management pack:

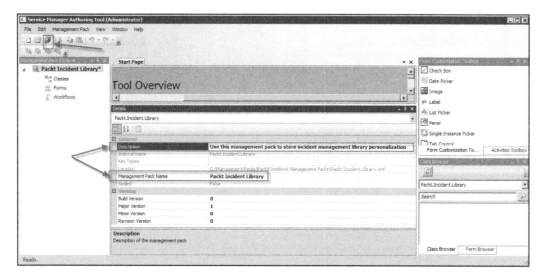

4. Repeat steps 1 – 3 to create additional management packs (for example, Packt.Change.Library).

5. Switch to the SCSM console to import the management pack(s).

6. Navigate to **Administration | Management Packs** and under the task pane on the right-hand side select **Import**:

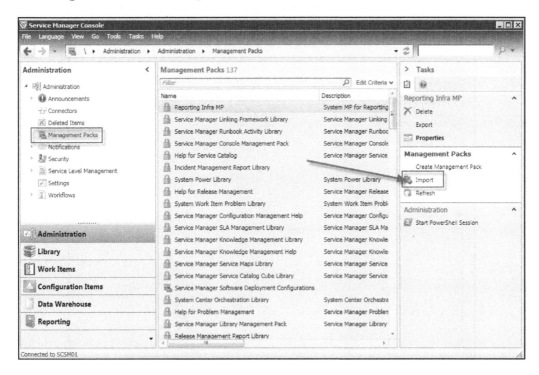

7. Navigate to the management pack file location. Select the management pack(s) to be imported and click on **Open**.

8. In the management pack window click on **Import**. Click on **OK** upon successful import.

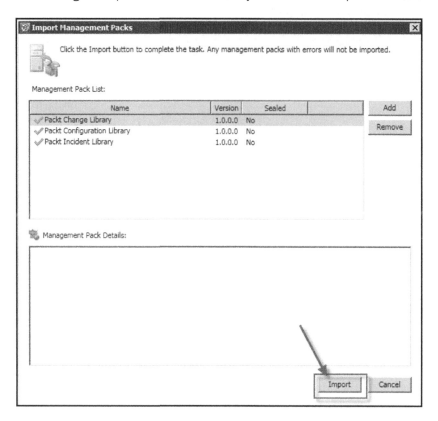

9. This completes the steps to create a management pack and import it into SCSM for personalization.

How it works...

SCSM stores its configuration in management packs. There are three types of management packs:

▶ **Unsealed**: This type of management pack is what you create when you create a management pack in the console, or when you create a management pack in the Authoring tool using the steps outlined in this recipe. Unsealed management packs have an .XML file extension. This type of management pack allows you to save your configuration or delete existing configurations that are stored in them using the SCSM console.

- **Sealed**: This is a management pack that is, in effect, a read-only configuration store. The settings stored in this type of management pack cannot be edited in the SCSM console. You have to store changes to the configuration associated with this MP in an unsealed management pack or edit the original unsealed version of the management pack.

- **Bundle**: This type of management pack is a special type of a sealed MP and has an .MBP file extension. A bundle typically contains more than one MP and associated resources like icons.

There's more...

The process of creating a management pack in the Authoring tool versus using the SCSM console is best practice for two core reasons. They are as follows:

- Initial baseline and standards
- Editing options and flexible customization

Initial baseline and standards

You have the option to create a management pack in the SCSM Console. Management packs created in the console are stored directly in the database. The management packs created in the console are always unsealed. Best practice is to create all your management packs in the Authoring tool. The recommended best practice will ensure you have a standard and proactively provision MPs before embarking on configuration changes.

Editing options and flexible customization

The only option when you create a management pack in the console is the display name and the description. The file name of a management pack that was initially created in the console is by default GUID.XML. Changing the file name can be error prone.

There are additional management pack configurations that can only be performed in the authoring tool (for example, creating a workflow using a PowerShell script with scheduling options).

Plan to use the authoring tool as a default option for creating management packs.

See also

- See *Appendix B, Useful Websites and Community Resources*, for some useful resource links with deep dives into the internals of SCSM Management packs

Creating formatted e-mail notification templates

This recipe discusses the steps required to create a rich text formatted e-mail template.

Getting ready

This procedure requires you to have a copy on Microsoft Word 2007 or above installed. You must be in the SCSM Administrators role and have the SCSM console open.

We will use an incident notification as an example. We will create a template for sending the affected user the following incident details:

- The ID
- Title
- Description
- Status

How to do it...

1. Create a new word document and type the details of the properties using new lines to separate each property:

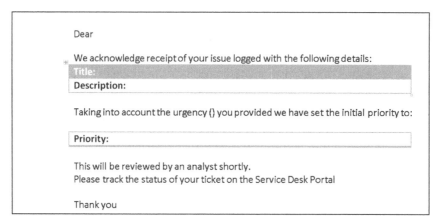

2. Save the file as a web page filtered file:

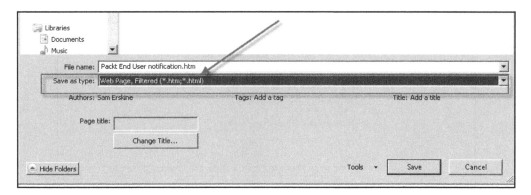

3. Navigate to the file location. Open the file with Notepad and copy the text.

4. Navigate to **SCSM Console | Administration | Notifications | Templates** and select **Create E-Mail Template** from the **Tasks** workspace:

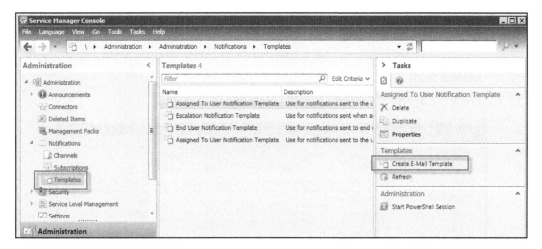

5. Configure the following for the general settings:

   ❏ **Notification template name**: **Packt End User Notification**

   ❏ **Description**: **HTML formatted message for new Incidents**

   ❏ **Target class**: Click on **Browse...** and select **Incident**

   ❏ Management pack: Select a custom management pack (for example, **Packt Incident Library**)

Click on **Next**.

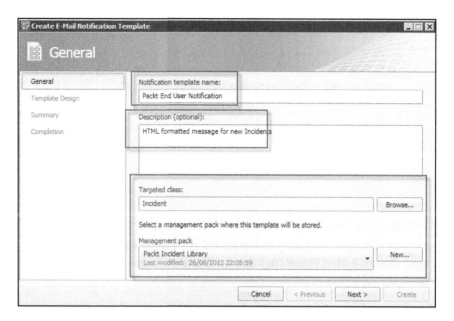

6. Tick the **Send as HTML** checkbox and type a descriptive message in the **Message subject** field.

7. Paste the details from step 3 into the **Message body** field:

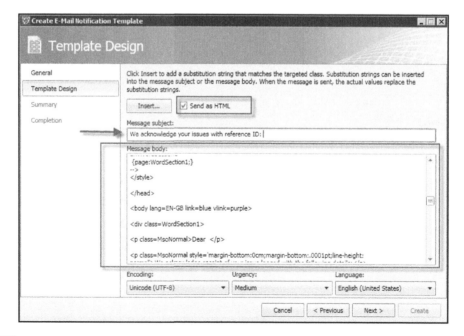

8. Find the various places where you want to insert the properties from the *Getting ready* section of this recipe. Click on **Insert...** to select the property and click on **Add**:

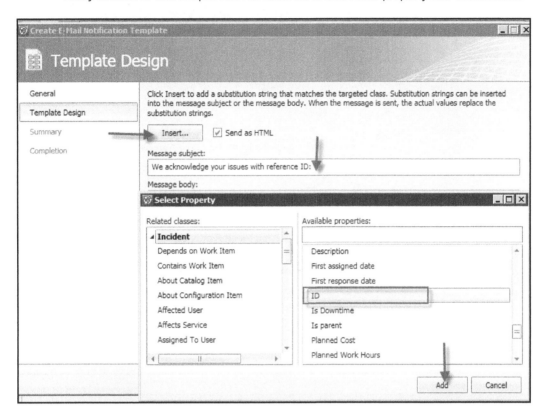

9. Repeat the previous step for all properties in scope:

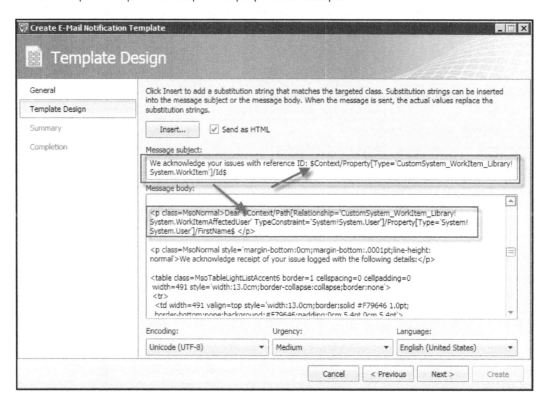

10. Click on **Next**. Verify the details and click on **Create**.

11. The template is created for use and can be selected for incident class notifications. For example, sending an e-mail to the affected user.

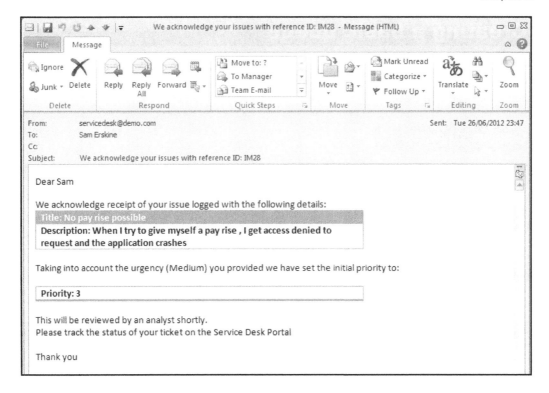

How it works...

By default, the e-mail notification templates you create in the SCSM console do not get formatted as HTML. This applies even if you select the **Send as HTML** option.

You have two choices if you want the message to be in true HTML format:

► Manually type the HTML tags to format the message

► Use an HTML capable editor to save the format as described in the recipe steps

See also

► The *Creating notifications for SLA warning and breaches* recipe in *Chapter 3, Configuring Service Level Agreements (SLAs)* discusses SLA notification and provides examples of using the notification templates you create

Creating a basic queue

This recipe details the steps for creating a SCSM queue. Queues in SCSM are specific to each process. You cannot combine classes, so in this example we will create a queue for a support group called *Service Desk*.

Getting ready

You need to ensure you have successfully installed the SCSM product, are a user in the SCSM Administrator's role, and have the SCSM console open.

Follow the list creation instructions in *Chapter 6, Working with Incident and Problem Management*, to create a new list item for the *Incident Tier Queue* list called *Service Desk*.

How to do it...

1. Open the SCSM Console. Navigate to **Library | Queues** and click on **Create Queue**:

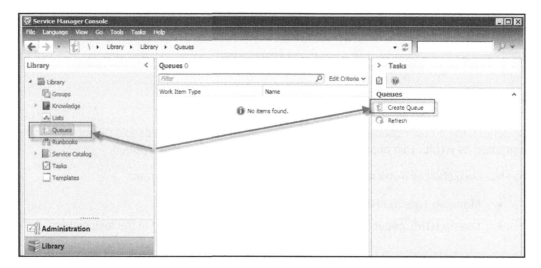

2. Click on **Next**. Provide a queue name and description.
3. Under **Work item type**, Click on **...** and select **Incident** as the work item type.
4. Under **Management pack** select a custom management pack (for example, **Packt Incident Library**). Click on **Next**.

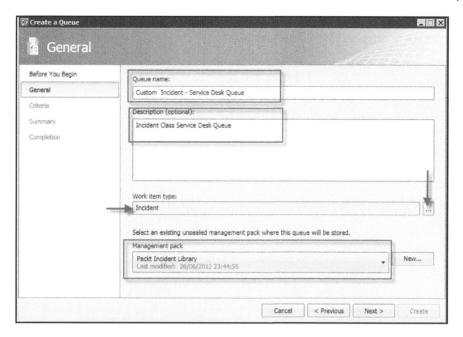

5. For the criteria, select **Support Group** under available properties on the right and click on **Add**:

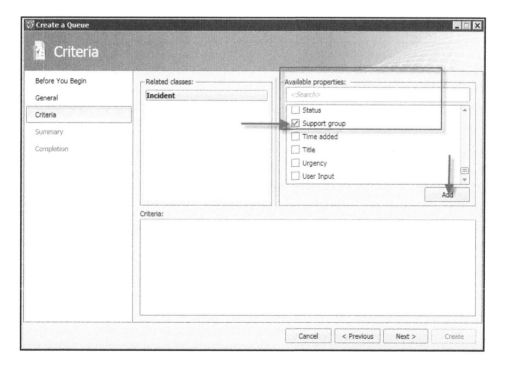

6. Set **Criteria** to **equals Service Desk**. Click on **Next**. Review **Summary** and click on **Create** to complete the Queue creation.

How it works...

In SCSM what you see in the console are called views. How much of what you see depends on your role and what your queue is allowed to see.

Think about a "Queue to a View". When you create a queue for a specific class (for example, incidents), you are able to filter and restrict what the users who match the queue criteria can see in the console, and what actions they can perform.

In the example steps, we can create a new Incident role where only the Service Desk queue is selected. This would have the effect of only showing users associated with that role incidents, with the support group set to Service Desk.

See also

► The *Creating Priority Queues* recipe in *Chapter 3, Configuring Service Level Agreements (SLAs)* for other scenarios related to the use of queues

3

Configuring Service Level Agreements (SLAs)

In this chapter we will provide recipes to tailor Service Manager to your environment. Specifically, we will cover the area of setting up the SLA functions of Service Manager with the following tasks:

- ▶ Creating Priority Queues
- ▶ Configuring business hours and non-working days
- ▶ Creating SLA metrics
- ▶ Creating Service Level Objectives
- ▶ Creating Incident Management SLAs
- ▶ Creating Service Request SLAs
- ▶ Viewing SLA warning and breaches
- ▶ Creating notifications for SLA warning and breaches
- ▶ Creating repeated notifications before SLA breaches with escalation

Introduction

Service Level Agreements in ITIL© and IT Service Management terms allow two parties to set out an agreement on how a specific service will be delivered by one to the other.

In this chapter we will provide recipes to configure Service Manager 2012's SLA engine. We will define how it will handle the tracking of Incidents and Service Requests against defined SLAs, how to view the progress of work items against these SLAs and how to configure Service Manager 2012 to alert users when work items are nearing, or have breached, these Service Level Agreements.

As with most areas of configuration within Service Manager 2012, the organization must define its processes before implementing the Service Manager feature. For example, this chapter assumes that Service Level Agreements are already in place and agreed with your customers and metrics relating to areas such as resolution time or response times, mapped to priorities are defined.

Creating Priority Queues

This recipe will define a number of queues related to your defined priority for work items such as incidents and service requests. These queues will then be mapped to Service Level Objectives (SLO).

Getting ready

For this recipe it is required that you have already followed the *Configuring Priority and Urgency for your SLA targets* recipe in *Chapter 2, Personalizing SCSM 2012 Administration* for configuring your priority matrix according to the Impact and Urgency definitions of your organization and that you have custom management packs in place to store your queue customizations.

How to do it...

The following steps will guide you through the process of creating priority queues:

1. Navigate to the **Queues** folder in the **Library** section of the **Service Manager 2012** console.

2. Choose **Create Queue** from the taskbar on the right-hand side of the console.

3. Review the information on the **Before You Begin** screen of the **Create Queue Wizard** and click on **Next**.

4. Enter a queue name that describes the queue. In this example, we will name it `Incident SLA Queue - Priority 1` to describe a queue holding Incidents with a priority of 1. Then click on the **...** selection button next to the **Work item type** textbox.

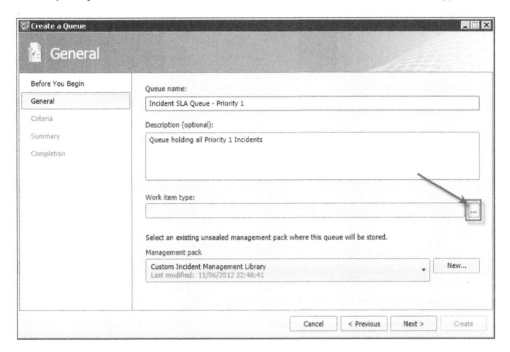

5. Use the filter box to scope the choices down to Incident Work Items, choose **Incident** and then click **OK**.

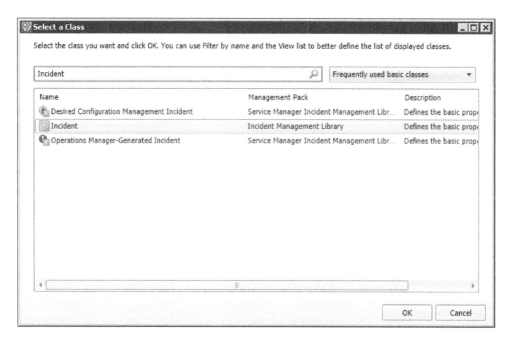

6. Choose your custom Incident Management Pack from the selection list and click on **Next**.

 Refer to *Chapter 2, Personalizing SCSM 2012 Administration* for more information on custom management packs.

7. Use the **Search** box under **Available properties** to scope the list down to **Priority**. Tick the box next to **Priority** and then click on **Add**.

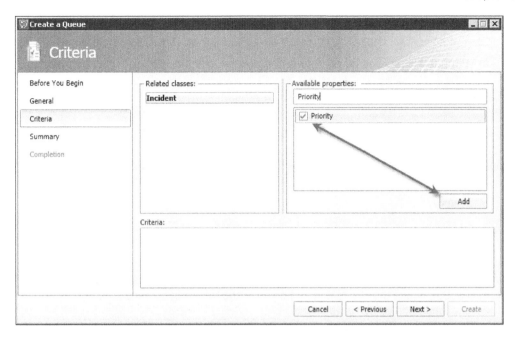

8. Change the criteria for **[Trouble Ticket] Priority** using the drop-down list to **equals** and supply the Priority value, in this example we will give a value of 1. Click on **Next**.

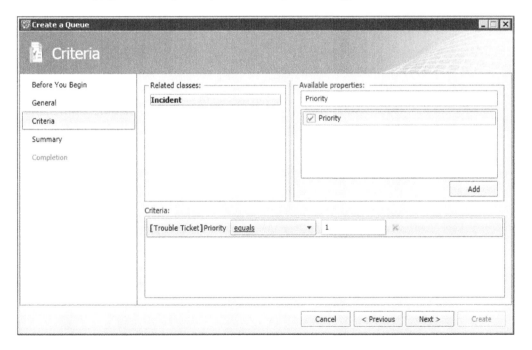

9. Review the **Summary** screen of the wizard and then click on **Create**.

10. You have now successfully created a queue. Click on **Close** to complete the wizard.

11. Repeat this process for each priority you want to link an SLO to.

How it works...

Creating a queue allows Service Manager to group similar work items that meet specified criteria, such as all Incidents with a priority of 1. Service Manager can use these queues to scope actions. Using this grouping of work items we have a target to apply an SLO to.

There's more...

This recipe requires you to repeat the steps for each priority you would like to apply an SLO to.

Repeat each step, but change key information such as the name, priority value, and description to reflect the priority you are creating the queue for. For example, for an Incident Priority 3 queue, make the changes as reflected in the following screenshots:

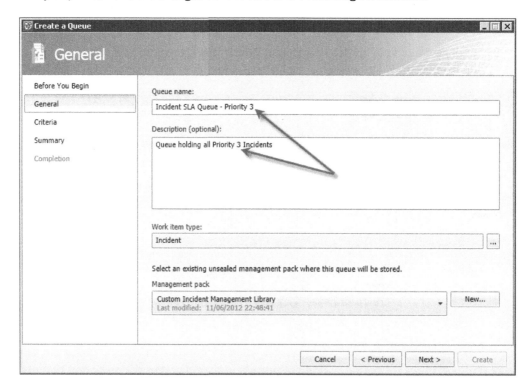

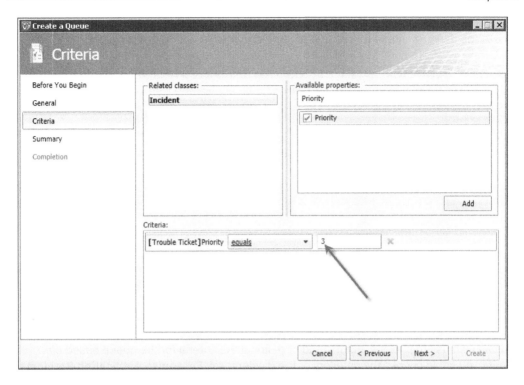

Service Request queues

Queues can be created to define any type of grouping of supported process work items in scope for SLA management.

For example, you may wish to repeat this recipe for the Service Request process class.

Repeat the recipe but select **Service Request** as the work item type in the wizard, and then choose the defining criteria for the queue related to the Service Request class.

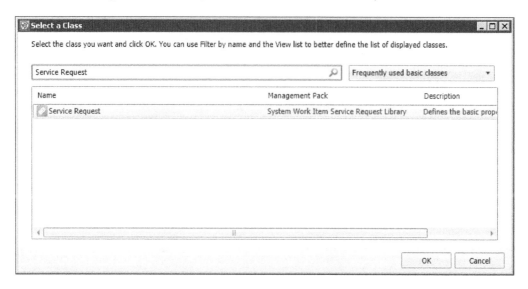

You can also use this recipe, but instead of defining the criteria for the queue based on priority, you could choose the category of the incident, say **Enterprise Application Problems**.

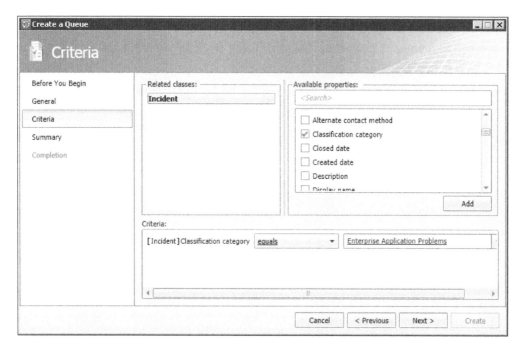

Further queue types

If the incident class was extended to capture whether the affected user was a VIP, you would be able to define a VIP queue and give those work items matching that criteria a different resolution time SLA.

See also

> ▸ The *Configuring Priority and Urgency for your SLA targets* recipe in *Chapter 2, Personalizing SCSM 2012 Administration*
>
> ▸ The *Creating Management Packs in the Authoring tool to save your SCSM personalization* recipe in *Chapter 2, Personalizing SCSM 2012 Administration*

Configuring business hours and non-working days

This recipe will define the hours that your business offers IT services, which allows calculation of resolution and response times against SLAs.

Getting ready

For this recipe it is required that you have already assessed the business hours that your IT services will offer to your organization, and that you have custom management packs in place to store your queue customizations.

How to do it...

The following steps will guide you through the process of configuring business hours and non-working days within Service Manager:

1. Under **Administration**, expand **Service Level Management** and then click on **Calendar**.
2. Under **Tasks** on the right-hand side of the screen click on **Create Calendar**.

3. Give the calendar a meaningful name, in this example we have used `Core Business Hours`:

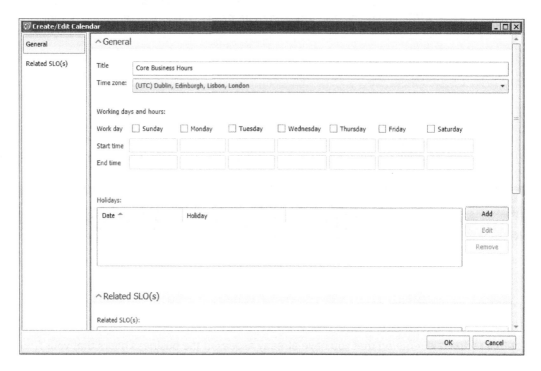

4. Choose the relevant time zone.

5. Place a check mark against all the days for which you offer services.

6. Under each working day enter a start time and an end time in the 00:00:00 format, for example 8 am should be entered as 08:00:00.

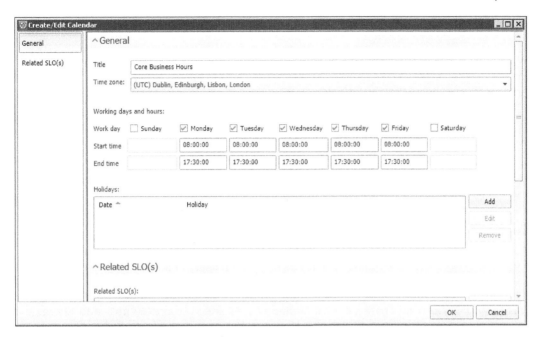

7. You can also specify the non-working days using the **Holidays** section; under the **Holidays** pane, click on **Add**.

8. In the **Add Holiday** window that opens enter a name for the Holiday, for example, Christmas Day.

9. Either manually enter the date in the format relevant for your regional settings (for example, for the United Kingdom regional settings use DD/MM/YYYY) or use the visual calendar by clicking on the button to the right of the date entry textbox.

10. Click on **OK** for each holiday, once all holidays have been added, click on **OK** to close the **Create/Edit Calendar** window.

How it works...

When you specify the business hours and non-working days, Service Manager will take these into consideration when calculating SLA metrics, such as resolution time and first response time for all work items that are affected by the calendar.

There's more...

A calendar on its own has no impact on service levels. The calendar is one part of the Service Level Objective configuration. The rest of this chapter provides additional recipes to complete the configuration.

Add holidays in bulk

Adding holidays manually can be a very time consuming process. Our co-author Anders Asp has automated the process using PowerShell to import a list of holidays.

You can download the script and read about the process on the TechNet Gallery at `http://gallery.technet.microsoft.com/Generate-SCSMHolidaysCSVps1-a32722ce`.

Creating SLA metrics

Using SLA metrics in Service Manager we can define what is measured within an SLA. For this recipe we will show how to create a metric to measure the resolution time of an Incident.

How to do it...

The following steps will guide you through the process of creating SLA metrics in Service Manager:

1. Under **Administration**, expand **Service Level Management** and then click on **Metric**.
2. Under **Tasks** on the right-hand side of the screen click on **Create Metric**.
3. Supply a title for the metric. In this example we will use `Resolution Time` and a description.
4. Click on the **Browse...** button next to the class field and use the filter box in the **Select a Class** window that opens to select **Incident**. Click on **OK**.
5. Use the drop-down list for **Start Date** and choose **Created date**.
6. Use the drop-down list for **End Date** and choose **Resolved date**.

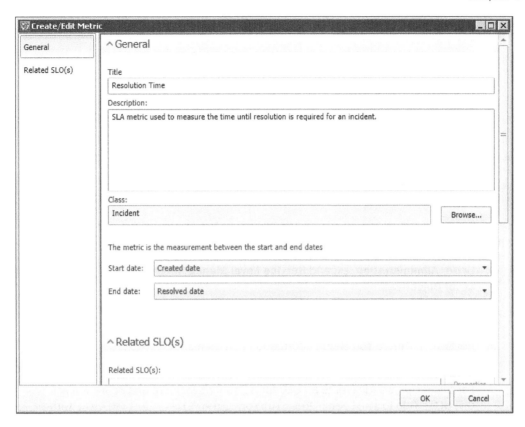

7. Click on **OK**.

How it works...

Creating a metric defines what you want Service Manager to track, within your SLA definition. So when an item falls outside the parameters, you can start a notification and escalation process.

Creating Service Level Objectives

This recipe will show you how to create a Service Level Objective, which is used within Service Manager to create the relationships between the queues, service levels, calendars, and metrics. The SLO will define the timings to trigger warnings or breaches of service levels.

Getting ready

To create an SLO you will need to have already created the following:

- ▸ Queues that correspond to each service level
- ▸ Metrics to measure differences in start and end times of an incident
- ▸ Calendar to define business working hours

You will also need custom management packs in place to store your SLO customizations.

How to do it...

The following steps will guide you through the process of creating service level objectives within Service Manager:

1. Under **Administration**, expand **Service Level Management** and then click on **Service Level Objectives**.

2. Under **Tasks**, on the right-hand side of the screen, click on **Create Service Level Objective**.

3. Review the **Before You Begin** information and then click on **Next**.

4. Provide a title and description relevant to the Service Level Objective you are creating.

   For this recipe we will create an SLO for a Priority 1 Incident and so we will set this SLO's Title to `Incident Resolution Time SLO - Priority 1` with a meaningful description.

5. Click on the **Browse...** button next to the **Class** textbox and use the filter box in the **Select a Class** window that opens to select **Incident**. Click on **OK**.

6. Use the drop-down list under the **Management pack** heading to select your custom management pack for storing SLA related customizations to.

7. If you are planning to use this SLO immediately then leave the **Enabled** checkbox ticked. Only untick this if you plan to create/stage SLOs before setting up SLA functions.

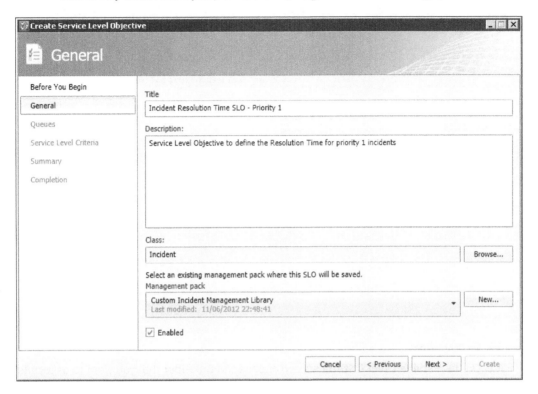

8. Click on **Next**.

9. Choose the queue you created previously in the *Creating Priority Queues* recipe of this chapter, which relates to the priority of incidents for this SLO.

In this recipe example use the queue named **Incident SLA Queue – Priority 1**.

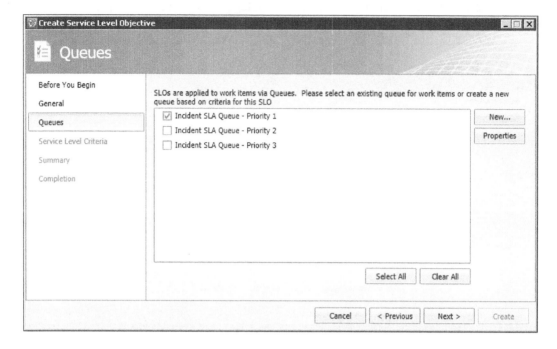

10. Click on **Next**.

11. On the **Service Level Criteria** screen choose the **Calendar** that you want to associate this SLO with.

    For this recipe example choose the **Business Hours** calendar that was created during the *Configuring business hours and non-working days* recipe in this chapter.

12. Under **Metric**, use the drop-down list to select the time metric you wish to measure against.

    Following along with the examples, select the **Resolution Time** metric.

13. Define the target time period before a breach would occur for this metric by entering a value under target.

    For our Priority 1 Resolution, enter **4 Hours** to define the time period before an incident would change to a breach SLA status.

14. Define the target time period before a warning would occur for this metric by entering a value under **Warning threshold**.

For our Priority 1 Resolution, enter **2 Hours** to define the time period before an incident would change to a warning SLA status.

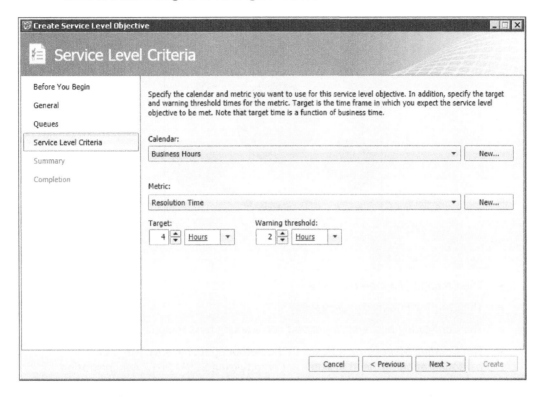

15. Click on **Next**.

16. Review the Information on the **Summary** page and when ready click on **Create**.

17. Once the SLO has been created and a successful message is displayed, click on **Close**.

How it works...

When you configure a Service Level Objective (SLO), you're pulling together three components, Queues, Calendars, and Metrics. These three components are defined and illustrated as follows:

▸ **Queues**: Work items this SLO will be applied to

▸ **Calendar**: Days and hours that services are offered on

▸ **Metric**: Items that are measured

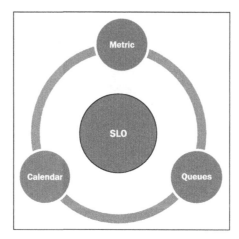

See also

▸ The *Creating SLA metrics* recipe

▸ The *Creating Priority Queues* recipe

▸ The *Configuring business hours and non-working days* recipe

▸ The *Creating Management Packs in the Authoring tool to save your SCSM personalization* recipe in *Chapter 2, Personalizing SCSM 2012 Administration*

Creating Incident Management SLAs

Service Manager has different classes of work items for which SLAs can be configured. This recipe will show how to set up SLA management of the Incident class for two common SLA categories, First Response Time and Resolution Time.

Getting ready

You should be familiar with the following recipes:

▸ *Creating SLA metrics*

▸ *Creating Priority Queues*

▸ *Configuring business hours and non-working days*

▸ *Creating Service Level Objectives*

▸ *Creating Management Packs in the Authoring tool to save your SCSM personalization* in *Chapter 2, Personalizing SCSM 2012 Administration*

How to do it...

The following steps will guide you through the process of creating the incident management SLAs.

Resolution time SLA

Perform the following recipes in this order:

1. **Creating Priority Queues**: Repeat the *Creating Priority Queues* recipe until you have a queue for each priority, usually this will be 5 queues for Priority 1 – 5 Incident types. Each time you create a new queue, ensure that the name, description, and value for priority change to reflect the priority.

2. **Configuring business hours and non-working days**: Only one calendar is required, based on the hours/days that you provide Incident Management services to your customers.

3. **Creating SLA metrics**: Use the example in the recipe for Resolution Time based on Created Date and Resolved Date.

4. **Creating Service Level Objectives**: Create a SLO for each priority; usually this will be 5 SLOs for Priority 1 – 5 Incident types. Each time you create a new SLO ensure that the name and description change to reflect the priority it is based upon and ensure that the correct priority queue is also selected.

   For each SLO, you will need to supply a target and warning threshold value. The following table shows common values that can be used, but it should reflect your organizations specifically defined requirements and/or agreements with your customers:

Priority	Target	Warning threshold
Priority 1	4 hours	2 hours
Priority 2	8 hours	4 hours
Priority 3	24 hours	12 hours
Priority 4	80 hours	40 hours
Priority 5	160 hours	80 hours

First Response Time SLA

Perform the following recipes in this order:

1. **Creating Priority Queues**: Keep repeating the *Creating Priority Queues* recipe until you have a queue for each priority, usually this will be 5 queues for Priority 1 – 5 Incident types. Each time you create a new queue, ensure that the name and description change to reflect the priority. You may have already created the queues for the Resolution Time SLA configuration. You can reuse the same queues; do not set up new queues based on the same priorities just with new names for response time SLAs.

2. **Configuring business hours and non-working days**: Only one calendar is required, based on the hours/days that you provide Incident Management services to your customers. Again the same calendar used for the Resolution Time SLA configuration can be reused.

3. **Creating SLA metrics**: Follow the recipe but instead of using Created Date and Resolved Date this time use the following:

   ❑ Start date:- Created date

   ❑ End date:- First Response date

4. **Creating Service Level Objectives**: Create a SLO for each priority; usually this will be 5 SLOs for Priority 1 – 5 Incident types. Each time you create a new SLO ensure that the name and description change to reflect the priority it is based upon and ensure that the correct priority queue is also selected. Select the First Response Time metric you created in the previous step.

   For each SLO, you will need to supply a target and warning threshold value. The following table shows common values that can be used, but should reflect your organizations specifically defined requirements and/or agreements with your customers.

Priority	Target	Warning threshold
Priority 1	30 minutes	15 minutes
Priority 2	2 hours	1 hours
Priority 3	8 hours	4 hours
Priority 4	16 hours	8 hours
Priority 5	24 hours	12 hours

How it works...

By defining the different parts that make up your organizations requirements and tying them together with a SLO, Service Manager now enables you to model your SLA requirements and keep track of how the service is performing. The ability to measure when incidents are nearing or have breached their SLA allows for escalations to be put in place, preferably before a breach, and for notifications to be sent to those people that need to be informed.

Creating Service Request SLAs

Service Manager has different classes of work items for which SLAs can be configured. This recipe will show how to set up SLA management for the Service Request class scoped to Implementation Time.

Getting ready

Be familiar with the following recipes:

- ▸ *Creating SLA metrics*
- ▸ *Creating Priority Queues*
- ▸ *Configuring business hours and non-working days*
- ▸ *Creating Service Level Objectives*
- ▸ *Creating Management Packs in the Authoring tool to save your SCSM personalization* in *Chapter 2, Personalizing SCSM 2012 Administration*

How to do it...

We will refer to the previous recipes. The main change is to ensure the work item class, where referenced, is changed to target the **Service Request** class as shown in the following screenshot:

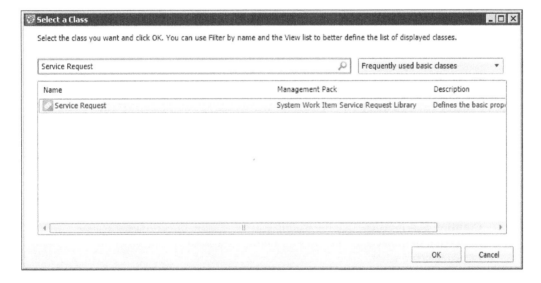

Implementation Time SLA

Perform the following recipes in this order:

1. **Creating Priority Queues**: Follow the *Creating Priority Queues* recipe, but each time you create a new queue ensure that the name and description are changed to reflect the priority and that they are for Service Requests.

   Ensure that during the creation the class is changed to Service Request.

   This will give you a different choice of priority for Service Requests.

With incidents you specified a numeric value. With Service Requests, use the drop-down selection list to choose the priority of **Low**, **Medium**, **High**, or **Immediate**.

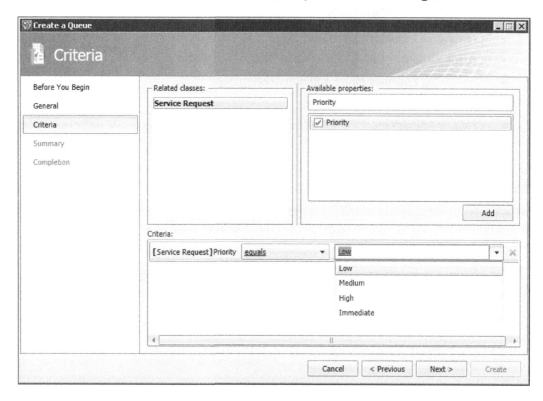

2. **Configuring business hours and non-working days**: Only one calendar is required based on the hours/days that you provide Service Request services to your customers. This could be the same calendar used for Incident Management, depending on your individual organization.

3. **Creating SLA metrics**: Use the example in the recipe, but change the class to **Service Request** and **End date:** to **Completed Date**, as shown in the following screenshot:

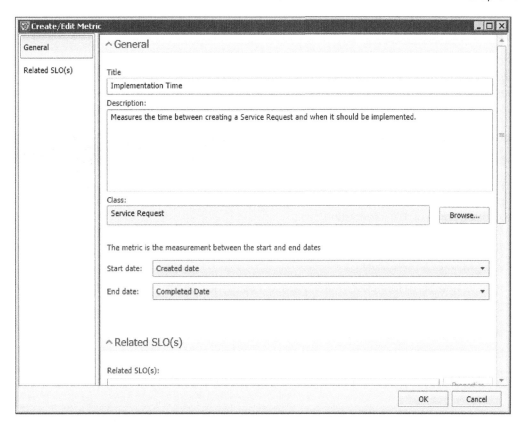

4. **Creating Service Level Objectives**: Create a SLO for each priority; usually this will be 4 SLOs for Priority **Low**, **Medium**, **High**, or **Immediate** Service Request types. Each time you create a new SLO ensure that the name and description change to reflect the respective Service Request SLO and its' Priority. Ensure that the correct priority queue for Service Requests is also selected.

    For each SLO, you will need to supply a target and warning threshold value. The following table shows common values that can be used, but should reflect your organization's specifically defined requirements and/or agreements with your customers.

Priority	Target	Warning threshold
Immediate	4 hours	2 hours
High	8 hours	4 hours
Medium	24 hours	12 hours
Low	48 hours	24 hours

How it works...

By defining the different parts that make up your organization's requirements and tying them together with a SLO, Service Manager now enables you to model your SLA requirements and keep track of how the service is performing. This recipe provides steps to implement Service Request specific SLAs using the unique properties of the service request process.

Viewing SLA warning and breaches

After setting up SLAs within Service Manager it would be rather useful to actually see how work items are performing against the SLAs you've defined. There are a few places where we can see some of this information.

Getting ready

In order to view SLA information in the SCSM console, you need to have completed the previous recipes in this chapter.

How to do it...

The following steps will guide you through the process of viewing SLA warnings and breaches within Service Manager:

1. Navigate to the **Work Items** node of the console, expand the **Incident Management** folder, and then click on **Incidents with Service Level Breached**.

2. This should display a list of all incidents that have breached their SLA in the center of the console.

3. Highlight an incident and either double-click it or choose **Edit** from the tasks pane on the right-hand side.

4. When the breached incident form opens it should be immediately obvious that there has been a breach of SLA on this incident from the yellow bar that is now present and the red exclamation mark next to the **Service Level** tab, as shown in the following screenshot:

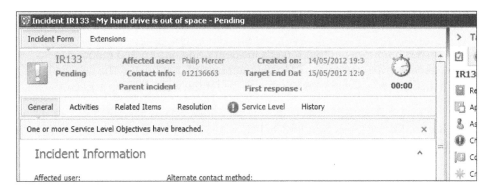

5. Clicking on the **Service Level** tab allows you to see more information related to the SLA, as shown in the following screenshot:

6. Depending on how the incident has been routed and the SLAs defined within you organization, it is possible to see multiple Service Levels displayed.

How it works...

Once a queue has been defined that target's incident's and has an SLO mapped to that queue, service levels are assigned to the members of that queue. The service level information is made available within the forms for the work items in scope of the configuration.

By default Service Manager has two views to help with Service Level monitoring/management: **Incidents with Service Level Breached** and **Incidents with Service Level Warning**.

There's more...

Service Manager provides you with the ability to display SLA information in a color-coded format.

RAG status in console

You can create custom views to get what is known as a Red, Amber, Green (RAG) status in the main console without having to open each incident.

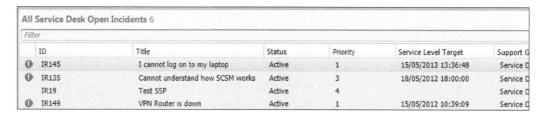

	ID	Title	Status	Priority	Service Level Target	Support G
		All Service Desk Open Incidents 6				
		Filter				
ⓘ	IR145	I cannot log on to my laptop	Active	1	15/05/2012 13:36:48	Service D
ⓘ	IR135	Cannot understand how SCSM works	Active	3	18/05/2012 18:00:00	Service D
	IR19	Test SSP	Active	4		Service D
ⓘ	IR149	VPN Router is down	Active	1	15/05/2012 10:39:09	Service D

Creating notifications for SLA warning and breaches

This recipe will show you how to configure Service Manager to send an e-mail notification when a work item moves into either an SLA warning or breach state.

Getting ready

Ensure Service Levels are fully configured by following the previous recipes in this chapter.

It is also assumed that you have set up an SMTP channel for e-mail.

How to do it...

The following steps will guide you through the process of creating notifications within Service Manager for when an SLA goes into warning or breach:

1. Navigate to the **Administration** node of the **Service Manager** console, expand the **Notifications** folder and click on **Templates**.

2. Click on **Create E-Mail Template** in the tasks pane on the right-hand side of the console.

3. Provide a title for the template and a description.

4. Click on the **Browse** button next to the targeted class box.

5. In the **Select a Class** window, use the drop-down box next to the search filter to change it from **Frequently used basic classes** to **All basic classes** and then filter the list to find **Service Level Instance Time Information**.

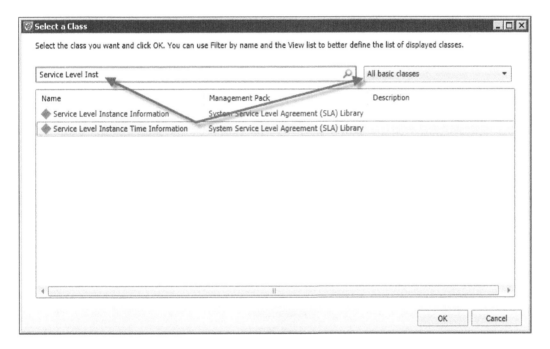

6. Choose the relevant custom management pack to store this customization in and click on **Next**.

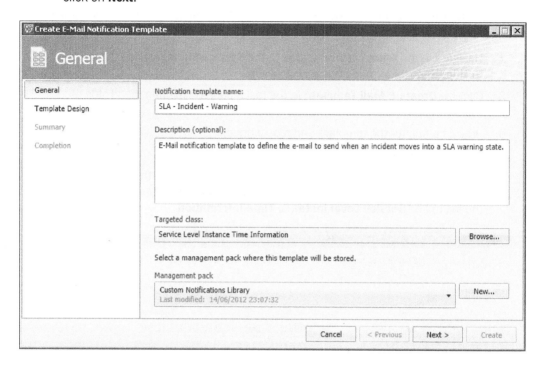

7. You can now design the template for the e-mail, including what information you would like to include.

   You can type custom text or you can use the **Insert...** button to insert Tokens or a combination of both.

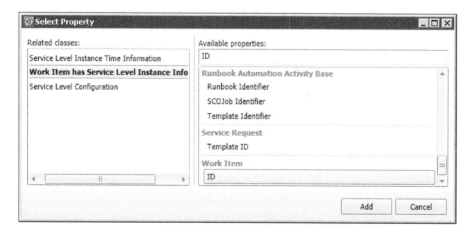

These tokens will dynamically resolve to information stored within Service Manager. For example, using the **Select Property** screen that opens and choosing **ID** under the **Work Item has Service Level Instance Information** Work Item will provide this token string back to the e-mail template design screen:

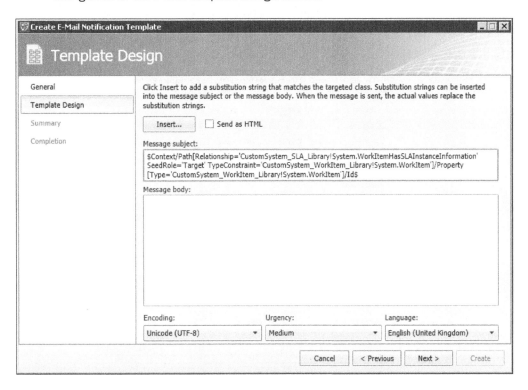

This long text will actually resolve the ID of the affected work item with the SLA breach, so if it was an incident the ID might be IR324 for example.

If you intend to use the Exchange Connector with Service Manager then it is advisable to wrap any incident IDs with square brackets for example, [IR324].

To do this just add the opening bracket "[" before the token and the closing bracket "]" after the token.

For example, using the token shown in the screenshot this would now look like the following:

```
[$Context/Path[Relationship='CustomSystem_SLA_Library!System.WorkI
temHasSLAInstanceInformation'SeedRole='Target'TypeConstraint='Cust
omSystem_SLA_Library!System.WorkItem']/Property[Type=CustomSystem_
SLA_Library!System.WorkItem]/Id$]
```

8. Add more meaningful text around any tokens used, for example in the message subject before the Work Item ID add something meaningful such as `SLA Warning - Incident:`.

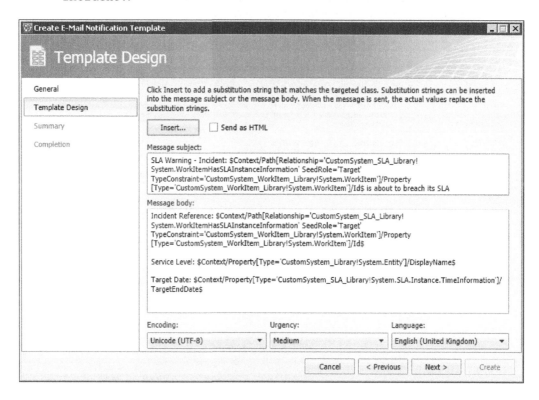

9. Click on **Next** when editing of the content is complete.

10. Review the **Summary** screen and click on **Create**.

11. Once it is completed click on **Close**.

12. Navigate to the **Administration** node of the **Service Manager** console, expand the **Notifications** folder and click on **Subscriptions**.

13. Click on **Create Subscription** in the tasks pane on the right-hand side of the console.

14. Click on **Next** on the **Before You Begin** screen.

15. Provide a title and a description for the subscription.

16. Use the drop-down list for **When to notify** and choose **When an object of the selected class is updated**.

17. Change the **Targeted** class to **Service Level Instance Time Information** using the **Browse...** button.

18. Select your custom management pack to store this subscription in and click on **Next**.

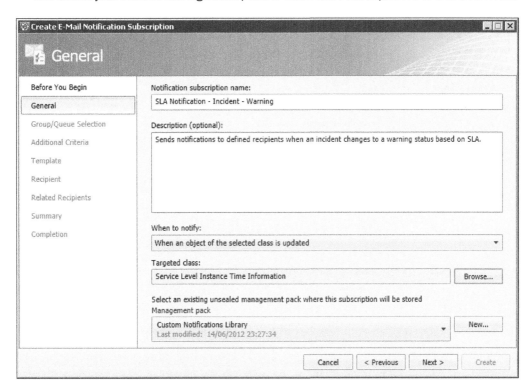

19. You can select specific groups/queues if it applies in your case, but we will skip it here and go to the additional criteria by clicking on **Next**.

   There are two tabs on the **Additional Criteria** screen, **Changed From** and **Changed To**.

20. In the **Changed From** tab filter the properties down to find **Status** and add it as a criterion.

21. Change the validation from **equals** to **does not equal** and set the value as **Warning**.

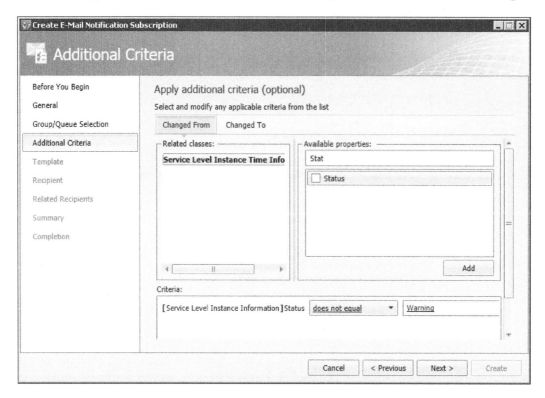

22. On the **Changed To** tab filter the properties down to find **Status** and add it as a criterion.

23. Set the value for the criteria to **Warning**.

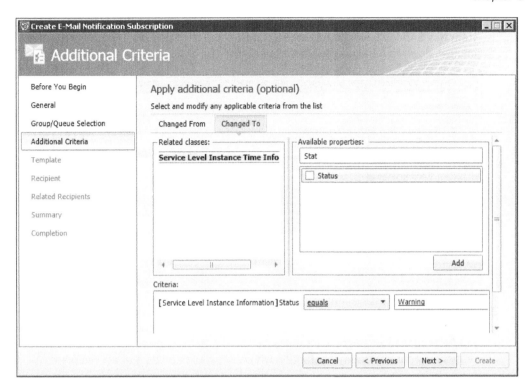

24. Click on **Next**.

25. Click on the **Select Button**, choose the e-mail notification template you created earlier in this recipe, and then click on **OK**. Click on **Next**.

26. You can either specify certain recipients to receive this notification by selecting their domain accounts from the CMDB, or click on **Next** to set up dynamic recipients.

27. Related recipients is a new feature for the 2012 release and allows you to use relational information within the CMDB. For example, you can send the same notifications to secondary recipients.

28. Click on **Add**. On the **Select Related Recipient** screen click on **[Work Item] Work Item has Service Level Instance Information** and then use the filter to narrow the choices down to **Assigned To User**. Select this and click on **Add**.

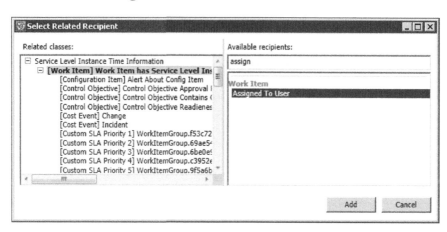

29. This adds a more dynamic nature to the e-mail subscriptions and provides flexibility. For example, we might want warning mails going to the assigned user for the incident, but for breaches we might want mails sent to the primary owner and the person responsible for customer satisfaction whom we would add as a direct recipient.

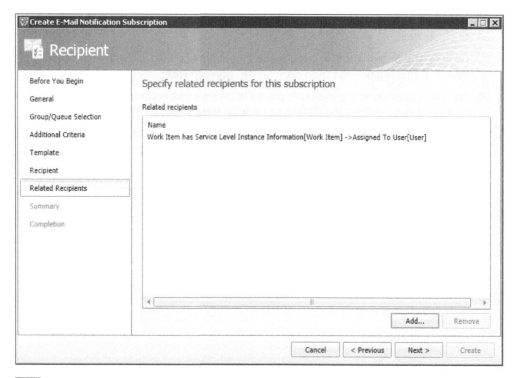

30. Click on **Next**.

31. Review the **Summary** screen and click on **Create**.

32. Once created click on **Close**.

How it works...

We created a template that defined the information and layout of the message we want to send and then we created a subscription that defines what event (change of SLA status to warning) causes the e-mail to be sent and to whom.

There's more...

This recipe can be followed for breaches of SLA rather than just warning, except for a couple of key changes.

Notification for breaches

When setting the additional criteria, we need the **Changed From** criteria setting as **equals Warning** and the **Changed To** criteria setting as **equals Breached**.

You must create a specific e-mail notification template just for breaches. Be sure to choose this template when creating the subscription.

Also, ensure names and descriptions are reflective of the intent of the notification.

Creating repeated notifications before SLA breaches with escalation

This recipe will show you how to set up a notification for incidents that are in a warning SLA status and send repeated notifications before a breach occurs, including sending a notification to an escalation point.

Getting ready

It would be advisable to perform the *Creating notifications for SLA warning and breaches* recipe in this chapter first, as some of the principles are the same.

It is also assumed that you have set up an SMTP channel for e-mail.

How to do it...

The following steps will guide you through the process of creating notifications that repeat before an SLA breach occurs, along with escalation:

1. Navigate to the **Administration** node of the **Service Manager** console, expand the **Notifications** folder and click on **Templates**.

2. Click on **Create E-Mail Template** in the tasks pane on the right-hand side of the console.

3. Provide a title and a description for the template.

4. Click on the **Browse...** button next to the targeted class box.

5. In the **Select a Class** window filter the list to find the **Incident** class, select it and click on **OK**.

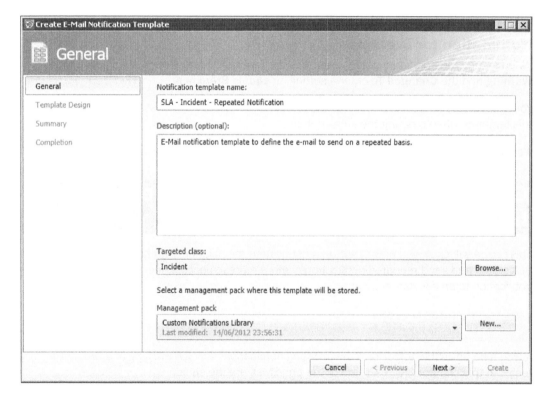

6. Choose the relevant custom management pack to store this customization in and click on **Next**.

7. You can now design the template for the e-mail, including what information you would like to include.

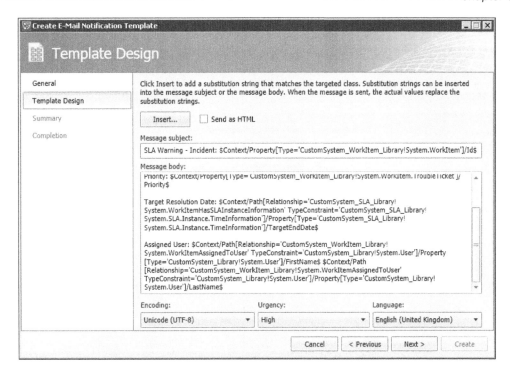

8. Click on **Next** when the content is complete.

9. Review the **Summary** screen and click on **Create**.

10. Once it is completed click on **Close**.

11. Navigate to the **Administration** node of the **Service Manager** console, expand the **Notifications** folder and click on **Subscriptions**.

12. Click on **Create Subscription** in the tasks pane on the right-hand side of the console.

13. Click on **Next** on the **Before You Begin** screen.

14. Provide a title and a description for the subscription.

    For repeated notifications for incidents you will need to configure one subscription for each priority queue, so adjust the subscription name appropriately.

15. Use the drop-down list for **When to notify:** and choose **Periodically notify when objects meet a criteria**.

16. Change the **Targeted class** value to **Incident** using the **Browse...** button.

17. Select your custom management pack to store this subscription in and click on **Next**.

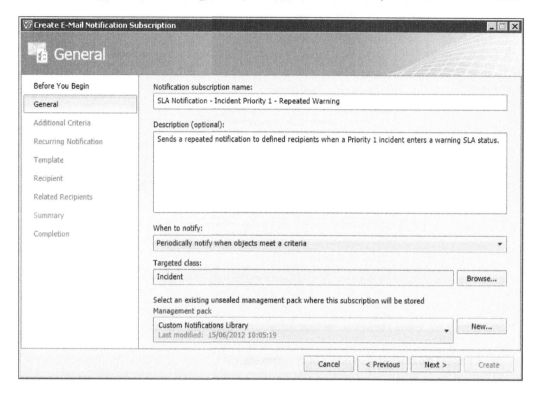

18. In the **Additional Criteria** tab filter the properties down to find **Priority** and add it as a criteria.

19. Change the validation to **equals** and set the value as 1.

20. Expand **Incident** in the **Related classes** window and scroll down to select **Work Item has Service Level Instance Information**.

21. Filter the available properties to find **Status** and add that as a criterion.

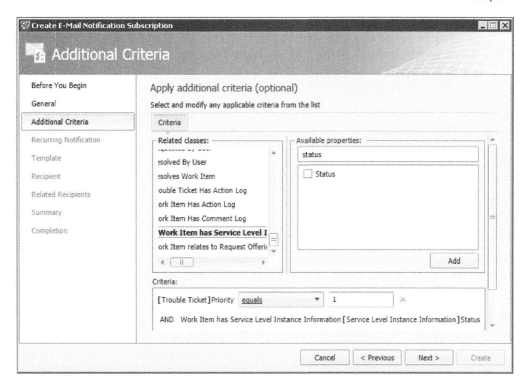

22. Change the value for **Work Item has Service Level Instance Information** to **equals Warning**.

23. Click on **Next**.

24. Depending on your **Priority time** definitions, set the frequency of the recurrence of the notification.

    In previous recipes in this chapter, we defined our Priority 1 SLA to be a warning state after 15 minutes and breach after 30 minutes.

This means I have a 15 minute time period after the incident changes to warning and before it breaches SLA, so it would be best to send a notification every three minutes for a total of four times. There isn't any point in sending a fifth notification, as that would be on or after 15 minutes at which point a breach notification should be sent, and not another warning mail.

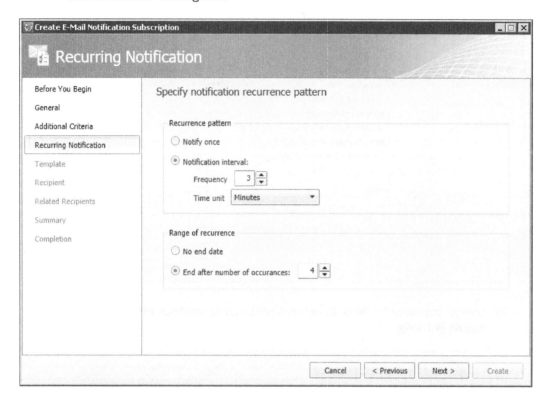

25. Click on **Next**.

26. Click on the **Select** button, choose the e-mail notification template you created earlier in this recipe, and click on **OK**. Then, click on **Next**.

27. You can either specify particular recipients to receive this notification by selecting their domain accounts from the CMDB, or click next to set up dynamic recipients.

28. Related recipients is a new feature for the 2012 release and allows you to use relational information within the CMDB. For example, you can send the same notifications to secondary recipients.

29. Click on **Add** and on the **Select Related Recipient** screen filter the available choices to **Assigned To User**. Select this and click on **Add**.

At this point we can also add in some escalation notifications by also adding for example the Primary Owner of the incident who may be a Line Manager, Service Desk Manager, or Team Leader for example.

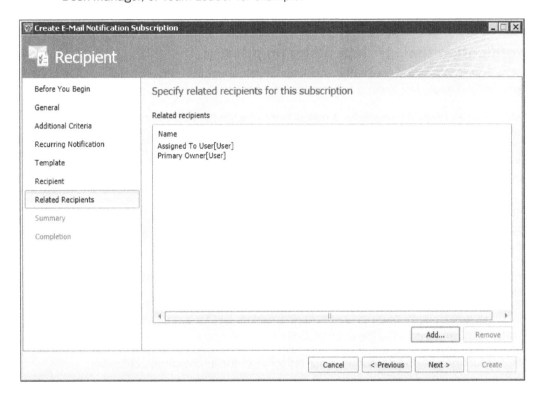

30. Click on **Next**.

31. Review the **Summary** screen and when you are happy click on **Create**.

32. Once created click on **Close**.

How it works...

We created a template that defined the information and layout of the message we want to send, and then we created a subscription that defines what, how often, and how many times the e-mail will be sent and to whom.

There's more...

The recipe provides steps for one priority. You may want to provide notifications for additional priorities.

Notification timings depending on priority

You will need to create a notification subscription following this recipe for each priority of work item that you would like to send out repeated notifications.

Each time you follow the recipe for a new priority, change the priority criteria to reflect the priority you are creating it for.

Also, change the notification interval and recurrence values to reflect the values for that specific priority.

Notification for breaches

This recipe can be followed for breaches of SLA rather than just warning, except for a couple of key changes.

When setting the additional criteria, the status criteria for **Work Item has Service Level Information** needs to be set to **equals Breached**.

You must create a specific e-mail notification template just for breaches. Be sure to choose this template when creating the subscription.

Also, ensure names and descriptions are reflective of the intent of the notification.

4

Building the Configuration Management Database (CMDB)

In this chapter we will have recipes for configuring the Service Manager with information about your environment. We will specifically cover the area of setting up the Configuration Management Database (CMDB) within Service Manager, with the following tasks:

- ▸ Adding configuration items manually
- ▸ Importing active directory configuration items
- ▸ Importing configuration manager configuration items
- ▸ Importing operations manager configuration items
- ▸ Importing virtual machine manager configuration items
- ▸ Importing orchestrator runbooks
- ▸ Using a CSV file to import items into the CMDB
- ▸ Creating a business Service
- ▸ Personalizing and organizing configuration item views
- ▸ Creating a configuration item group

Introduction

In this chapter, Service Manager administrators are shown how to build the CMDB, with various options ranging from a manual approach, right through to automating the importing of information from external systems.

A **Configuration Management Database** (**CMDB**) is a store of information related to all the components of information systems used in an organization's IT environment. It contains the details of the **Configuration Items** (**CI**) within the IT infrastructure. CI can be types of components such as, software, hardware, users, clouds and are typically stored in the CMDB with their important attributes and relationships between other CIs.

Service Manager has the ability to create CIs through the following methods:

- ▶ Manual creation
- ▶ Importing from CSV
- ▶ Connection to active directory
- ▶ Connection to configuration manager
- ▶ Connection to operations manager
- ▶ Connection to virtual machine manager
- ▶ Connection to orchestrator

Adding configuration items manually

This recipe will show you how to use the Service Manager console to manually create a computer configuration item without using the connector framework or by importing any information.

How to do it...

The following steps will guide you through the process of adding CIs manually to the Service Manager CMDB.

1. In the Service Manager console navigate to **Configuration Items | Computers | All Windows Computers**.
2. Click on **Create Computer** in the task pane on the right-hand side of the console.
3. A new form screen will open.
4. Fill out the form with relevant data, ensuring any field marked with a red asterisk is filled in as they are mandatory fields.
5. Click on **OK**.

How it works...

Filling in the form submits the data to the database, creating the CI and a unique GUID identifier within the database.

There's more...

This method can be repeated for any configuration item within Service Manager. For a basic installation, this includes CIs such as the following:

- ▸ Computers/servers
- ▸ Software
- ▸ Users
- ▸ Business services
- ▸ Environments

Importing active directory configuration items

This recipe will show you how to set up the active directory connector, which will allow you to import users, groups, and printers from your active directory forest as CIs within Service Manager.

Getting ready

Before you set up the connector you will need an account within your active directory forest that has Read permissions to the organizational units containing the items you would like to import.

How to do it...

The following steps will guide you through the process of importing data from Active Directory into the Service Manager CMDB.

1. In the **Service Manager** console, navigate to **Administration | Connectors**.
2. In the task pane on the right-hand side click on **Create Connector** and select **Active Directory Connector**.
3. Review the information on the **Before You Begin** screen and click on **Next**.

4. Enter a name and description for the connector. In this example I've called it **demo. local Active Directory Connector**.

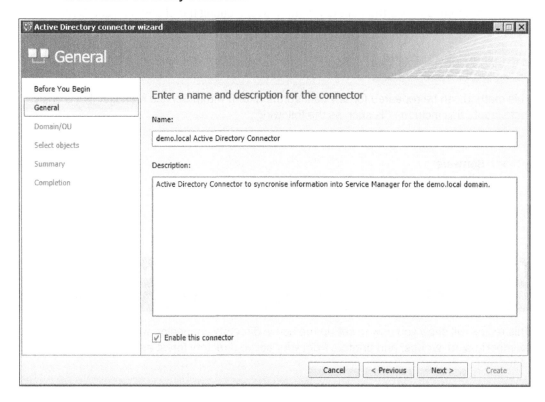

5. Ensure the **Enable this connector** box is checked and then click on **Next**.
6. Choose to either synchronize the entire domain or a specific OU.

   In this example I've chosen to synchronize the entire domain.

A specific OU may be a more appropriate choice where the active directory structure may contain lots of non-relevant information and you require a more targeted import of data.

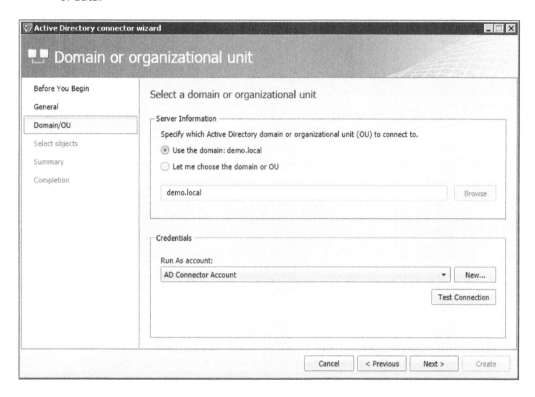

7. Next to the **Run As Account** drop-down options, click on **New** and enter the details of the account you set up before starting this recipe, which has Read rights to active directory. Click on **Next**. When prompted, supply the password for the account used for the connector.

8. The **Select objects** screen allows you to drill down and choose either specific objects to synchronize with this connector or provide an LDAP query to select the objects based on a custom criteria. As shown in this example, just select **All computers, printers, users and user groups**.

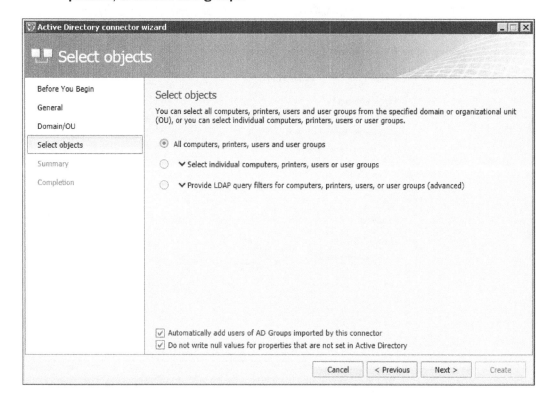

9. Ensure that both options at the bottom of the screen are selected and click on **Next**.

10. Review the summary and then, click on **Create**.

11. When the completion screen shows that the connector was successfully created, click on **Close**.

How it works...

By default the active directory connector polls active directory every 24 hours for new objects. If new objects are present, they are inserted into Service Manager as new configuration items, otherwise the connector becomes dormant until the next 24 hour interval.

By default the AD connector schedule is not configurable via the GUI console but can be changed via PowerShell.

There's more...

The active directory connector can be accessed via the `Connectors` folder under the Administration Workspace of the **Service Manager** console. Select the connector and click on **Properties** from the tasks pane on the right-hand side of the console.

Mapping active directory domain attributes to Service Manager properties

The following link is to the Service Manager TechNet library documentation and shows the active directory attribute and the corresponding Service Manager property that it maps to.

```
http://technet.microsoft.com/en-us/library/hh524307
```

Changing the active directory connector schedule via PowerShell

Unfortunately, changing the schedule of a connector isn't an easy PowerShell cmdlet and requires the use of the SDK via PowerShell.

Anton Gritsenko has a good blog post here that explains how to achieve this:

```
http://blog.scsmsolutions.com/2012/03/update-ad-and-sccm-connector-
scheduler-with-powershell/
```

Importing Configuration Manager configuration items

This recipe will show you how to set up the Configuration Manager connector, which will allow you to import information such as hardware and software information from your configuration manager system as CIs within Service Manager.

Getting ready

Before you set up the connector you will need an account within your active directory forest for the connector that has the following permissions:

- Configuration Manager SQL Database—`smsdbrole_extract&db_datareader` roles
- Service Manager—advanced operator

How to do it...

The following steps will guide you through the process of importing data from System Center Configuration Manager into the Service Manager CMDB.

1. In the **Service Manager** console, navigate to **Administration | Connectors**.

2. In the task pane on the right-hand side, click on **Create Connector** and select **Configuration Manager Connector**.

3. Review the **Before You Begin** screen and then click on **Next**.

4. On the **General** screen, enter a name and a description for the connector. In this example, shown as follows), I've called it **demo.local Configuration Manager Connector**.

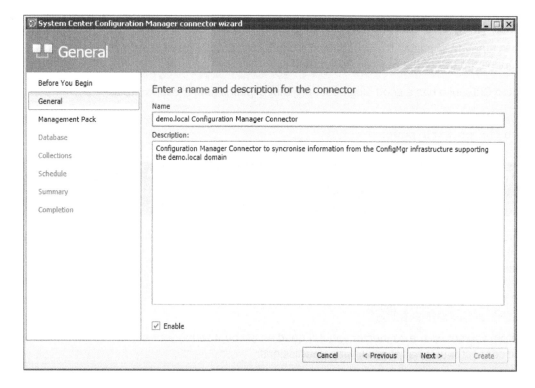

5. Ensure the **Enable** is ticked so that this connector box is enabled and then click on **Next**.

6. On the **Select Management Pack** screen, use the drop-down list under **Management Pack** to select the appropriate version of **Configuration Manager** that you wish to connect to, and then click on **Next**.

7. On the **Connect to System Center Configuration Manager Database** screen, supply the name of the server hosting the SQL site database (including any instance information if applicable). Then supply the name of the database. In this example, I've used **SCCM01** as the name of the server holding the site database and **SMS_DL1** as the database name.

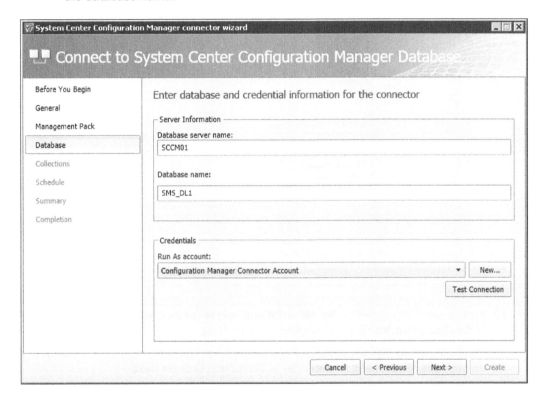

8. Next to the **Run As Account** drop-down selection, click on **New** and enter the details of the account you had set up before starting this recipe, which is a member of `smsdbrole_extract` and the `db_datareader` groups for the site database.

9. Click on **Test Connection** and enter the password for the account, when prompted.

10. Click on **Next**.

11. On the **Collections** screen select the collection containing the CIs you would like to synchronize, for this example, **All Systems**.

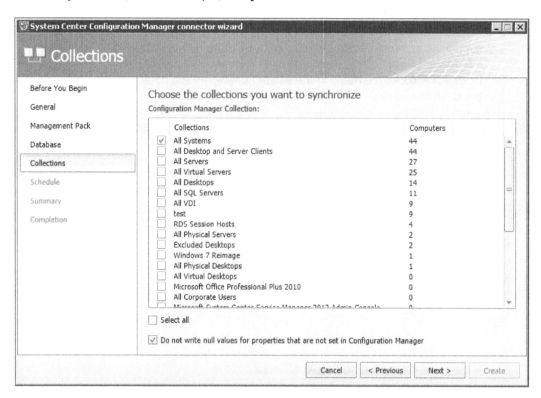

12. Ensure that the box next to **Do not write null values for properties that are not set in Configuration Manager** is checked. Click on **Next**.

13. On the **Schedule** screen, select when and how often you would like the connector to run. For this recipe, set it to every day at 06:00 and click on **Next**.

14. Review the information on the **Summary** screen then click on **Create**.

15. Review the information on the **Confirmation** screen the click on **Close**.

How it works...

The Service Manager connector queries the configuration manager database and extracts information related to computers, software, hardware, operating systems, software updates, users, and DCM baselines, and stores it within the CMDB.

There's more...

The Configuration Manager connector can be accessed via the `Connectors` folder under the Administration Workspace of the **Service Manager** console. Select the connector and click on **Properties** from the task pane on the right-hand side of the console.

Mapping Configuration Manager attributes to Service Manager properties

The following link is to the Service Manager TechNet library documentation and shows the Configuration Manager attribute and the corresponding Service Manager property that it maps to.

```
http://technet.microsoft.com/en-us/library/hh519741
```

Importing Operations Manager configuration items

This recipe will show you how to set up the Operations Manager connector, which will allow you to import information such as server IP addresses, SQL databases, and distributed application information from your operations manager system as CIs within Service Manager.

Getting ready

Before you set up the connector you will need an account within your Active Directory forest for the connector that has the following permissions:

- ▶ Operations Manager—operator privileges
- ▶ Service Manager—advanced operator

For the Operations Manager connector to know what to synchronize with Service Manager, it is required that the management packs containing the classes that define the information are imported into Service Manager.

The Service Manager installation directory contains the base management packs required to get started with the Operations Manager connector.

For Operations Manager 2007:

1. Open a PowerShell window.

2. Type the following commands:

   ```
   Set-ExecutionPolicy Unrestricted

   Set-Location \"Program Files\Microsoft System Center 2012\Service
   Manager\Operations Manager Management Packs"

   .\installOMMPs.ps1
   ```

3. Close the PowerShell window.

4. This will import the Operations Manager 2007 Management Packs required for a basic connector.

For Operations Manager 2012:

1. In the **Service Manager** console navigate to the **Administration | Management Packs**.

2. In the tasks pane on the right-hand side under **Management Packs** click on **Import**.

3. On the **Select Management Packs to Import** screen, click on **Add** and navigate to the drive where Service Manager is installed:

   ```
   Program Files\Microsoft System Center 2012\Service Manager\
   Operations Manager 2012 Management Packs.
   ```

4. Click on the **Change the File Type** drop-down menu to select **MP Files (*.mp)**.

5. Select all the management packs displayed and click on **Open**.

6. On the **Import Management Packs** screen, click on **Import**.

7. When the import process is complete, click on **OK**.

How to do it...

The following steps will guide you through the process of importing data from System Center Operations Manager into the Service Manager CMDB.

1. In the **Service Manager** console navigate to **Administration | Connectors**.

2. In the task pane on the right-hand side, click on **Create Connector** then select **Operations Manager CI Connector**.

3. Review the **Before You Begin** screen then click on **Next**.

4. On the **General** screen, enter a name and a description for the connector. In this example I've called it **demo.local Operations Manager Connector**.

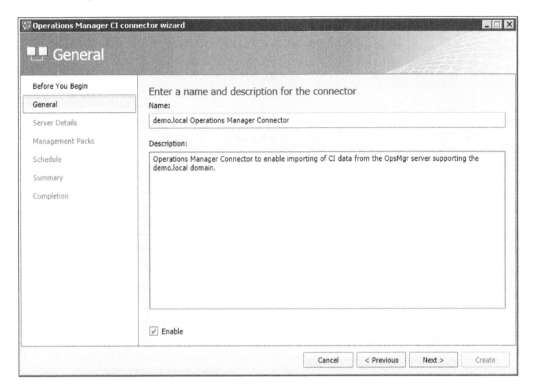

5. Ensure the **Enable** box is checked and then click on **Next**.

6. On the **Server Details** screen in the **Server Name** box, supply the name of the server that the Operations Manager Management Server is installed on.

7. Next to the **Run As Account** drop-down menu, click on **New** and enter the details of the account you had set up before starting.

8. Click the test connection and enter the password for the account, when prompted.

9. Click on **Next**.

10. On the **MP Selection** screen, check the **Select all** box and ensure that the **Do not write null values for properties that are not set in Operations Manager** box is checked. Click on **Next**.

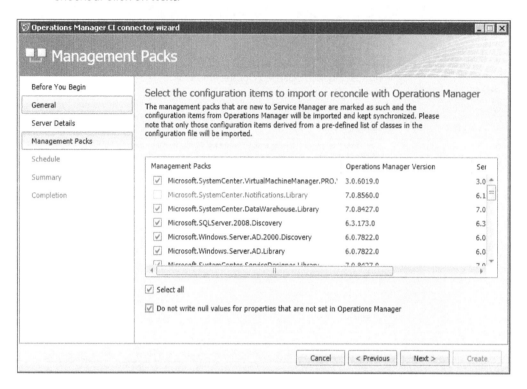

11. On the **Schedule** screen, select when and how often you would like the connector to run. For this recipe, set this to every day at 05:00 and click on **Next**.

12. Review the information on the **Summary** screen then click on **Create**.

13. Review the information on the **Confirmation** screen the click on **Close**.

How it works...

The Service Manager connector queries the Operations Manager Management Server and extracts information related to servers and related items and stores it within the CMDB according to the schedule specified.

There's more...

The Operations Manager connector can be accessed via the `Connectors` folder under the Administration Workspace of the **Service Manager** console. Select the connector and click on **Properties** from the task pane on the right-hand side of the console.

Adding new Operations Manager CIs

Every so often you will import new management packs into Operations Manager to extend its monitoring capabilities and/or update its management packs with newer versions. These will require importing into Service Manager to either allow these new classes of data to be brought across as CIs or to ensure that any changes to the classes within the management packs are mirrored across both systems.

First use the same method described in the *Getting ready* section of this recipe to import and browse for the updated/new management packs.

Next you must edit the Operations Manager CI connector, as follows:

1. In the Service Manager console, navigate to the **Service Manager** console to **Administration | Connectors**.

2. Select the **Operations Manager CI Connector**, named **demo.local Operations Manager Connector** in this recipe.

3. In the task pane on the right-hand side, click on **Properties**.

4. In the **Edit** screen on the left-hand side, click on **Management Packs** and then click on **Refresh**.

5. Enter the password for the account used by the Operations Manager CI Connector and click on **OK**.

6. In the **Management Packs** list, select the new management packs that you have just imported or check the **Select All** box, and click on **OK**.

Importing Virtual Machine Manager configuration items

This recipe will show you how to set up the Virtual Machine Manager connector, which will allow you to import information about your virtualization CIs and your private cloud environment.

Getting ready

Before you set up the connector you will need an account within your Active Directory forest for the connector that has the following permissions:

- ▸ Virtual Machine Manager—SCVMM Administrator Role and Local Administration Rights on the Virtual Machine Manager server
- ▸ Service Manager—Advanced Operator

You must also ensure that an Operations Manager CI connector has been created first and that the following management packs are imported:

- ▸ IIS 2003
- ▸ IIS 7
- ▸ IIS Library
- ▸ SQL Server Core Library

After these are imported, import the Virtual Machine Manager Management Pack (Microsoft. SystemCenter.VirtualMachineManager.2012.Discovery) into Service Manager and all the management packs are synchronized with the Operations Manager CI Connector.

See the *Operations Manager CI Connector* recipe for information on importing management packs, setting up the Operations Manager CI connector, and synchronizing management packs with the connector.

How to do it...

The following steps will guide you through the process of importing data from System Center Virtual Machine Manager into the Service Manager CMDB:

1. In the **Service Manager** console, navigate to **Administration | Connectors**.
2. In the task pane on the right-hand side, click on **Create Connector**. Then select **Virtual Machine Manager Connector**.

3. Review the **Before You Begin** screen then click on **Next**.

4. On the **General** screen enter a name for the connector and a description. In this recipe I've called it **demo.local SCVMM Connector**.

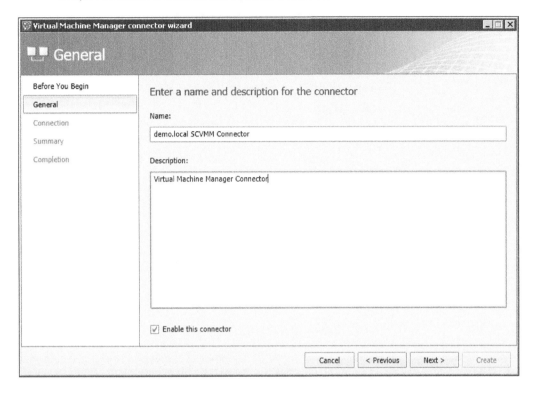

5. Ensure that the **Enable this connector** box is checked, and then click on **Next**.

6. On the **Connection** screen in the **Server Information** box, supply the name of the server that the Virtual Machine Manager is installed on. In this recipe I've used **SCVMM01** as the name of the Virtual Machine Manager Server.

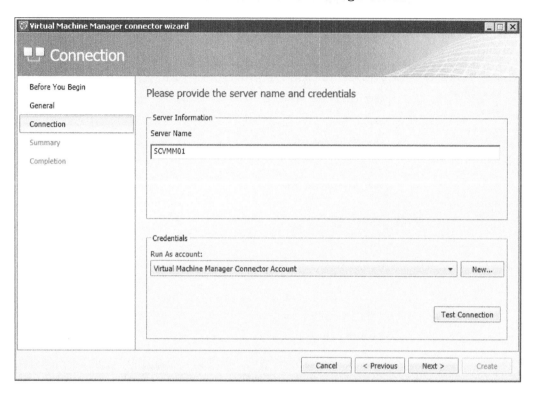

7. Next to the **Run As Account** drop-down menu click on **New** and enter the details of the account that you had set up before starting.
8. Click **Test Connection** and enter the password for the account when prompted.
9. Click on **Next**.
10. Review the information on the **Summary** screen and then click on **Create**.
11. Review the information on the **Confirmation** screen and then click on **Close**.

How it works...

Most of the CI information related to virtualization is actually brought across by the Operations Manager CI connector, which is why it is a prerequisite to have that connector set up before creating the Virtual Machine Connector. The Virtual Machine Connector syncs information relating to the Virtual Machine Manager Library to complete the CMDB information.

The items the connector syncs are as follows:

- Service templates
- VM templates
- Storage classifications
- Logical networks
- Load balancers
- Load balancer VIP templates

This extra information allows you to create items such as Service Requests that might allow a user to provision a Virtual Machine by referencing a VM Template.

There's more...

The Virtual Machine Manager connector can be accessed via the `Connectors` folder under the Administration Workspace of the Service Manager Console. Select the connector and click on **Properties** from the task pane on the right-hand side of the console.

Need to use an account that isn't a local Administrator?

If you have a policy that prohibits the use of local administrator accounts, you need to manually adjust a few permissions to allow for remote PowerShell usage by the account used for the Virtual Machine Manager connector.

1. Log on to the server hosting Virtual Machine Manager as a user with administrative rights.

2. Open a PowerShell window (ensure it's elevated with administrative rights).

3. Type the following and press *Enter*:

    ```
    Set-PSsessionConfigurationMicrosoft.Powershell -
    ShowSecurityDescriptorUI
    ```

4. When prompted whether "you are sure you want to perform this action", type *Y* and press *Enter*.

5. Add the account being used for the connector and grant it **Execute (Invoke)** permission by checking the **Allow** box.

6. Click on **OK**.

7. If prompted to confirm whether "WinRM can be restarted", type *Y* and press **Enter**.

Setting up a Virtual Machine Manager and Operations Manager integration

Because most of the information about your virtualization CIs comes through the Operations Manager CI Connector it is also advisable to set up the integration feature between Virtual Machine Manager and Operations Manager via the Virtual Machine Manager console.

1. Within Operations Manager ensure that the following management packs are imported:

   ❑ IIS 2003

   ❑ IIS 7

   ❑ IIS Library SQL

   ❑ Server Core Library

2. In the **Virtual Machine Manager** console, navigate to **Settings** workspace.

3. Click on **System Center** settings and Operations Manager Server.

4. If no connection exists, a wizard will start.

5. Follow the wizard through and the connection will be made.

Importing Orchestrator runbooks

This recipe will show you how to setup the Orchestrator connector, which will allow you to import information about your runbooks to allow them to be used within automation activities in Service Request processes.

Getting ready

Before you set up the connector you will need an account within your Active Directory forest for the connector that has the following permissions:

▸ Read Properties

▸ List Contents

▸ Publish permissions to the root Runbook folder and all child objects

These permissions are granted via the **Runbook Designer** console.

How to do it...

The following steps will guide you through the process of importing runbook information from System Center Orchestrator into the Service Manager CMDB to allow runbooks to be used as automation activities during Service Requests.

1. In the **Service Manager** console navigate to **Administration | Connectors**.

2. In the task pane on the right-hand side click on **Create Connector** then select **Orchestrator Connector**.

3. Review the **Before You Begin** screen then click on **Next**.

4. On the **General** screen enter a name for the connector and a description. In this recipe I've called it **demo.local Orchestrator Connector**.

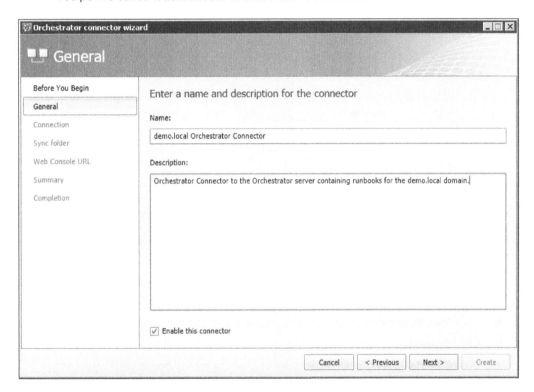

5. Ensure that the **Enable this connector** box is checked, and then click on **Next**.

6. On the **Connection** screen in the **Server Information** box, supply the URL of the Orchestrator Web Service. This is in the form of `http://<Server>:81/Orchestrator2012/Orchestrator.svc`. In this example I've used `http://SCORCH01:81/Orchestrator2012/Orchestrator.svc` as the URL of the Orchestrator Web Service.

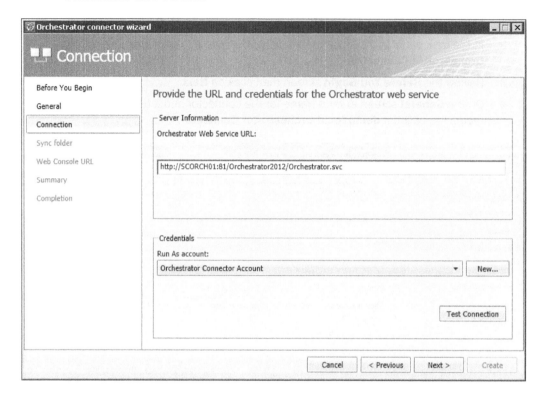

7. Next to the **Run As Account** drop-down menu, click on **New** and enter the details of the account you set up before starting.

8. Click **Test Connection** and enter the password for the account when prompted.

9. Click on **Next**.

10. On the **Folder** screen select the folder containing the runbooks you require to synchronize to Service Manager. For this recipe select the root folder (shown as a \ ) to synchronize all runbooks.

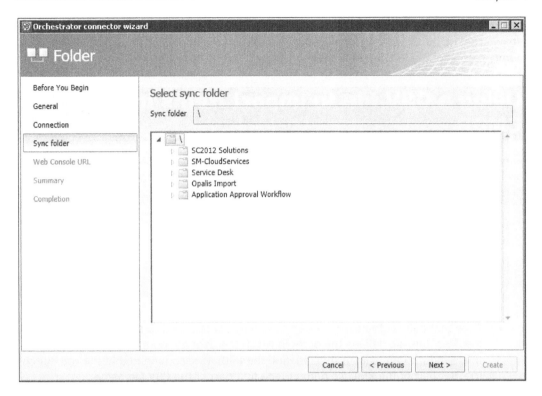

11. On the web console URL screen type the URL for the Orchestrator web console. This is usually in the form of `http://<Server>:82`. For this recipe I've used `http://SCORCH01:82`.

12. Review the information on the **Summary** screen then click on **Create**.

13. Review the information on the **Confirmation** screen the click on **Close**.

How it works...

The connector pulls information from the web Service regarding what runbooks are available and the input parameters that each runbook contains. These runbooks and their parameters can then be used with automation activities. The automated activities are invoked by workflows which use the the parameters specified in the runbook CIs.

There's more...

After creating the connector, the imported information regarding the runbooks will be available for use within activities for use with Service Requests.

Where are my runbooks?

After you set up the Orchestrator connector, you will find the imported runbooks under the **Library** section of the **Service Manager** console.

Using a CSV file to import items into the CMDB

Sometimes you may want to bulk import configuration items into the CMDB. One way to do this is to import them using a **Comma-Separated Value** (**CSV**) file containing the CIs that relate to any class type or projection type already existing within Service Manager.

Getting ready

To import data using this method, two files are required, as follows:

▸ A file containing the CIs to be imported; structured in a comma-delimited method and saved with a `.csv` extension.

▸ A file that defines the class types or projection types used by all items in the CSV file. Also, this file defines the order in which the data appears as columns. The file must end with an `.xml` extension, and the authors recommend that the you match the first part of the XML file name to the first part of the CSV file name.

How to do it...

First we need to create the data file. In this recipe we will create a CSV file that will allow us to import some computer/server configuration items into Service Manager.

1. Open Microsoft Excel or similar spreadsheet application.

    On the first row create the following headers:

    ❑ Computer Name

    ❑ Number of Physical Processors

    ❑ Number of Logical Processors

    ❑ IP Address

2. Then provide data, like the following table:

Computer Name	Number of Physical Processors	Number of Logical Processors	IP Address
WKST01	1	2	172.16.1.50
WKST02	1	4	172.16.1.52
WKST03	1	2	172.16.1.57
WKST04	1	2	172.16.1.60
WKST05	1	6	172.16.1.68
Server01	2	4	172.16.1.200
Server02	2	8	172.16.1.201
Server03	4	16	172.16.1.202
Server04	4	24	172.16.1.203
Server05	1	1	172.16.1.204

3. Remove the first row with the column headings and then save the data as a CSV file called `ComputerCIs.csv`.

4. The resulting CSV file contents should look like the following:

   ❑ WKST01,1,2,172.16.1.50

   ❑ WKST02,1,4,172.16.1.52

   ❑ WKST03,1,2,172.16.1.57

   ❑ WKST04,1,2,172.16.1.60

   ❑ WKST05,1,6,172.16.1.68

   ❑ Server01,2,4,172.16.1.200

   ❑ Server02,2,8,172.16.1.201

   ❑ Server03,4,16,172.16.1.202

   ❑ Server04,4,24,172.16.1.203

   ❑ Server05,1,1,172.16.1.204

Next we need to create the XML file that defines the format and structure.

1. The information stored in the data file is aimed at creating/updating CIs of the class Windows Computer, which is defined within Service Manager as a class `Microsoft. Windows.Computer`.

2. We also have four columns of data that need mapping to the appropriate properties of the `Microsoft.Windows.Computer` class. You can either use the Authoring tool to locate the class and view the properties or you can use PowerShell.

3. Use an XML editor to create the required XML file (for example `Notepad.exe`). The following table shows the appropriate properties for our data that we need to map the columns to:

Property	Property name
Computer Name	PrincipalName
Number of Physical Processors	PhysicalProcessors
Number of Logical Processors	LogicalProcessors
IP Address	IPAddress

4. Every XML definition file for CSV import starts with the following line:

   `<CSVImportFormat>` and ends with a similar closing line: `</CSVImportFormat>`

5. The next line defines the class type to be imported. For this recipe that needs to be the `Microsoft.Windows.Computer` class.

   ```
   <Class Type="Microsoft.Windows.Computer">
   ```

   This again requires a closing tag after the properties:

   ```
   </Class>
   ```

6. For each column of data within the data file, we need to specify the property of the class it requires mapping to and in the order in which they are listed within the CSV file.

   ```
   <Property ID="PrincipalName" />
   <Property ID="PhysicalProcessors" />
   <Property ID="LogicalProcessors" />
   <Property ID="IPAddress" />
   ```

7. This will give a completed XML definition file that looks like this:

   ```
   <CSVImportFormat>
   <Class Type="Microsoft.Windows.Computer">
   <Property ID="PrincipalName" />
   <Property ID="PhysicalProcessors" />
   <Property ID="LogicalProcessors" />
   <Property ID="IPAddress" />
   </Class>
   </CSVImportFormat>
   ```

8. Save this XML file as `ComputerCIs.xml`.

Finally these two files can now be used to import data into Service Manager by following these next steps:

1. In the **Service Manager** console navigate to the **Administration** workspace.

2. Expand **Administration** and the click on **Connectors**.

3. In the tasks pane on the right-hand side, click on **Import from CSV File**.

4. On the **Import Instances from CSV File** screen that opens, use the **Browse** buttons to locate and open the XML and CSV files previously created.

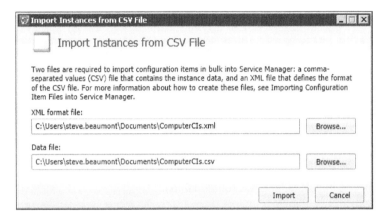

5. Click on **Import**.

6. The **Importing Instances** screen will now open and give you a progress bar for the import. If importing a large number of objects, this could take a considerable time.

How it works...

By mapping the columns of data to the properties of the class you define within the XML file it's possible to bulk import lots of data and have Service Manager match the data to the classes and properties so it can create the configuration items for you.

There's more...

The previous recipe shows the steps required to import data using a CSV file and the CSV connector but below are some additional tips.

Using PowerShell to find the properties

Rather than having to open the Authoring tool and create a temporary management pack to view the different classes and their properties PowerShell can be used to quickly look these up using the SCSM PowerShell Cmdlets available from CodePlex here: http://smlets.codeplex.com/.

For this recipe we needed the properties for the `Windows Computer` class.

Open a PowerShell session and type the following:

```
Import-Module SMLets
$CI = Get-SCSMClass -Name Microsoft.Windows.Computer$
$CI.PropertyCollection
```

This will list all the properties directly used by the class (but not relationships).

Is CSV import just for configuration items?

No, CSV import is not just for configuration items. The CSV import method can also be used to create work items such as incidents by targeting the data at the `System.WorkItem.Incident` class by using the XML definition file and defining the properties for the data such as `Title`, `Description`, `Impact`, and `Urgency`.

This can be very useful especially for scenarios such as migrating Service Desk tools.

Complex CI importing

Sometimes you will want to import data that isn't held by just a single class but maybe spans multiple classes and in particular class relationships.

For example, you may want to import a new computer CI, but specify the Asset Custodian for that device.

This can be achieved through the use of Type Projection and defining these in the XML definition file rather than just a single class type.

Apart from using the previous recipe and creating a new computer CI based on the information such as Computer Name, Number of Physical Processors, Number of Logical Processors, and IP Address, we also now need to specify the user details for the custodian.

The original XML definition file started with the following code:

```
<CSVImportFormat>
<Class Type="Microsoft.Windows.Computer">
```

This time the Type Projection needs to be specified first:

```
<CSVImportFormat>
<Projection Type="Microsoft.Windows.Computer.ProjectionType">
<Seed>
<Class Type="Microsoft.Windows.Computer">
```

Specify the properties as before, close the class section with the `</Class>` tag and then ensure the seed section is also closed with a `</Seed>` tag.

Next, the additional class information for the Custodian can be added by starting a new section with a <Component Alias> tag:

```
<Component Alias="Custodian">
<Seed>
<Class Type="System.Domain.User">
<Property ID="Domain"/>
<Property ID="UserName"/>
</Class>
</Seed>
</Component>
```

This allows the data to be added to the data file in the format of the Domain Name in the column after IP Address and then the username of the custodian that should be assigned.

Finally the </Projection> tag must be placed towards the bottom to close the Type Projection definition.

The final XML would look like the following:

```
<CSVImportFormat>
<Projection Type="Microsoft.Windows.Computer.ProjectionType">
<Seed>
<Class Type="Microsoft.Windows.Computer">
<Property ID="PrincipalName"/>
<Property ID="PhysicalProcessors"/>
<Property ID="LogicalProcessors"/>
<Property ID="IPAddress"/>
</Class>
</Seed>
<Component Alias="Custodian">
<Seed>
<Class Type="System.Domain.User">
<Property ID="Domain"/>
<Property ID="UserName"/>
</Class>
</Seed>
</Component>
</Projection>
</CSVImportFormat>
```

See also

There are third-party tools that make CSV import and data mapping easier. See the *Appendix* for information about Provance and their Data Management Pack.

Creating a business service

This recipe shows how to create a business service within Service Manager. A **business service** is a collection of information relating to an IT service such as an e-mail system, a payroll system, or other line of business service. The information about the service consists of information such as the components that make up the service (servers, databases, websites) and properties such as availability of the service, affected users, and owner information for example.

Getting ready

You can either manually create a business service in which case review the manually creating CIs recipe or you can have them synchronized with information relating to distributed applications from within Operations Manager, in which case review and set up the Operations Manager CI Connector as shown in the recipe within this chapter.

This recipe will show how to create a business service based on a distributed application. Before attempting this recipe you will need a distributed application and save it to management pack.

You will also need all the management packs that contain items that your distributed application references, such as SQL and IIS.

How to do it...

The following steps will guide you through the process of creating a business service within Service Manager:

1. Within Operations Manager export the management pack containing the distributed application you want to create as a business service.

2. Within the **Service Manager** console navigate to **Administration | Management Packs**.

3. On the task pane on the right-hand side of the console click on **Import**.

4. On the **Select Management Packs to Import** screen, navigate to the management pack you exported earlier, select it, click on **Open**, and then click on **Import**.

5. If the import fails, review the error details and mostly likely it will reference a management pack that the one you are trying to import relies on. If so, repeat the import process but navigate to the required management pack and import that first before the one containing your distributed application.

6. Once you have the management pack imported navigate in the **Service Manager** console | **Administration** | **Connectors**.

7. Select the **Operations Manager CI Connector** and in the task pane click on **Properties**.

8. In the **Edit** screen, in the left-hand side, click on **Management Packs**, and then click on **Refresh**.

9. Enter the password for the account used by the Operations Manager CI Connector and click on **OK**.

10. In the Management Packs list, select the new management packs you imported and click on **OK**.

11. With the **Operations Manager CI connector** selected click on **Synchronize Now** in the task pane.

12. Navigate in the **Service Manager** console | **Configuration Items** | **All Business Services**.

13. Your distributed application should now be displayed under **All Business Services**.

14. Select your business service and click on **Edit** on the task pane on the right-hand side.

15. From the form screen that opens you can add additional information such as availability, operational status, owner and affected users, as well as view the components that make up the business service as defined within Operations Manager as your distributed application.

How it works...

Service Manager uses the information in the exported management pack, from operations manager to create the business service CI. The business service definition in Service Manager matches the distributed application in Operations Manager due to the use of this shared management pack.

There's more...

The business services are great for storing information related to a service so they're available when creating work items, but they can also be used to automatically raise incidents.

Raising related incidents

By default, Service Manager will not connect related incidents raised from Operations Manager to Business Services. For example an alert about a database being offline that is part of a business service will not add the business service as a related item to the incident.

This can be enabled, but requires the alert to be generated with the same name as the business service. This requires some planning and the use of rollup monitors in the related Operations Manager instance.

Personalizing and organizing configuration item views

This recipe is designed to show you how to personalize and organize your configuration item views.

How to do it...

The following steps will guide you through the how to organize CI information into personal views within Service Manager.

1. Navigate in the **Service Manager** console to **Configuration Items** workspace, expand **Configuration Items**, and click on **Computers**.

2. Click on **Create View** on the task pane on the right-hand side.

3. Specify a name and description for the view. For this recipe give the view a name of **All Virtual Servers**.

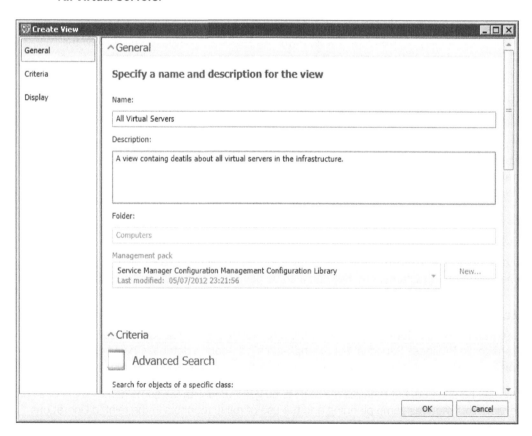

4. Click on **Criteria** on the left-hand side of the **Create View** screen.

5. Next to the **Search for objects** of a specific class click on the **Browse** button.

6. On the **Select a Class** screen use the drop-down list to select **Combination classes** and use the filter box to find the **Computer (typical)** type projection, select it, and click on **OK**.

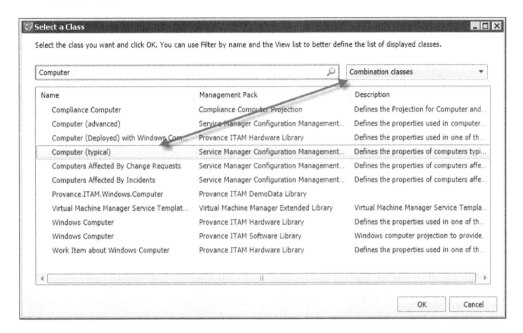

7. Under **Available properties** select the relevant property to filter the information shown in the view. For this recipe choose **Virtual Machine** and click on **Add**. Ensure that the criteria for **Virtual Machine** is set to **equals** to **True**.

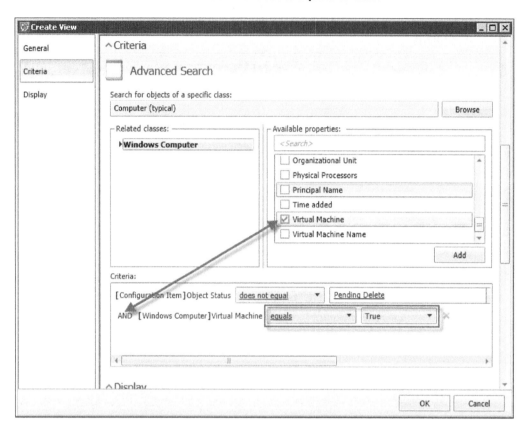

8. Click on **Display** on the left-hand side of the **Create View** screen.

9. Use this section to select the columns to display in the view. For this recipe select only the following:

   - NetBIOS Computer Name
   - - Expand Hosts Windows Operating System
   - Operating System Version Display Name
   - Physical Memory (MB)
   - Service Pack Version

10. Click on **OK**.

How it works...

This recipe walked you through the process of creating a view to display information related to the virtual servers contained within your CMDB. This recipe can be repeated to create new views based on any class or combinations of classes you select and the visible columns of data you choose to display by choosing different classes and columns in steps 6,7, and 9.

Creating a configuration item group

You can use groups within Service Manager to logically group and manage configuration items (CIs). Groups can contain either CIs of the same class or mixed classes and can be either a static group by manually adding certain CIs or a dynamic group by specifying the rules.

How to do it...

The following steps will guide you through the process of creating a CI group.

1. In the **Service Manager** console navigate to the **Library** workspace, expand **Library** and click on **Groups**.

2. In the task pane on the right-hand side click on **Create Group**.

3. Review the information on the **Create Group Wizard** screen then click on **Next**.

4. On the **General** screen provide a name for the group and a description. For this recipe name the group **VIP Users** and provide a description of **All VIP IT Service Users**.

5. Under **Management pack**, drop the list down and select your custom management pack to store this group in, and then click on **Next**.

6. If you wish to manually specify any specific objects, on the **Included Members** screen, click on **Add**. For this recipe, simply click on **Next** on the screen to skip.

7. On the **Dynamic Members** screen click the **...** button next to the box under the text **Specify the class and add criteria to build your query**.

8. On the **Select a class** screen that opens filter the list by typing in the box and select the **User** class. Click on **OK**.

9. Use the filter box under **Available properties** to find **Department**, select it, and click on **Add**. Then alter the **Criteria** to **contains** and type **Management**.

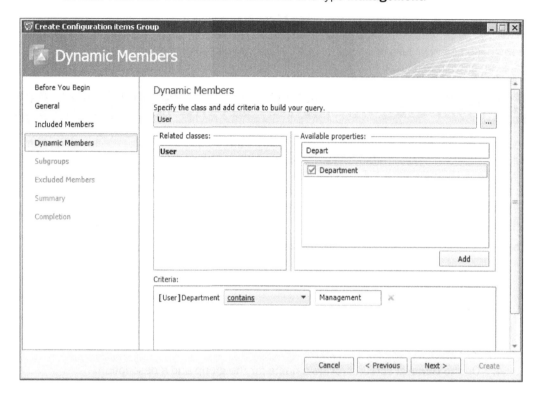

This will create a group containing all users that have management as part of their department description which is either pulled from Active Directory or manually specified.

10. Click on **Next**.

11. On the **Subgroups** page you can specify other groups that already exist to combine them into one group. For example if you had two separate groups, one for the senior managers and one for the line managers, you could create an all managers group and use this to simply add both the groups without having to use the dynamic members section. For this recipe, just click on **Next** to skip the screen.

12. On the **Excluded Members** screen you can choose objects to specifically exclude from the list that might get picked up by any dynamic rules or other groups that you don't want in this list. For this recipe just click on **Next** to skip the screen.

13. Review the information on the **Summary** screen then click on **Create**.

14. Once the **Completion** screen shows that the group has been created successfully, click on **Close**.

How it works...

A **group** is a logical grouping of configuration items stored within the CMDB. Once you have created a group, you can use it within security roles to restrict access, as criteria for notification subscriptions or even as criteria for reports.

There's more...

This recipe showed how to create a group containing users but you can create groups for other CIs too.

Creating other groups containing other CI types

You can use this recipe and change the object type to select anything stored within the CMDB to build groups containing other CIs such as a group to hold all the virtual servers by varying steps 8 and 9. Also, you can manually assign items by adding them in step 6 and skipping steps 7, 8, and 9 instead.

5
Deploying Service Request Fulfillment

In this chapter we will provide recipes to configure Service Manager to your environment. Specifically we will cover the Service Request Fulfillment of Service Manager 2012 with the following tasks:

- Creating Support Groups for Service Requests
- Creating Service Request templates
- Creating Service Request activities
- Creating Service Offering categories
- Creating Service Catalog Request offerings
- Creating Service Catalog Service offering
- Publishing Service offerings and Request offerings
- Working with Service Requests in the portal
- Creating Service Request notifications

Introduction

System Center 2012 Service Manager supports the ITIL© process, Service Request Fulfillment.

Service Request Fulfillment provides services to users created by the IT department. Typical Service Request and Service Offerings are: Requests for new hardware (computers, printers, smartphones), software, user management (create, modify, or delete/disable users), requests for new virtual machines in a cloud, and many more.

The ability of SCSM 2012 to use Review Activities, Manual Activities, and Orchestrator Runbook Activities in a sequential and/or parallel order offers the opportunity to design individual process workflows for different Service Offerings.

In this chapter we will provide the recipes to configure the basics of the Service Catalog, Service Offerings, and Request Offerings. Also, we will explain how to use the SCSM 2012 portal to create Service Requests.

Creating Support Groups for Service Requests

Using different Support Groups of Service Requests offers the opportunity for detailed and filtered reporting as well as the routing of Service Requests. The Service Request Support Groups can also be used to create different views to filter Service Requests in the SCSM2012 console.

This recipe will show how to create the Service Request Support Groups in SCSM 2012.

Getting ready

To create Service Request Support Groups open the SCSM 2012 console and navigate to **Library | Lists**. In the filter field type `Service Request Support Group` and the list we need will be shown.

How to do it...

The following steps will show you how to create Support Groups for Service Requests:

1. Double-click on the list named **Service Request Support Group**.

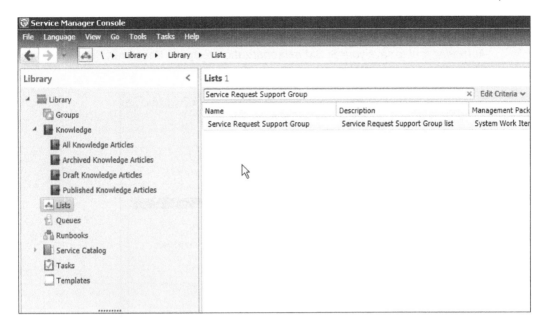

2. Click on the **Add Item** button, as shown in the following screenshot:

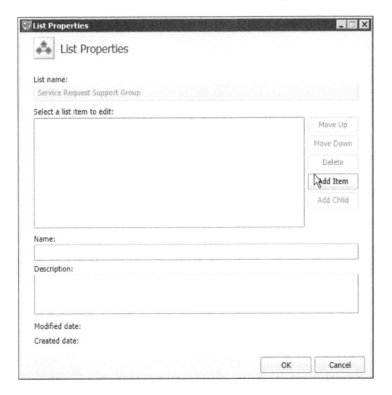

3. Choose a management pack to store the modification. Best practice and how to work with management packs is explained in the *Creating Management Packs in the Authoring tool to save your SCSM personalization* recipe in *Chapter 2, Personalizing SCSM 2012 Administration*.

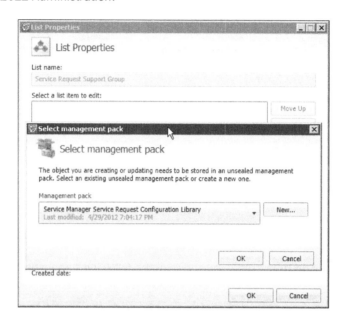

4. Select the **List Value** entry and provide a name to suit your requirements. We will choose **User Management Service Request Support Group** in this recipe.

5. Add as many Service Request Support Groups as required. After you have added the required groups click on **OK** to close the **List Properties** window.

How it works...

Service Request Support Groups can be used for filtering reports, views, as well as criteria for workflows and routing of Service Requests.

There's more...

In addition, to the steps provided for creating Support Groups, here is some more information about child list items, the use of Support Groups for filtering Reports, and the use of this particular support group in service level management.

Creating sub (child) list items

You can also create a sub list item. Just select the list item you want to create a child item below, and click on the **Add Child** button

Using Support Groups for filtering in reports

The *Viewing SCSM reports* and *Analyzing data with Microsoft Excel* recipes in *Chapter 9, Reporting*, show you how to work with different criteria for filtering.

Working with management packs

The *Creating Management Packs in the Authoring tool to save your SCSM personalization* recipe in *Chapter 2, Personalizing SCSM 2012 Administration* describes how to store your customizations in management packs, as well as best-practice for naming the XML files.

The Service Request Groups and Service Level Agreements

The Service Request Groups can be used as a criterion in Service Level Agreements (SLA)/Service Level Objectives (SLO) to filter Service Requests that belong to a SLO.

For more information on how they work please take a look at *Chapter 3, Configuring Service Level Agreements (SLAs)*.

See also

> ▶ Microsoft TechNet Library: Using the Service Catalog in System Center 2012 - Service Manager: `http://technet.microsoft.com/en-us/library/hh495624`

Creating Service Request templates

Service Request templates can be used to auto-fill information in the Service Request form. These can be a predefined Title, Description, Urgency, Priority, and Service Request Support Group. This recipe will describe the steps needed to create a new Service Request template.

Getting ready

To create Service Request templates open the SCSM 2012 console and navigate to **Library | Templates**.

How to do it...

The following steps explain how to create a new Service Request template:

1. Click on **Create Template**.
2. Fill in the name and description of the new template.

3. Click on the **Browse...** button besides the **Class** textbox and pick **Service Request** from the list.

4. Choose a management pack to store the Service Request template. We will use a custom management pack in this case (`Custom.ServiceRequest.Library`). Click on **OK** to close the window.

5. Fill out the fields in the **General** tab of the **Service Request Template** window.

   We will enter the **Title**, **Urgency**, **Priority**, **Area**, and **Support Group** we created in the previous recipe.

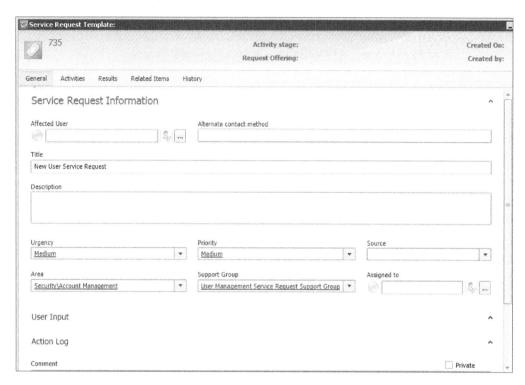

How it works...

Basically a pre-filled template in SCSM 2012 can be used to create new Work Items (for instance Incident Records, Change Requests, and Service Requests). Using templates keeps the required and optional information of Service Request forms consistent and also saves time.

There's more...

In a Service Request Template you can add different types of activities. How to work with mandatory fields in a Service Request is described in the following topic.

Configuring the Service Request activities in a template

In this recipe we filled out the fields of the **Service Request General** tab only. How to work with the activities on the **Activities** tab of a Service Request is described in the next recipe.

Configuring required fields of a Service Request

The fields **Urgency** and **Priority** are required fields in a Service Request. If you don't fill the fields in the Service Request template you have to provide this information in each Service Request (you have to add two questions for **Urgency** and **Priority** in a **Request Offering**).

See also

> ▸ Microsoft TechNet Library: Using the Service Catalog in System Center 2012 - Service Manager: http://technet.microsoft.com/en-us/library/hh495624

Creating Service Request activities

With activities you can define the process steps that are needed to fulfill the Service Request. This recipe shows how to work with different activities such as Approval Activity and Manual Activity.

Getting ready

To create Service Request activities open the SCSM 2012 console and navigate to **Library | Templates**. Open the Service Request template we created in the previous recipe.

How to do it...

The following are different steps needed to create Service Request Activities:

1. In the opened **Service Request Template** click on the **Activities** tab. Click on the **+ Activities** icon and choose **Default Review Activity** from the list. Click on **OK**.

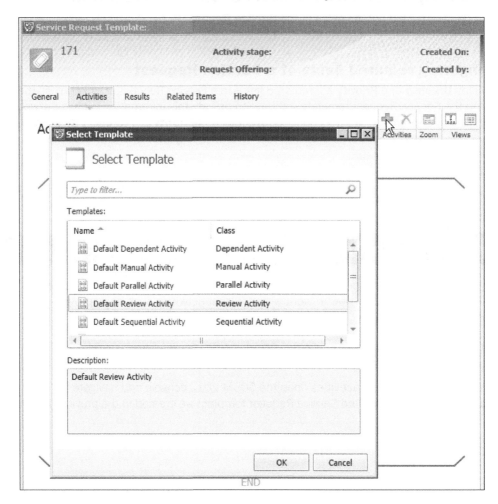

2. In the **Review Activity** form fill the necessary fields. We will provide a **Title** and **Description**. If approval is required from the manager of the requesting user check the **Line Manager should review** checkbox. The Line Manager is the synced Manager attribute of the Active Directory.

In the **Approval Condition:** drop-down box you can choose between **Automatic** (the approval will be done automatically), **Percentage Approval Threshold (%):** (A calculation is performed using the number of reviewers selected and the percentage for example in the instance where we have 3 reviewers with a 50% threshold, 2 reviewers must approve) or **Unanimous** (only one reviewer needs to approve). You can add reviewers manually by clicking on **Add** and choosing the reviewer by name from the list. Click on **OK** to close the form.

3. Click on the **+ Activities** icon again. Choose **Default Manual Activity** from the list. Click on **OK** to close the window.

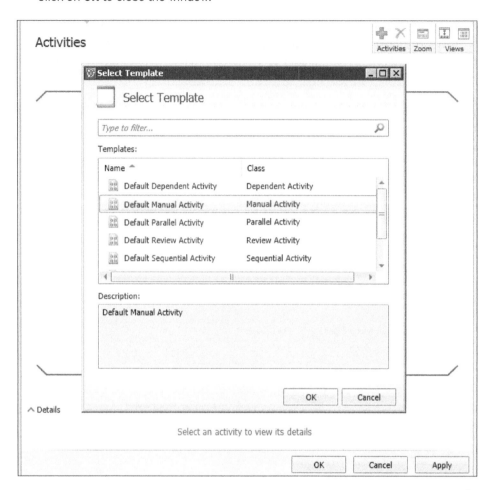

4. Fill the necessary fields in the form. We will fill the **Title**, **Description**, **Area**, and **Priority** for this example. Click on **OK** to close the form.

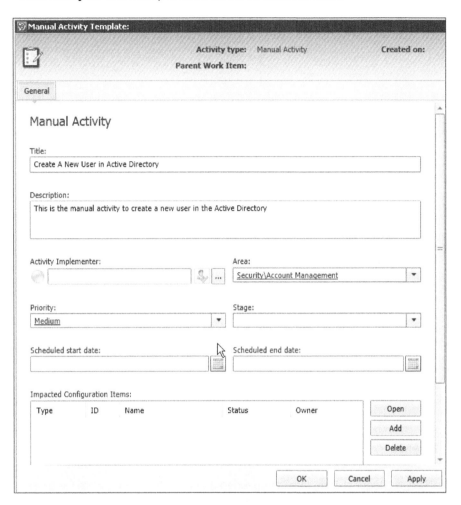

5. Add more activities related to your process requirements. Once complete click on **OK** in the **Service Request Template** form.

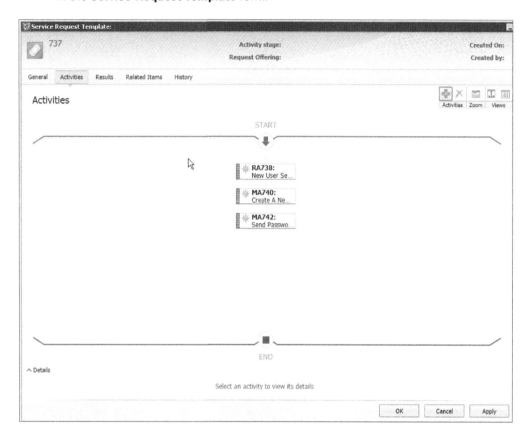

How it works...

When the Service Request Template is applied to a Service Request, all pre-filled fields and all activities are in the newly created Service Request.

A SCSM 2012 workflow will set the first activity to the status **In Progress**, all other activities will be set to a status **Pending**. The Service Request will get the status **In Progress**.

There's more...

You can add different types of activities in a Service Request Template.

How to configure the other activity types

For more information regarding other types of activities please take a look at the following Change and Release Management recipes in *Chapter 7, Designing Change and Release Management*:

- ▶ *Creating and managing Change Management Review Activities*
- ▶ *Creating Manual Activities for Change Management*
- ▶ *Creating and managing Dependent Activities in Change Management*
- ▶ *Creating and personalizing Change Management Parallel Activities*
- ▶ *Creating and personalizing Change Management Sequential Activities*

Add more activities to a Service Request created on a template

You can add additional activities to Service Requests that are based on a template, during the process of working with the request. Importantly, you can add more activities as long as the last activity in the Service Requested isn't completed.

See also

- ▶ Microsoft TechNet Library: Using the Service Catalog in System Center 2012 - Service Manager: `http://technet.microsoft.com/en-us/library/hh495624`

Creating Service Offering categories

Service Offering categories in SCSM 2012 can be used to sort Service Offerings in the SCSM 2012 portal. The categories offer the opportunity to filter Service Requests in reports as well as views. The steps to create the Service Offering categories are shown in this recipe.

Getting ready

To create Service Offering categories open the SCSM 2012 console and navigate to **Library | Lists**. In the filter field type `Service Offering Category` and the list we need will be shown.

How to do it...

1. Open the **Service Offering Category** list.
2. Click on **Add Item**.

3. Choose a management pack to store the new Service Offering category. We will choose the same management pack we used in the previous recipes, `Custom.ServiceRequest.Library.mp`.

4. Choose a name of the new category. In this recipe we will use `User Management`.

5. Click on **OK**.

How it works...

Choosing Service Offering categories as an attribute in Service Offerings provides the opportunity to combine and sort these offerings in the SCSM 2012 portal. These categories are the first tier used to combine related types of Service Offerings/Service Requests in the SCSM 2012 portal.

There's more...

Service Request Offering categories can be used as filters in reports.

Using Service Offering categories in reports (filtering)

How filtering of reports works is described in the *Viewing SCSM reports* recipe in *Chapter 9, Reporting*.

How to work with Excel and Analysis Services for reporting is described in the *Analyzing data with Microsoft Excel* recipe in *Chapter 9, Reporting*.

See also

▶ Microsoft TechNet Library: Using the Service Catalog in System Center 2012 - Service Manager: `http://technet.microsoft.com/en-us/library/hh495624`

Creating Service Catalog Request offerings

Request offerings in the SCSM 2012 Service Catalog are the different services the users can request. In the Request offerings the required questions to fulfill the service request are defined and mapped within the different forms of a Service Request.

This recipe will provide the steps required to create a Request offering in the Service Catalog of SCSM 2012.

Getting ready

To create Request offerings in the SCSM 2012 Service Catalog open the SCSM 2012 console and navigate to **Library | Service Catalog | Request Offerings**.

How to do it...

To create a Service Catalog Request offering, follow these steps:

1. Click on **Create Request Offering** in the **Tasks** pane of the SCSM 2012 console.
2. In the **Create Request Offering** wizard read the **before You Begin** information and click on **Next**.
3. In the **General** page fill in a title (for example, `Request A New User In Active Directory`)
4. Optionally choose an icon. This icon will be shown in the SCSM 2012 Self-Service portal.
5. Add a short description (for example, `This Service Offerings is for requesting a new user in Active Directory`).
6. Choose a Service Request template. We will choose the Service Request template **New User Service Request Template** we created in the previous recipe.

7. Choose a management pack to store the Request offering. In this recipe we will use the same management pack as we used previously, `Custom.ServiceRequest.Library`.

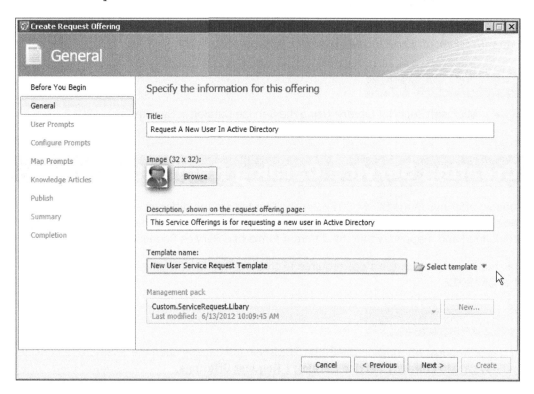

8. Click on **Next**.

9. In the **User Prompt** page fill out **Forms Instructions**. This information will be shown in the SCSM 2012 portal to the end user.

10. Add `Prompts` or `Information Text` in the next fields. For each prompt you can define different types.

Supported prompt types are:

□ **Date**

□ **Decimal**

□ **File Attachment**

□ **Integer**

□ **MP Enumeration List** (content of a SCSM 2012 list you have to specify in the next step)

- ❑ **Query Result** (Query on the SCSM 2012 CMDB. For instance list of users, computers, and so on.)
- ❑ **Simple List** (A simple list available only in this Request offering. No relation to any other list in SCSM 2012.)
- ❑ **Text**
- ❑ **True/False**

You can choose if the prompt is required, optional, or only displayed (for information).

Importantly, all prompts need to be mapped to fields in the Service Request or Activity forms in a later step. The type of the prompts must match the type of fields in the forms: **Text | String**, **Date/Time | Date/Time field** in a form, and so on.

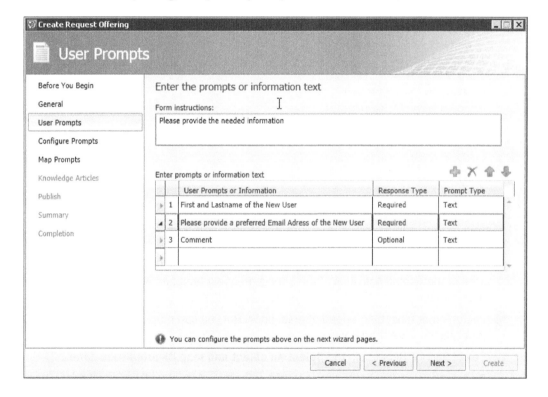

11. Click on **Next**.
12. On the next page you can configure each prompt. For this select the prompt and click on **Configure**. In this recipe we will configure the text prompt of **Please provide a preferred Email Address of the New User** to be a valid e-mail format.

13. Configuring the text prompt is optional. Some of the prompt types must be configured. For instance, if you choose **Simple List** on the previous page for a prompt you have to configure the values of **Simple List**. Also the **MP Enumeration List** and **Query Result** prompts need to be configured (which SCSM 2012 list you want to refer to and which SCSM 2012 class in the CDMB you want to query). Click on **OK** to close the **Configure Text Control** window.

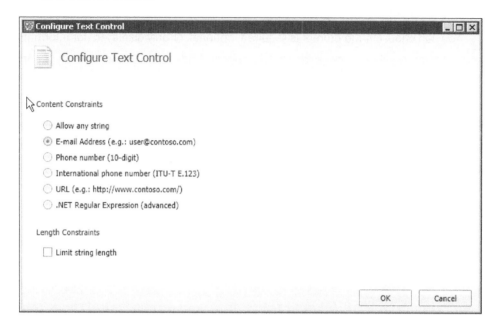

14. Click on **OK** and then on **Next** in the wizard.

15. On the **Map Prompts** page you have to map the prompts to the **Service Request** form or the related Activities of the Service Request template we chose in step 6 of this recipe.

16. Each prompt must be mapped at least once. But you can map a prompt in different forms/fields more than once.

17. Select Service Request in the **Select an object and map its properties** pane.

    By default you will only see the common properties. Activating **Display all properties** will show all fields of the selected object.

18. Select **Description** of the Service Request and map the prompt to the **Comment** field.

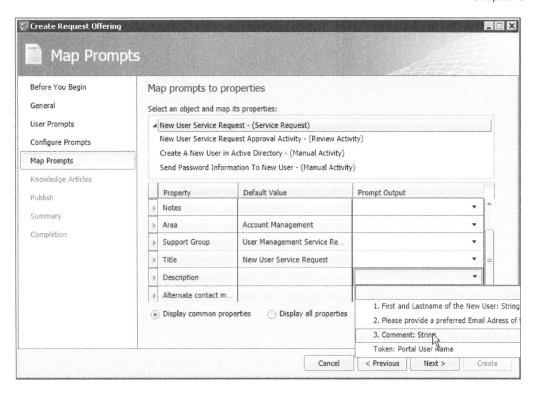

19. Select the **New User Request Service – (Service Request)** Request Approval activity and map **Description** to the prompt **First and Lastname of the New User: String**. Select the **Create A New User in Active Directory – (Manual Activity)** activity and map **Description** to the prompt **Please provide a preferred Email Address of the New User: String**.

20. In the selection form all prompts that are mapped at least once show a tick next to them. The mapping of **Token: Portal User Name** is optional (the user who created the Service Request in the SCSM 2012 portal).

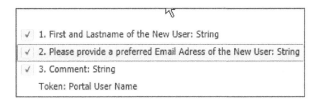

21. Click on **Next**.

22. In the **Knowledge Articles** page relate an existing article to the Request offering. This step is optional.

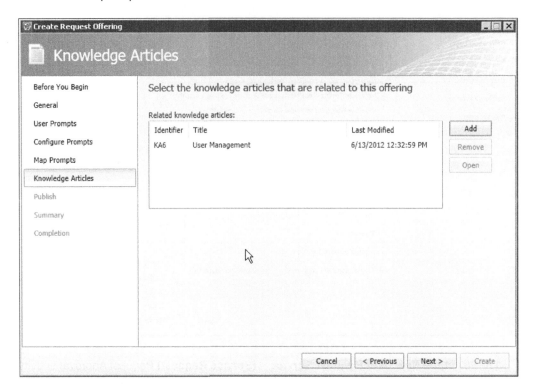

23. Click on **Next**.

24. In the **Publish** page add an Offering owner. This owner will be responsible for this Service Offering.

    We will publish the Service offering in a later recipe named *Publishing Service offerings and Request offerings*

25. Click on **Next**.

26. On the **Summary** page verify the information and click on **Create**.

How it works...

Request Offerings when scoped to the Service Request class, provide you with the ability to map all fields in the Service Request template form and its Activity templates to user friendly questions. These user friendly questions are displayed in the SCSM 2012 Self-Service Portal and will also include, the Name, Description, and an icon image of the Request Offering.

There's more...

Request offerings can be copied. This is helpful if you need to create similar Request offerings, for instance in different languages.

Copying Request offerings

You can create copies of Request offerings, for instance to use different languages or create almost similar Request offerings. Follow these steps to copy an existing request offering:

1. Select a Request offering you would like to copy.
2. Click on the **Create a copy** task. You can choose if you would like to create a corresponding Service Request template.
3. Open the newly created copy and make your changes.

Views for different status of Request offerings

In the SCSM 2012 console there are different views of Request offerings. This offers the opportunity to quickly navigate through the filtered list of Request offerings.

The following views are default in SCSM 2012:

- All Service Request Offerings
- Published Request Offerings
- Draft Request Offerings
- Standalone Request Offerings

Take look at the *Publishing Service offerings and Request offerings* recipe.

Standalone Request offerings

If a Request offering isn't related to a Service Request it is called a Standalone Request offering.

This type of Request offering is only visible in the List View of the SCSM 2012 portal.

There is a special view available for Standalone Request offerings. You must navigate to **SCSM 2012 Console | Library | Service Catalog | Request Offerings | Standalone Request Offerings** to view this type of offering.

Adding a Request offering to an existing Service offering

To add a Request offering to an existing Service offering in the SCSM 2012 console navigate to **Library | Service Catalog | Request Offerings** (**Draft**, **Published**, or **Standalone Request Offering**).

1. Select the Request offering and click on **Add to Service Offering** in the **Tasks** pane.

2. Select a Service offering from the list.

3. Click on **Add**.

4. Click on **OK** to close the window.

To control the access of Request offerings use groups and user roles in SCSM 2012

To control the access to Request offerings to a specific group of users you can use groups and user Roles in SCSM 2012.

1. In the SCSM 2012 console navigate to **Library | Groups**.

2. Click on **Create Catalog Group**.

3. Provide a name and choose a management pack.

4. Click on **Next**.

5. In the **Included Members** page add Request offerings from the list.

6. Click on **Next**.

7. In the **Dynamic Members** page you can specify a criteria for dynamically selecting the offerings (for example, dynamically include **Request Offering** class where "Display Name" contains "Active Directory").

8. Click on **Next**.

9. Add existing catalog groups if needed.

10. Click on **Next**.

11. Add offerings to the excluded members (if they are added dynamically as a dynamic member).

12. Click on **Next**.

13. Verify the **Summary** screen and click on **Create**.

See also

▸ Microsoft TechNet Library: Managing Service Requests in System Center 2012 - Service Manager: `http://technet.microsoft.com/en-us/library/hh519681`

▸ How to create and configure user roles in SCSM 2012 is described in the *Creating and managing Service Request roles*, *Creating and managing Incident Management roles*, *Creating and managing Problem Management roles*, *Creating and managing Change and Release Management roles*, and *Creating hybrid roles* recipe names in *Chapter 8, Implementing Security Roles*

Creating Service Catalog Service offerings

Service offerings in the SCSM 2012 Service catalog are the second tier to sort and combine Service offerings. SCSM 2012 groups and user roles can be used to control the permission through which users are able to see and use request offerings in the SCSM 2012 portal.

This recipe shows the necessary configuration and steps to create Service offerings in SCSM 2012.

Getting ready

To create Service offerings in the SCSM 2012 Service catalog, open the SCSM 2012 console and navigate to **Library | Service Catalog | Service Offerings**.

How to do it...

To create a Service Catalog Service offering, follow these steps:

1. Click on **Create Service Offering** in the **Task** pane of the SCSM 2012 console.
2. Read the **Before You Begin** information and then click on **Next**.

3. In the **General** page fill in all the information. Choose the **User Management** category we created in an earlier recipe. Choose an image.

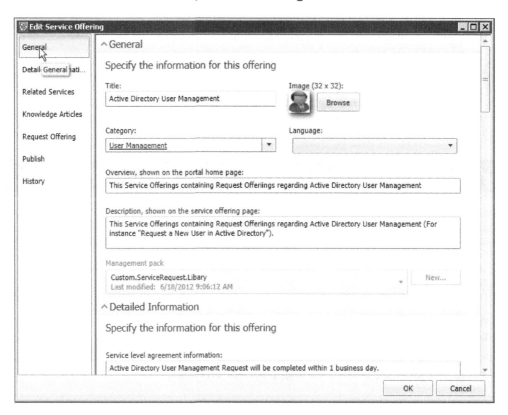

4. Click on **Next**.

5. Fill in all information in the **Detailed Information** page. This information is optional but will be helpful to the end user in the SCSM 2012 portal.

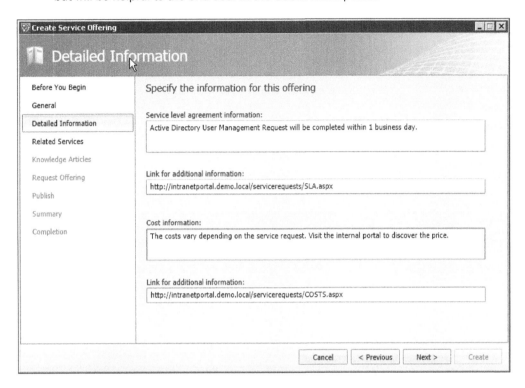

6. Click on **Next**.

7. In the **Related Services** page you can add a Business Service of SCSM 2012. In this recipe we will not add any related service.

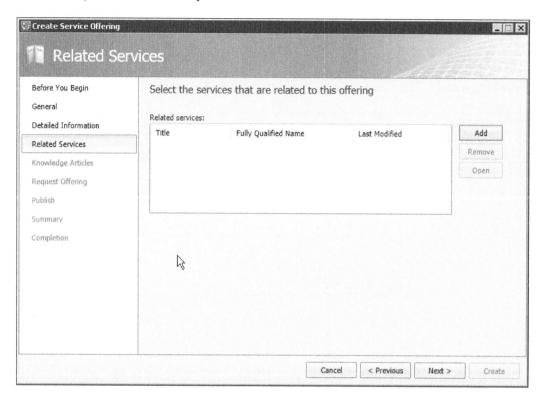

8. Click on **Next**.

9. Add a knowledge article to the Service offering in the **Knowledge Article** page. In our recipe we will add the **User Management** article.

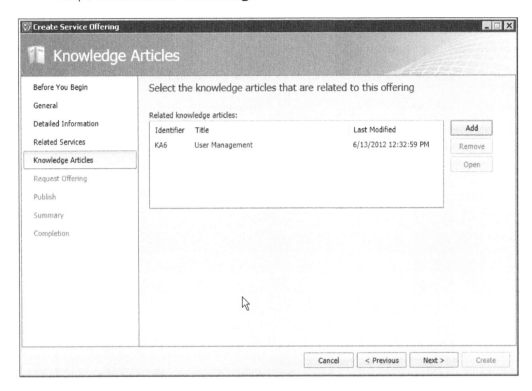

10. Click on **Next**.

11. In the **Request Offering** page add the Request offering we created in the previous recipe. Use the filter to find the **Create New User in Active Directory** request.

12. Select the Request offering, click on **Add**, and then click on **OK**.

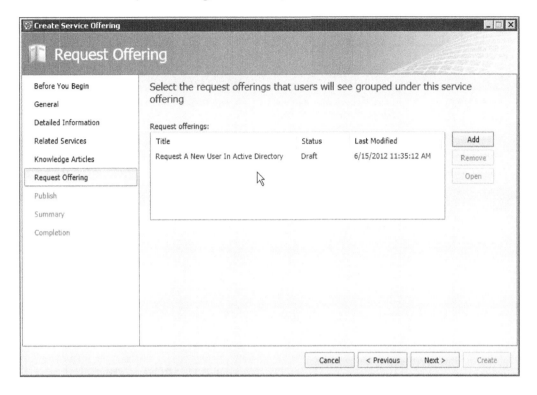

13. Click on **Next**.

14. In the **Publish** page fill in the owner of the offering. Leave the status as **Draft**. We will work with the publishing of offerings in the next recipe.

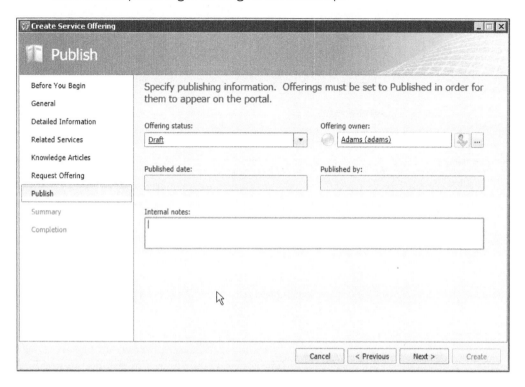

15. Click on **Next**.
16. Verify the **Summary** page and click on **Create**.

How it works...

All the information in the different pages of a Service offering will be used to display the Request offerings grouped in categories in the SCSM 2012 portal.

There's more...

Different views can be used in the SCSM 2012 console to filter Service offerings in different statuses.

Views for different status of Service offerings

In the SCSM 2012 console there are different views of Service offerings. This offers the opportunity to quickly navigate through the filtered list of Service offerings.

The following views are default in SCSM 2012:

- ▸ All Service Offerings
- ▸ Draft Service Offerings
- ▸ Published Service Offerings

You could also take a look at the *Publishing Service offerings and Request offerings* recipe.

Controlling access of Service offerings using groups and user roles

To control the access of Service offerings to a specific group of users you can use groups and user roles in SCSM 2012.

1. In the SCSM 2012 console navigate to **Library | Groups**.
2. Click on **Create Catalog Group**.
3. Provide a name and choose a management pack.
4. Click on **Next**.
5. In the **Included Members** page add offerings from the list.
6. Click on **Next**.
7. In the **Dynamic Members** page you can specify a criteria for dynamically selecting the offerings (for example, dynamically include Service Offering class where "Display Name" contains "Active Directory").
8. Click on **Next**.
9. Add existing catalog groups if needed.
10. Click on **Next**.
11. Add offerings to the excluded members (if they are added dynamically as a dynamic member).
12. Click on **Next**.
13. Verify the **Summary** screen and click on **Create**.

How to create and configure user roles in SCSM 2012 is described in *Chapter 8, Implementing Security Roles.*

See also

> ▶ Microsoft TechNet Library: Managing Service Requests in System Center 2012
> - Service Manager: `http://technet.microsoft.com/en-us/library/hh519681`

> ▶ Microsoft TechNet Library: Using the Service Catalog in System Center 2012 - Service Manager: `http://technet.microsoft.com/en-us/library/hh495624`

Publishing Service offerings and Request offerings

After creating Request and Service offerings as described in the previous two recipes you need to publish both types of offerings. As long as the offerings are in the **Draft** status they will be not visible in the SCSM 2012 portal to the end users.

A best practice for publishing request and Service offerings is to use Change Management with approvals for the publishing. This recipe discusses how you use Change Management with approvals to change a draft offering into a published offering visible in the SCSM 2012 Self Service portal. This will be done in two steps to publish the different offerings. The first step is for publishing Service offerings. The second one is for publishing Request offerings.

Getting ready

To publish Service offerings in the SCSM 2012 Service catalog open SCSM 2012 and navigate to **Library | Service Catalog | Service Offerings**.

To publish Request offerings in the SCSM 2012 Service catalog open SCSM 2012 and navigate to **Library | Service Catalog | Request Offerings**.

How to do it...

To publish a Service offering select the related Service offering (Active Directory User Management) in the list in **SCSM 2012 Console | Library | Service Catalog | Service Offerings**:

1. Click on **Create Change Request to Publish** in the **Tasks** pane.

2. Choose the **Publish Offering** template from the list in the **Select Template** window and click on **OK**.

3. In the **Change Request** form fill in the information regarding the publishing of the Service offering (**Title**, **Description**, **Reason**, **Created By**, **Area**, **Assigned To**, **Priority**, **Impact**, and **Risk**). For more information regarding Change Request and how they work please take a look at *Chapter 7, Designing Change and Release Management*.

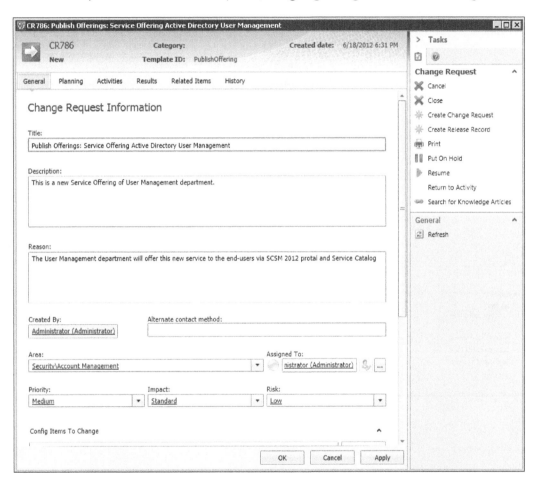

4. Click on the **Activities** tab. Verify that two activities are listed. The first Review Activity (RA-suffix) is the approval, the second (AC-suffix) is an automated activity to publish the Service offering.

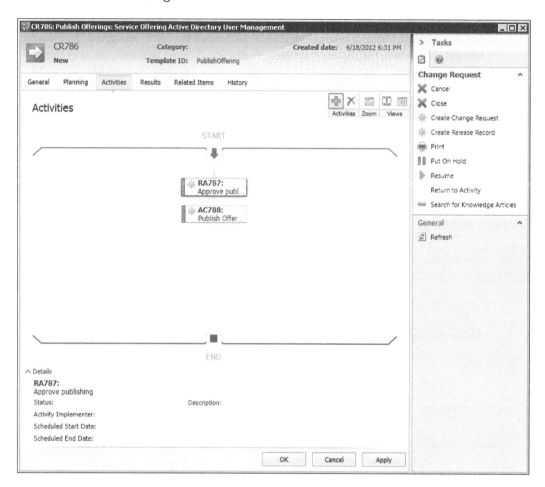

5. Add the reviewer and click on **OK** in the **Review Activity** page.

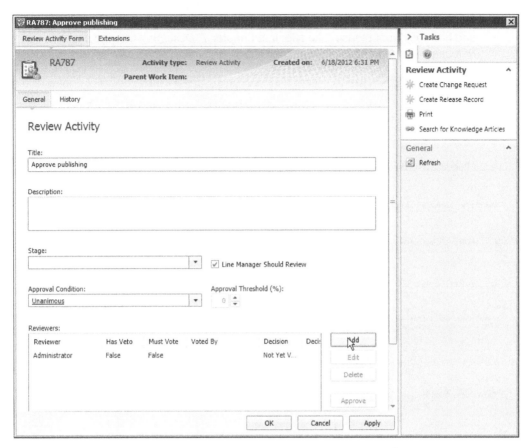

6. Close the Change Request by clicking on **OK**.

To publish a Request offering select the related Request offering (Request A New User in Active Directory) in the list in **SCSM 2012 Console | Library | Service Catalog | Request Offerings**:

1. Click on **Create Change Request to Publish** in the **Tasks** pane.

2. Choose the **Publish Offering** template from the list in the **Select Template** window and click on **OK**.

3. In the **Change Request** form fill in the information regarding the publishing of the Request offering (**Title**, **Description**, **Reason**, **Created By**, **Area**, **Assigned To**, **Priority**, **Impact**, and **Risk**). For more information regarding Change Request and how they work please take a look at *Chapter 7, Designing Change and Release Management.*

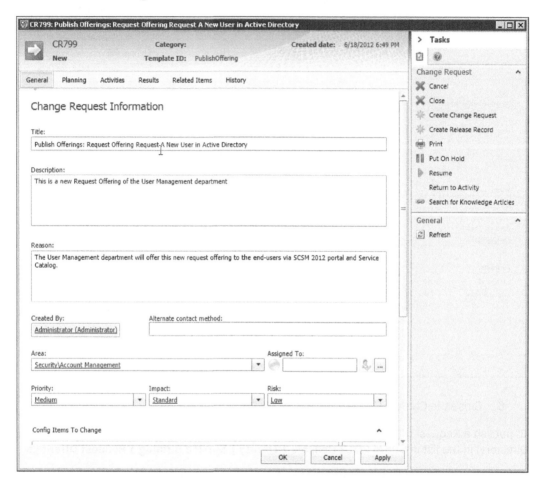

4. Click on the **Activities** tab. Verify that two activities are listed. The first Review Activity (RA-suffix) is the approval, the second (AC-suffix) is an automated activity to publish the Request offering.

5. Add the reviewer and click on **OK** in the **Review Activity** page. (as described in the part to publish the Service offering).

6. Close the Change Request by clicking on **OK**.

Approving both Change Requests to publish the Service offering and the Request offering:

1. In the SCSM 2012 console navigate to **Work Items | Activity Management | Review Activities | In-Progress Activities**.

2. Select the first Review Activity named **Approve publishing** and click on **Approve** in the **Tasks** pane.

3. Enter a comment (required) and click on **OK** to close the window.

4. Select the second Review Activity named **Approve publishing** and click on **Approve** in the **Tasks** pane.

5. Enter a comment (required) and click on **OK** to close the window.

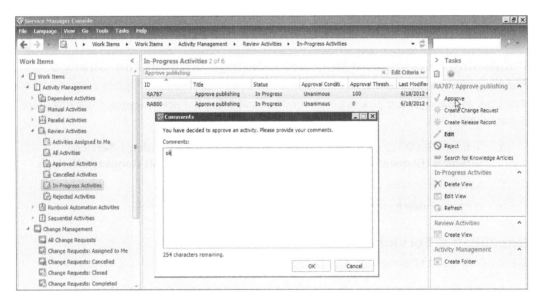

Verify the result:

1. After both Review Activities are approved wait for a few minutes. SCSM 2012 workflows will trigger the Automated Activities to change the status for the Service offering and Request offering to **Published** after a few minutes.

2. In the SCSM 2012 console navigate to **Library | Service Catalog | Service Offerings | Published Service Offerings**. The Service offering we created and published during the recipes in this chapter should be listed.

3. In the SCSM 2012 console navigate to **Library | Service Catalog | Request Offerings | Published Request Offerings**. The Request offering we created and published during the recipes in this chapter should be listed.

How it works...

Change Management can be used for the publishing process of Service or Request offerings.

After creating a related Change Request two activities are added to the Change Request record. The first activity is for reviewing and approving. The second, automated activity will be triggered by an internal SCSM 2012 workflow after the reviewer approves the first activity. The workflow will set the status of the offering to **Published**.

There's more...

The publishing and unpublishing of Service and Request offerings can be done without involving the Change Management process.

Publishing Service and Request offerings without the Change Management process

If no Change Management process is needed to publish the Service or Request offering there is a shortcut:

1. In the SCSM 2012 console navigate to **Library | Service Catalog | Service Offerings/Request Offerings | Draft Service Offerings/Draft Request Offerings**.
2. Select the Service offering or Request offering.
3. Click on **Publish** in the **Tasks** pane.

Unpublish a Service offering or Request offering

Service or Request offerings can also be unpublished:

1. In the SCSM 2012 console navigate to **Library | Service Catalog | Service Offerings/Request Offerings | Published Service Offerings/Published Request Offerings**.
2. Select the Service offering or Request offering.
3. Click on **Unpublish** in the **Tasks** pane.

See also

> ▸ Microsoft TechNet Library: Managing Service Requests in System Center 2012 - Service Manager: `http://technet.microsoft.com/en-us/library/hh519681`

> ▸ Microsoft TechNet Library: Using the Service Catalog in System Center 2012 - Service Manager: `http://technet.microsoft.com/en-us/library/hh495624`

Working with Service Requests in the portal

After publishing the Request offering and Service offering end users can start creating Service Requests in the SCSM 2012 Self Service portal based on this offering.

This recipe shows how to work with the SCSM 2012 portal to submit a Service Request.

Getting ready

Open the SCSM 2012 Self Service portal in Microsoft Internet Explorer.

By default the URL is `https://<portalservername>:<port>/SMPortal/`.

How to do it...

1. The following is the SCSM 2012 portal entry page:

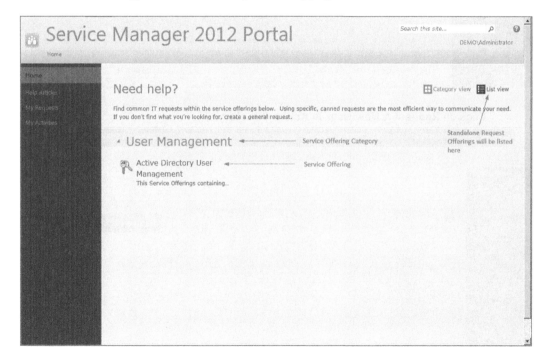

2. Click on the Service offering **Active Directory User Management**.

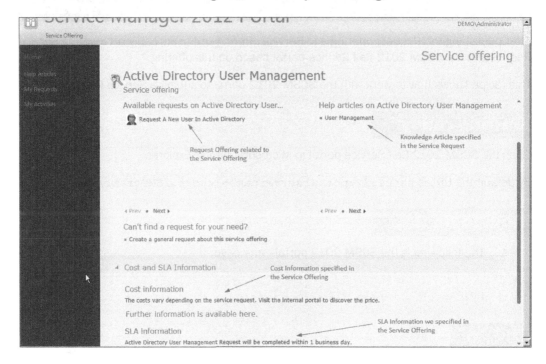

3. Click on **Request A New User in Active Directory**.

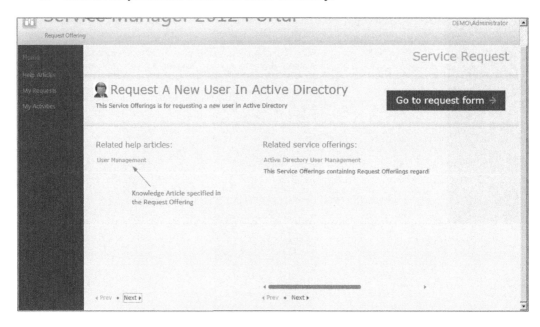

4. Click on **Go to request form**.

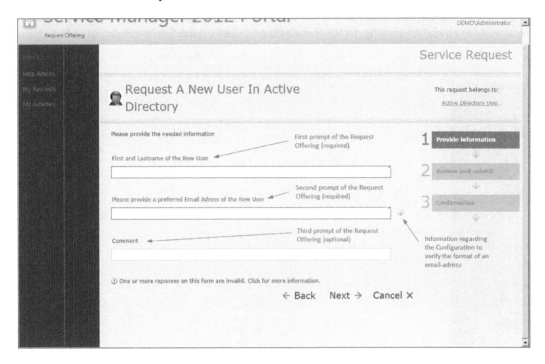

5. Provide the information in the form. Click on **Next**.

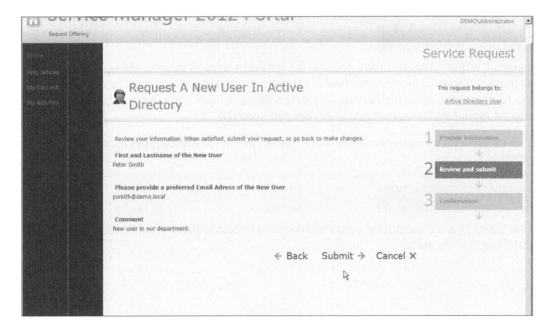

6. Verify the input and click on **Submit**.

7. After the Service Request is submitted the end user can follow the progress of his/her request by clicking on **My Requests** and then on the Service Request in the list.

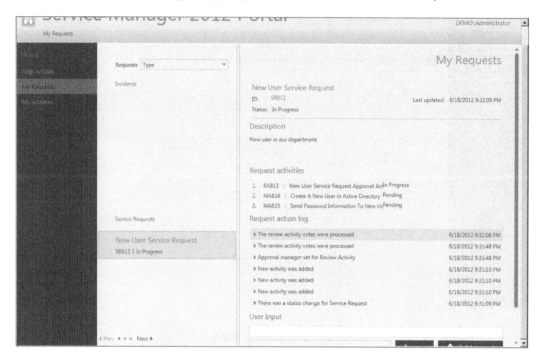

How it works...

Using the SCSM 2012 portal it is possible for end users to raise service requests. Based on all the information in the Service offering and Request offering the user will be able to get as much information about the Service Request as possible (SLA, costs, Knowledge Articles, and the required information to fulfill the Service Request).

Also, he/she can follow the progress of his/her request in the **My Request** section of the SCSM 2012 portal.

There's more...

After submitting a Service Request the end user can add additional input by using the SCSM 2012 Self Service portal.

Additional User Input after the Service Request is submitted

As long as the status of a Service Request request is in the progress the end user can provide additional information to the Service Request in the SCSM 2012 portal by following these steps:

1. Open the SCSM 2012 portal in a supported SCSM 2012 web browser.
2. Click on **My Request**.
3. Click on the Service Request in the list.
4. Write the information in the **User Input** field and click on **Update Request**.

See also

▶ Microsoft TechNet Library: Managing Service Requests in System Center 2012 - Service Manager: `http://technet.microsoft.com/en-us/library/hh519681`

▶ Microsoft TechNet Library: Using the Service Catalog in System Center 2012 - Service Manager: `http://technet.microsoft.com/en-us/library/hh495624`

Creating Service Request notifications

In this recipe we will configure the notification of an end user if a Service Request that he/she submitted is completed.

Getting ready

Create a notification template as described in the *Creating formatted e-mail notification templates* recipe in *Chapter 2, Personalizing SCSM 2012 Administration*. For example, *Service Request Completed Notification Template*.

In the SCSM 2012 console navigate to **Administration | Workflow | Configuration**.

How to do it...

To create a Notification workflow for completed Service Requests select **Service Request Event Workflow Configuration** and click on **Configure Workflow Rules** in the **Tasks** pane.

1. Click on **Add** in the **Configure Workflows** window.
2. Read the **Before You Begin** information and click on **Next**.
3. Provide a name and description.
4. Choose **When an object is updated** in the **Check for events** section.

5. Choose a management pack to store the information in.

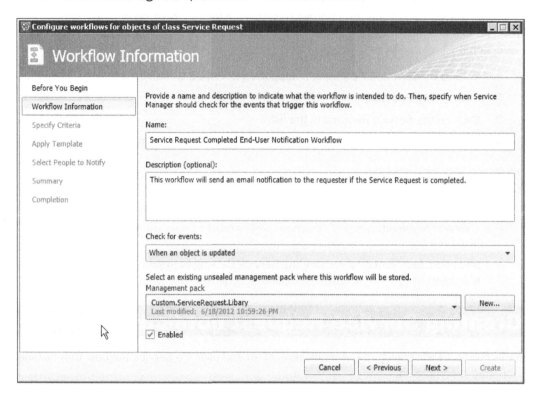

6. Click on **Next**.

7. Specify the criteria **Changed from**, **Status**, **does not equal**, and **Completed** in the **Specify Criteria** page.

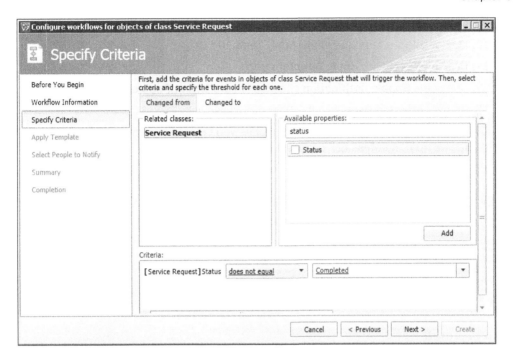

8. Specify the criteria **Changed to**, **Status**, **equals**, and **Completed** in the **Specify Criteria** page.

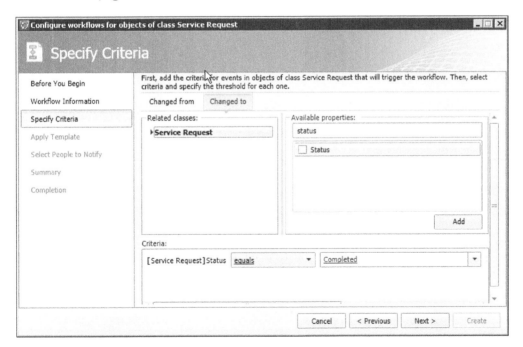

9. Click on **Next** in the **Specify Criteria** page.

10. Do not select a template in the **Apply Template** page.

11. Click on **Next** in the **Apply Template** page.

12. Check the **Enable notification** checkbox in the **Select People to Notify** page.

13. Choose **Affected User** from the **User** drop-down list.

14. Choose the message notification template you created before starting this recipe from the **Message template** drop-down list.

15. Click on **Add**.

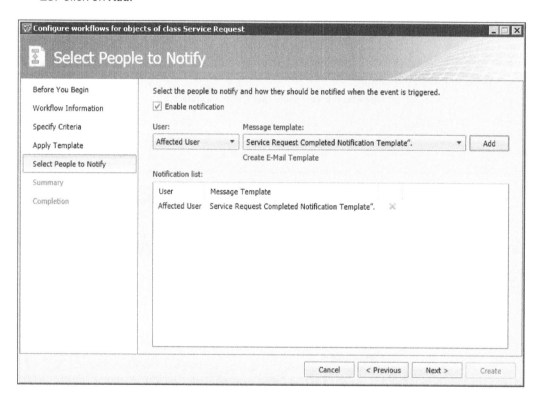

16. Click **Next** on the **Select People to Notify** page.

17. Verify the **Summary** page and then click on **Create**.

18. Click on **Close** in the **Completion** page.

19. The workflow will be visible in the list in the **Configure Workflows** window.

20. Click on **OK** to close the **Configure Workflows** window.

How it works...

The SCSM 2012 workflow engine checks in intervals to see if a condition of a defined workflow is met. If the status of a Service Request is changed from **not Completed** to **Completed** the workflow we created in this recipe will be executed. The specified e-mail template will be used to send a message to the requester (affected user). The requester will be informed that his Service Request is completed.

There's more...

In SCSM 2012 you can configure additional notification workflows based on the status of service requests.

Send different notifications regarding a Service Request

Based on different criteria in additional workflows and different templates, the end user can also be informed if a Service Request fails (for instance if a Service Request is "rejected" in the "Review Activity" step for some reason).

Notification for activities in Service Requests

To send notifications on different types of Activities (Review and Manual Activities) take a look at *Chapter 7, Designing Change and Release Management*. There are some recipes to notify the reviewer (Review Activity) or the implementer (Manual Activity).

See also

▶ TechNet Library: How to View Workflow Success or Failure: `http://technet.microsoft.com/en-us/library/hh524277`

6
Working with Incident and Problem Management

In this chapter, we will cover:

- ▶ Configuring Incident and Problem lists
- ▶ Creating an Incident template
- ▶ Adding a task to the Incident form
- ▶ Creating a workflow to notify the affected user upon the creation of an Incident
- ▶ Creating a view to display the Problem Records created in the last 30 days
- ▶ Configuring the Global Operators Group
- ▶ Downloading, installing, and configuring the Exchange Connector
- ▶ Making the description field in the Incident form to auto grow
- ▶ Extending the Incident class with a new property

Introduction

In this chapter we will look at recipes for two of the core processes within ITIL©, Incident and Problem Management.

Any company following the ITIL© framework probably started their journey with the Incident process, as it is one of the easiest processes to adapt and understand. Since the Incident process is central to both ITIL© and Service Manager (SCSM), this is one of the areas where you might find yourself spending some extra time to fine tune SCSM.

Configuring Incident and Problem lists

Lists are widely used in Service Manager and appear in almost any form. These lists are used to offer the analysts predefined choices rather than having them enter text manually. This is really handy for fields where you want to limit the input options, to save time for the analyst and to make sure that the input is standardized.

Getting ready

Make sure that Service Manager is up and running and that you have sufficient privileges to edit a list. In order to complete this and the rest of the recipes in this chapter, you need to be a member of the Author or Administrator user role within Service Manager.

How to do it...

The following lists are available in Incident and Problem Management:

- Incident Tier Queue
- Incident Status
- Incident Source
- Incident Classification
- Incident Resolution
- Problem Status
- Problem Resolution
- Problem Classification
- Problem Source
- Urgency
- Impact

Any of these lists can be configured through the Service Manager console. Here's an example of how to add a hardware option to the Problem Classification list:

1. Open the Service Manager console and go to the **Library** workspace.
2. Select **Lists** in the navigation pane.

3. To locate the **Problem Classification** list, enter `Problem classification` in the **Filter** field, as shown in the following screenshot:

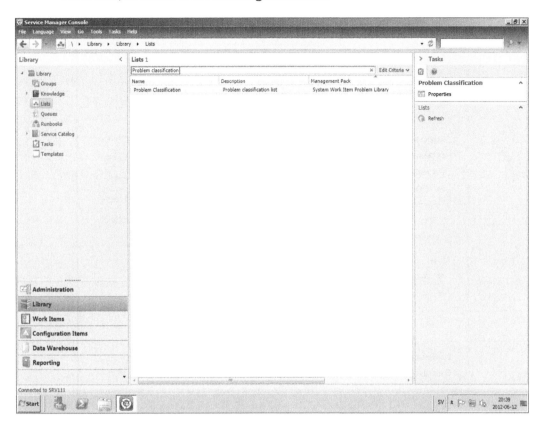

4. Double-click the **Problem Classification** list to open it.

5. Click on **Add Item** to add a new value to the list.

6. At the bottom of the list, a new value named **List Value** should appear. Select this item and change the name to `Hardware`.

7. With **Hardware** still selected, click on the **Add Child** button.

8. A child item with the name **List Value** should appear under **Hardware**. Select this item and change the name to `Client`.

9. Select **Hardware** and click on **Add Child** again. Change the name of the new list item to `Server`.

10. Now select **Hardware** again, and click on the **Move Up** button until the **Hardware** option is placed right under **Facilities**.

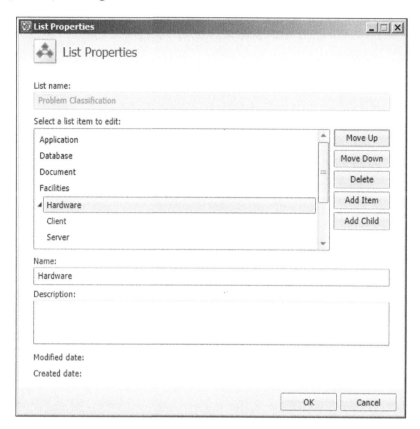

11. Click on **OK** when you are done.

All these lists come predefined out of the box but most of them will need to be modified by you to fit your organization. Every time you edit a list, this change is reflected in a Management Pack. This makes it easy to work with lists in a pre-production environment and then copy them all to production by exporting, copying, and importing the Management Pack.

There's more...

This way of working with lists applies to all the lists in Service Manager, and not only lists related to the Incident and Problem processes. If you add your own list to the system, by creating it in the Authoring Tool or by writing your own XML code, you will be able to see and edit it in the same fashion.

If there's a predefined list item that you do not want, you should avoid renaming it to something different that you would like to have in your list. Instead, remove the list item and add a new one. The reason for this is that you are only changing the display strings for that particular list item in the language that you are running the console.

> For instance, if you are running a Swedish console and rename the list item named **Configuration Data Problems** in the Incident Classification list to **Terminal Server Problems**, any users running a console in another language than Swedish will still see **Configuration Data Problems**!

When working with lists for the Incident and Problem processes, there are two lists that are special, Impact and Urgency. These two lists are shared between the two processes, so you are unable to have different Impact and Urgency lists between the two processes.

If you modify any of these lists, this will be reflected in the Priority Matrix under Incident and Problem settings.

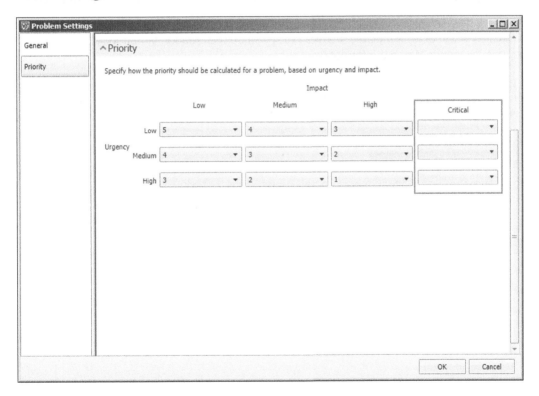

See also

▶ For more information regarding Management Packs, please see the *Creating Management Packs in the Authoring tool to save your SCSM personalization* recipe in *Chapter 2, Personalizing SCSM 2012 Administration*

▶ For more information regarding the Authoring Tool, please see *Using the SCSM Authoring Tool* in *Chapter 10, Extending SCSM with Advanced Personalization*

▶ For more information regarding Impact, Urgency and Priority, please see the *Configuring Priority and Urgency for your SLA targets* recipe in *Chapter 2, Personalizing SCSM 2012 Administration*

▶ For more information regarding lists, please see the *Creating Support Groups for Service Requests* recipe in *Chapter 5, Deploying Service Request Fulfillment*

Creating an Incident template

There are certain types of incidents that occur frequently and this is where the use of templates is valuable. Templates are used to speed up the creation of new incidents and give us a way to standardize the information in them.

A template consists of one or more predefined properties of a certain class. For instance, an incident template used for registering local printer incidents might have the Title, Description, Classification Category, Impact, and Urgency predefined.

Getting ready

Make sure that Service Manager is up and running and that you have sufficient privileges to create new templates.

How to do it...

As an example, we will create a template for registering local printer issues. In order to do so, follow these steps:

1. Start the Service Manager console and go to the **Library** workspace.
2. Select **Templates** in the navigation pane.

3. A list of all available templates should now be displayed. Click on **Create Template** in the task pane on your right-hand side.

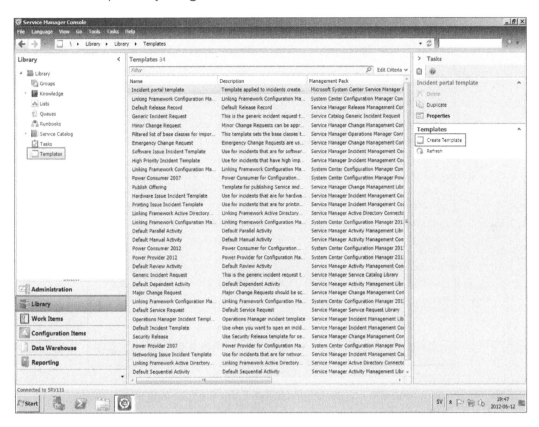

4. This will launch a new dialog form where you have to enter the **Name** and **Description** of the template. You also have to choose a targeted class and a management pack to store this template in.

5. Enter `Local Printer Incident` as the **Name** of the template.

6. Enter `Use this template to register any issues related to Local Printers` as the **Description** of the template.

7. Click on the **Browse...** button, select the Incident class, and click on **OK**.

8. Choose between storing your template in an existing management pack or creating a new management pack to store it in; then click on **OK**.

9. An Incident form should now be displayed. Enter the following information:

   ❑ **Title** = Local Printer issue

   ❑ **Classification Category** = Printing Problems

   ❑ **Impact** = Low

   ❑ **Urgency** = Low

10. Then click on **OK**.

How it works...

After you have created a template, you can use this template to create a new Incident with the **Create Incident from Template** task. If you do so, all the fields that you entered information in when creating the template will be pre-populated with that piece of information.

It is also possible to apply a template to an already existing Incident with the **Apply Template** task. Just bear in mind that all the fields that you have specified within your template will be written into the incident regardless of the information currently in those fields.

There's more...

Templates can be used in other ways as well. For instance, the Exchange Connector will base new Incidents or updates to Service Request upon a template. It will also apply a template when updating an existing Work Item.

You may also apply templates to Work Items from a workflow. This can be useful to route specific Incidents to a person or group, for instance.

[The Problem Management process within Service Manager does not support templates. It's possible to create templates for problems, but there is no way to apply these from the console.]

See also

- ▶ For more information regarding templates, please see the *Creating Service Request templates* recipe in *Chapter 5, Deploying Service Request Fulfillment*
- ▶ For more information regarding management packs, please see the *Creating Management Packs in the Authoring tool to save your SCSM personalization* recipe in *Chapter 2, Personalizing SCSM 2012 Administration*
- ▶ For more information regarding the Exchange Connector, see the *Downloading, installing, and configuring the Exchange Connector* recipe
- ▶ For more information regarding applying templates with workflows, see the *Routing Incidents automatically using workflows* recipe in *Chapter 11, Automating Service Manager 2012*

Adding a task to the Incident form

Tasks are different type of actions that you can perform on an object from the Service Manager console. Some tasks are essential for Service Manager to work, such as the Create and Edit tasks, other tasks are used to facilitate the troubleshooting process. A good example of this is the Ping Related Computer or Remote Desktop tasks that are available when selecting an Incident.

Getting ready

Make sure that Service Manager is up and running and that you have sufficient privileges to create a new task.

How to do it...

In this example, we will create a custom task for executing an `nslookup` on a computer related to an incident.

1. Start the Service Manager console and go to the **Library** workspace.

2. Select **Tasks** in the navigation pane.

3. If you have created any tasks previously, these tasks should now be displayed, otherwise you should get the **No items found** message. To create a new task, click on the **Create Task** console task.

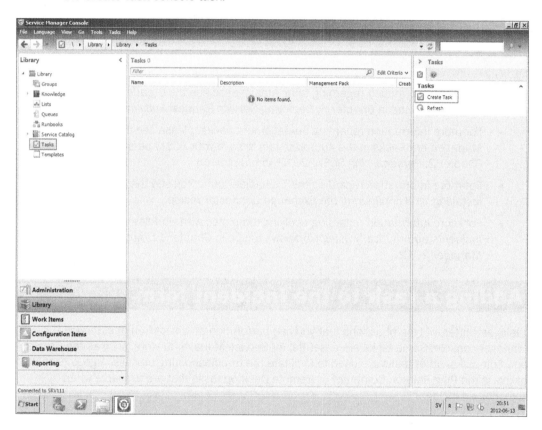

4. The **Create Task** wizard should now launch. In the **Before You Begin** step, click on **Next**.

5. Enter a name for your task; in this example we will give the task the name `Nslookup`.

6. As a description, enter `Perform an Nslookup on a computer related to the Incident.`

7. Click on the **Browse...** button next to **Target Class**.

8. Select the **Incident** class and click on **OK.**

9. Specify whether you want to save this task in an existing management pack or if you want to create a new one to save it in. Then click on **Next.**

10. You will be asked to specify where this task should be visible in the console. If you don't choose anything specific here, it will only show up when an object of the selected class is selected.

   Don't select anything and click on **Next.**

11. Now, we have to specify where the executable is located, and which parameters we want to launch the program with. In the **Full path to command** field, enter `%windir%\System32\nslookup.exe`.

12. Now click on the **Insert Property** button, select **About Configuration Item**, then enter `principal name` in the search field for **Available properties**. Select **Principal Name** under the **Windows Computer** heading and click on **Add**.

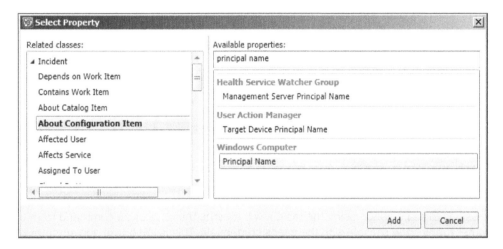

13. Make sure that the checkboxes for **Log in action log when this task is run** and **Show output when this task is run** are checked. Then click on **Next**.

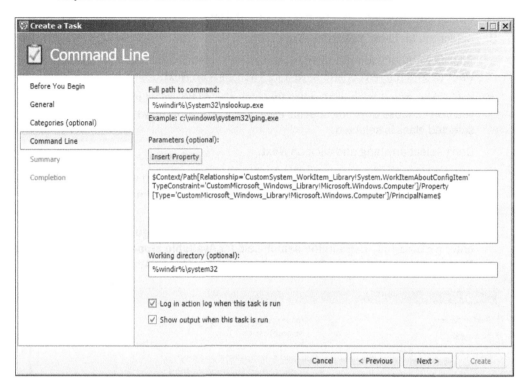

14. Review the summary, and then click on **Create** followed by **Close**.

How it works...

This task will be available in all consoles as long as the user running the console has the permissions to see it. When using the task, it will execute the `nslookup` command from the computer running the console with the user's credentials. This is important and something to keep in mind when creating new tasks.

Before creating a new task, make sure that the executable is located in the same path on the computers where the Service Manager console is used. Otherwise the task won't work.

There's more...

The tasks created from Service Manager are simply an easier way of executing a command. There are, however, more advanced tasks that you configure using Visual Studio. Those kinds of tasks require developer skill and knowledge of the Service Manager SDK, and are not covered in this book.

If your tasks are using input properties and the fields used for this don't contain any information, you will be asked to enter this manually. Additionally, if your field contains more than one object, you will be asked to select which object to run this task against.

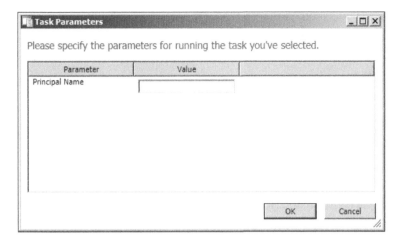

See also

▸ For more information on how to create custom tasks in Visual Studio, please see this blog post on the official Service Manager blog: `http://blogs.technet.com/b/servicemanager/archive/2010/12/22/tasks-part-2-custom-console-tasks-for-create-edit-delete.aspx`

Creating a workflow to notify the affected user upon the creation of an Incident

Many IT departments often hear that they need to improve their information flow to the customer during the troubleshooting process. To improve this we can create workflows or subscriptions to automatically send e-mail notifications during the lifecycle of a Work Item, such as an Incident. Workflows and subscriptions can be triggered when a Work Item fulfills a criterion. This could be when the status of an Incident changes from Active to Resolved or when the Escalated checkbox is checked.

Getting ready

In order to send outgoing mails from Service Manager, you need to configure a Notification Channel. If you haven't done so, follow these steps:

1. Open the Service Manager console and go to the **Administration** workspace.

2. Expand **Notifications** and select **Channels**.

3.   Double-click on the **E-mail Notification Channel** to open the properties.

4.   Enable e-mail notifications by checking the **Enable e-mail notifications** checkbox.

5.   Enter the **Return e-mail address** (if you are using the Exchange connector, the reply address should match the address for the workflow account).

6.   Now click on the **Add...** button.

7.   Enter the SMTP server address and set **Authentication Mode** to **Windows Integrated**.

8.   Click on **OK** to close the **Add SMTP server** dialog.

9.   Click on **OK** to close the **Configure E-Mail Notification Channel** dialog.

How to do it...

In this example, we will take a look at how to create a workflow to notify the affected user that a new incident has been created. To do so, follow these steps:

1.   Open the Service Manager console and go to the **Administration** workspace.

2.   Expand **Workflows** and select **Configuration**.

3.   Double-click on **Incident Event Workflow Configuration**.

4.   In the **Configure Workflows** dialog, click on **Add**.

5.   Skip the **Before You Begin** step by clicking on **Next**.

6.   Enter `Incident - New Incident Notification` as the name of the workflow.

7.   In the **Description** field, enter `This workflow is used to notify the affected user upon creating a new incident`.

8.   Make sure that the **Check for events** drop-down box has **When an object is created** selected.

9. Specify in which management pack you want to save this workflow and then click on **Next**.

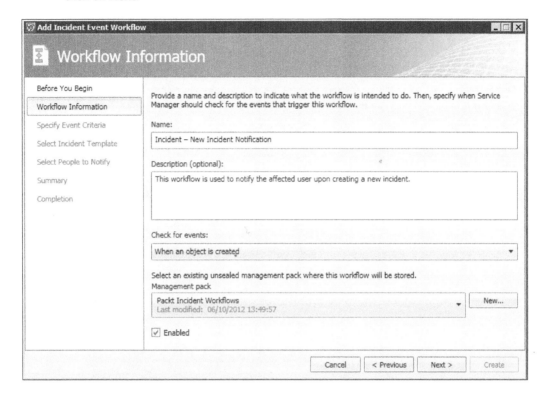

10. In the **Specify Event Criteria** step, don't enter anything and click on **Next**.

11. In the **Select Incident Template** step, click on **Next**.

12. In the **Select People to Notify** step, check the checkbox next to **Enable notification.**

13. In the **User** drop-down box select **Affected User**, and in the **Message template** drop-down box select **End User Notification Template**. Then click on **Add**.

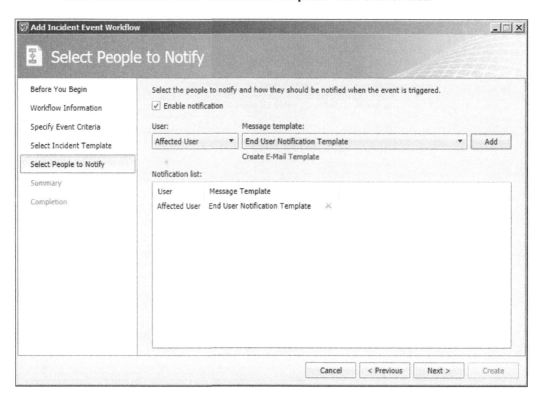

14. Click on **Next** followed by **Create** and **Close**.
15. Close the **Configure Incident Event Workflows** by clicking on **OK**.

How it works...

Whenever a new Incident is created and fulfills the criteria specified in our workflow, Service Manager will send an e-mail to the affected user using the End User e-mail notification template. Since we didn't specify a criteria, this workflow will trigger on the creation of all Incidents.

There's more...

When creating the workflow as described, we used an out of the box notification template to send your e-mail. Even though this works, you should consider creating your own e-mail notification templates for workflows and subscriptions.

When creating your own e-mail notification template you can specify the exact wording and format of the e-mail, and you can choose to insert some properties of the Incident that triggered the outgoing e-mail into the template.

If you are using the Exchange Connector to handle incoming e-mails, you are required to add the ID of the Work Item within square brackets (for instance, [IR319]) in the subject of the e-mail, otherwise the Exchange Connector won't work properly.

If you have configured the Notification Channel in Service Manager and created the workflow as described previously, and still don't receive an e-mail, there might be an issue with your e-mail server or Antivirus application. Many e-mail servers won't allow other servers to send e-mails and would require an authorizing configuration by an administrator.

Additionally, some Antivirus applications block outgoing e-mails from servers. You may have to configure exceptions in the relevant Antivirus application to allow the Service Manager workflow server to send e-mails.

Workflows and subscriptions

Workflows and subscriptions are mentioned in this recipe but we only looked at creating a workflow. Both of these can be used to send outgoing e-mail notifications.

So when should you use one or the other? To start with, workflows can only be created for Activities, Change Requests, Incidents, Release Records, and Service Requests, while subscriptions can be created for any class in the system (including Configuration Items). Next, workflows can use different notification templates for different recipients; in subscriptions, all recipients will get the same notification template.

On the other hand, subscriptions can send notifications to a certain user even if that user does not have a relation to the actual item triggering the subscription. This can be useful for sending notifications to the management team when an SLA is breached for instance. The Workflow option has an advantage over subscriptions due to the ability to apply templates to the Work Item when a criterion is fulfilled.

So the answer to the question is, it depends on the situation. If the notification you want to configure can be triggered from either of these, use the most appropriate option.

See also

▶ For more information regarding notification channels and notification templates, please see *Creating formatted e-mail notification templates* and *Configuring global e-mail notification infrastructure settings* recipes in *Chapter 2, Personalizing SCSM 2012 Administration*

▶ For more information regarding workflows and notifications, please see the *Creating Service Request notifications* recipe in *Chapter 5, Deploying Service Request Fulfillment*

Creating a view to display the Problem Records created in the last 30 days

Views are used everywhere in the Service Manager console to display objects of a certain class and for a given criteria. If you take a look at the views for the Problem Management process, there are a couple of predefined views, as follows:

- ▶ Active Known Errors
- ▶ Active Problems
- ▶ Closed Problems
- ▶ My Problems
- ▶ Needing Review
- ▶ Resolved Problems

These are all good and useful views, but there's a good chance that you might want to create a couple of additional views. For instance, you might want a view that shows all the Problem records that's been created for the last 30 days, regardless of their status.

Getting ready

Make sure that Service Manager is up and running and that you have sufficient privileges to create a new view.

How to do it...

Here's how you create a view to display all the Problem Records that have been created in the last 30 days:

1. Open the Service Manager console and go to **Work Items**.
2. Select **Problem Management**.
3. Click on the **Create View** task in the task pane.
4. Enter `All Problems last 30 days` as the name of the view.
5. Enter `This view displays all Problem Records created in the last 30 days` as the description.
6. Select a **Management Pack** to store this view in.
7. In the **Criteria** section, click on the **Browse** button, select the **Problem** class, and click on **OK**.
8. In the search field for **Available Properties**, enter `created date`.

9. Check the **Created date** property and click on **Add**.

10. **Created date** should now appear in the **Criteria** section. Click on the drop-down box next to **Created date** and select **is greater than or equal to**.

11. Now check the **relative** checkbox and enter [now-30d] in the text field, as shown in the following screenshot:

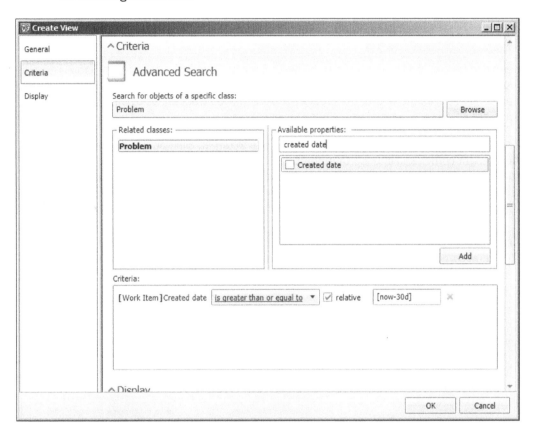

12. Now go to the **Display** section and make sure that the only Columns that are selected are:

- ❑ **Created date**
- ❑ **Id**
- ❑ **Known Error**
- ❑ **Status**
- ❑ **Title**

13. Click on **OK** to create the view.

How it works...

The view will display all objects for the given class and criteria. In our example we created a view targeting the Problem class. We used a special criteria property "now" for creating the view which is known as a token. Because we used [now-30d], Service Manager will deduct thirty days from the current date and use that as the criteria when querying the database.

There's more...

Views can be created for any class in the system using a similar series of steps. You could even create a view to display all Incidents where the affected user belongs to the marketing department. In order to create such a view, you would have to base your view on a Combination class instead of the regular Incident class.

When creating your view and choosing which class to target, click on the drop-down menu at the top-right corner and choose **Combination classes**. You will then get a list of all available Combination classes. If you would like to create the view for all Incidents where the affected user belongs to the marketing department, you could base your view on the **Incident (typical)** Combination class for instance.

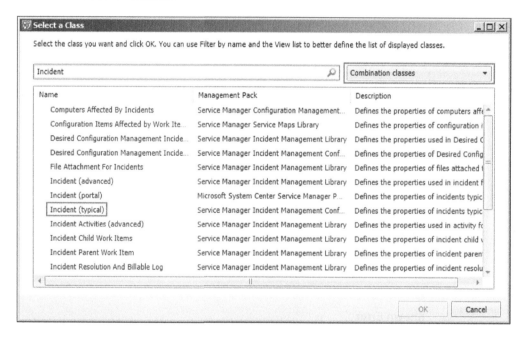

There's a catch in using Combination classes for your views; the bigger your Combination class is, the more objects will have to be retrieved from the database, which in turn decreases the performance for loading the view. Because of this, you should avoid using Combination classes if it's not necessary, and if you need to use them, always use the narrowest one.

Combination classes are actually another name for Type Projections, and the Type Projection term is far more common when searching for more information regarding this on the Web.

Available tokens in Service Manager

Currently there are three tokens available in Service Manager:

▸ [me]

▸ [mygroups]

▸ [now]

All three tokens can be used when creating views. If you take a look at the views displaying My Incidents or My Problems, you can see how these tokens are used. Tokens cannot be used for anything other than view criteria.

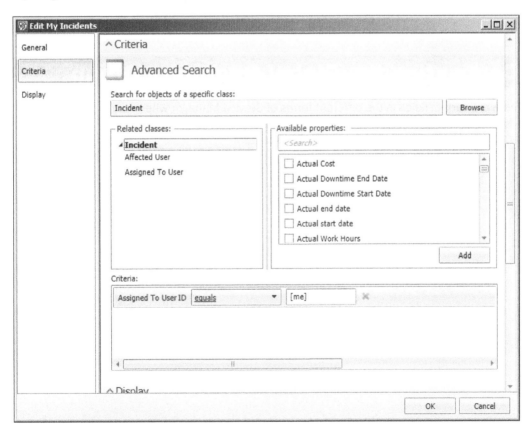

See also

- ► For more information regarding views, please see the *Personalizing and organizing configuration item views* recipe in *Chapter 4, Building the Configuration Management Database (CMDB)*

- ► For more information regarding Combination Classes/Type Projections and views, please see these blog posts on the official Service Manager blog:

    - ❑ http://blogs.technet.com/b/servicemanager/
      archive/2010/02/02/creating-views-that-use-related-
      property-criteria-type-projections-software-views-
      example.aspx

    - ❑ http://blogs.technet.com/b/servicemanager/
      archive/2010/12/02/faq-why-is-my-custom-incident-view-
      so-slow.aspx

    - ❑ http://blogs.technet.com/b/servicemanager/
      archive/2011/04/06/faq-why-can-t-i-add-some-columns-
      that-i-want-to-views.aspx

Configuring the Global Operators Group

There are certain fields in the different forms of Service Manager where you are supposed to add a user or group. These fields are called User Pickers and if you take a look at the Incident form there are three User Pickers on the **General** tab:

- ► **Affected user**
- ► **Assigned to**
- ► **Primary owner**

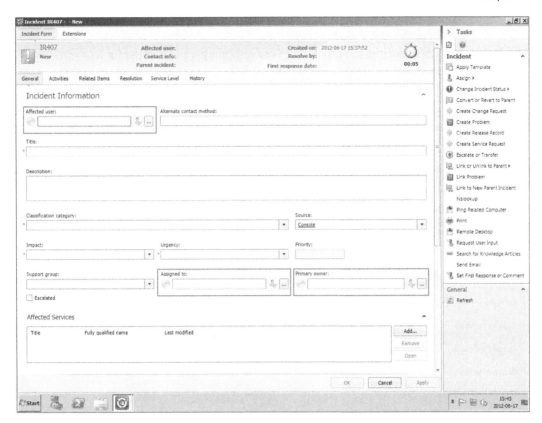

Some of these User Pickers target the end users, such as the **Affected user** field, while others target users or groups from the IT department, such as the **Assigned to** and **Primary owner** fields. When searching for a user to add to the User Picker, Service Manager will by default search the whole CMDB for users and groups. This is exactly what we want for the User Pickers targeting the end users, but for the User Pickers targeting the IT department, we are not interested in retrieving any users outside of the IT department.

It's very unlikely that we will assign an Incident to a person outside of the IT department for instance. To narrow the scope of the User Pickers targeting the IT department you will have to configure something called the Global Operators Group.

Getting ready

Make sure Service Manager is running and that you have sufficient privileges to configure the Global Operators Group.

How to do it...

The Global Operators Group is pre-created in Service Manager but in order for it to work properly you will have to configure it. To configure the Global Operators Group to include dynamic members, follow these steps:

1. Start the Service Manager console, go to the **Library** workspace, and select **Groups** in the navigation pane.

2. Double–click on **Global Operators Group** to view its properties.

3. Go to the **Dynamic Members** section and locate **Department** in the list of available properties.

4. Select **Department** and click on **Add**.

5. Change the value of the list next to **Department** in the criteria section to **equals** and then enter IT in the text field right next to it.

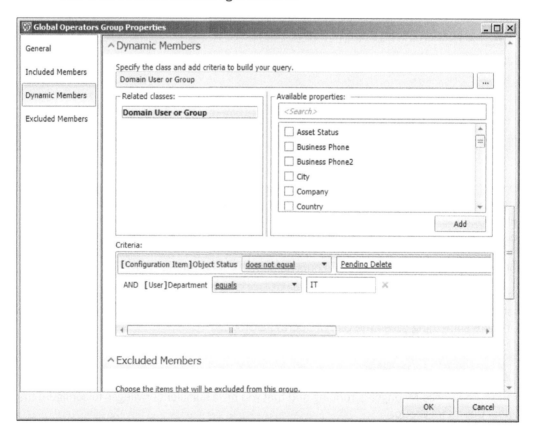

6. Click on **OK** to save your changes and close the **Global Operators Group** properties.

How it works...

After the internal group calculation has occurred in Service Manager (which can take a couple of minutes), the Global Operators Group will include all users, which fulfill the criteria specified in the Dynamic Members. This means that if you now browse a User Picker targeting the IT department (such as the Assigned to field in an Incident), you will now only see users where the department is set to IT. You must ensure that the target property for your criteria is populated in Active Directory. In the example we use the department of the user (the field data in the example is "IT"), which is a field in the Organization property of the active directory user.

You can of course specify another criteria than the one used in the previous example.

There's more...

When configuring the Global Operators Group, you have two options for membership:

- ▸ Static Members (Included Members)
- ▸ Dynamic Members

Static Members are added in the Included Members section. Here you get the option to specify exactly which users and groups to include in the Global Operators Group. The downside of this is that you will have to maintain this manually.

Dynamic Members are added in the Dynamic Members section. Here you have the option to create a criterion for the Domain User or Group class. Any user or group that fulfills this criterion will automatically be added to the Global Operators Group. If a user or group doesn't fulfill the criteria anymore, it will be removed as a member of the Global Operators group.

You also have the option to exclude members from the Global Operators Group. This is only useful when you use Dynamic Membership.

 You can temporarily disable the Global Operators Group scope in a User Picker by deselecting the **Scope users by global operators group** checkbox when browsing for users or groups.

See also

- ▸ For more information regarding Groups in general, please see the *Creating a configuration item group* in *Chapter 4, Building the Configuration Management Database (CMDB)*

Downloading, installing, and configuring the Exchange Connector

Service Manager has a built in function to handle incoming e-mails. Unfortunately this built-in function can be challenging to configure and is also very limited. Just to mention a few limitations:

▸ It can only handle Incidents

▸ It doesn't handle updates to existing Work Items

▸ It requires an SMTP server to drop e-mails as a file in a folder within Windows

Because of these limitations and the need to have a working incoming e-mail channel, the Exchange connector was developed. The Exchange Connector is able to create new Incidents or Service Requests based on incoming e-mails. It's also able to update existing Work Items. Upon creating or updating Incidents/Service Requests it can also apply a template to that record.

 Please note that even though the Exchange Connector is available on the Microsoft website for download, it's not supported as of the time of writing this book. Microsoft aims to add this connector to the product, but until then it will remain officially unsupported. Even though it's not officially supported, almost all organizations running Service Manager use this connector.

Getting ready

Make sure Service Manager is running and that you have sufficient privileges to create a new connector.

Download the Microsoft Exchange Web Service Managed API from Microsoft at `http://www.microsoft.com/en-us/download/details.aspx?id=28952`.

Download the Exchange connector from Microsoft at `http://www.microsoft.com/en-us/download/details.aspx?displaylang=en&id=29423`.

How to do it...

Here is how to install and configure the Exchange connector for Service Manager. The process of installing the connector is split into three parts.

Part 1 – Install the Exchange Web Service Managed API

1. Log on to the Service Manager Management Server and make sure you have downloaded the Exchange Web Service Managed API installer.

2. Double-click on the `EwsManagedApi.msi` file to start the installation.

3. In the first page of the installation wizard, click on **Next**.

4. Read the EULA, select **I accept the terms in the License Agreement**, and click on **Next**.

5. Make a note of the installation folder and click on **Next** followed by **Next** again.

6. Once the installation is finished, click on **Close**.

7. Now browse to the installation folder of the Exchange Web Service Managed API and copy the `Microsoft.Exchange.WebServices.dll` file.

8. Browse to the installation folder of Service Manager and paste this DLL file. (The default installation folder for Service Manager 2012 is `C:\Program Files\ Microsoft System Center 2012\Service Manager.`)

Part 2 – Install the Exchange Connector

1. Log on to the Service Manager Management Server. Make sure that you have downloaded the Exchange Connector.

2. Double-click on the `System Center 2012 - Service Manager Exchange Connector 3.0 RC.exe` file to extract it.

3. Read and accept the EULA by clicking on the **Accept** button.

4. Choose a **Destination** folder and click on **Extract**.

5. Go to the extracted folder and open the `ExchangeConnector` folder.

6. Copy the `Microsoft.SystemCenter.ExchangeConnector.dll` file.

7. Browse to the installation folder of Service Manager and paste this DLL file. (The default installation folder for Service Manager 2012 is `C:\Program Files\ Microsoft System Center 2012\Service Manager.`)

8. Open the Service Manager console and go to the **Administration** workspace. Then select **Management Packs** in the navigation pane.

9. Click on the **Import** task in the task pane.

10. Browse to the `Microsoft.SystemCenter.ExchangeConnector.xml` file that's located in the `ExchangeConnector` directory from where you extracted the Exchange Connector.

11. Select the `Microsoft.SystemCenter.ExchangeConnector.xml` file and click on **Open**.

12. The **Import Management Packs** dialog should now be displayed. Click on the **Import** button to import the management pack.

13. Once the import has finished, click on the **OK** button.

Part 3 – Configure the Exchange Connector

1. In the Service Manager console, go to the **Administration** workspace and select **Connectors** in the navigation pane.

2. Click on the **Create Connector** task in the task pane and select **Exchange Connector**.

3. Click on **Next** in the Welcome step.

4. Give the Exchange Connector a name, such as `Exchange Connector -` `helpdesk@mycompany.com`.

5. Enter the e-mail address to monitor. Note that this address must be the e-mail address of the workflow account, which should also be the Return Address for you notification channel. Click on **Next**.

6. You will now be asked to enter a number of parsing keywords. The title of each field gives a good indication of what each keyword is used for. If you are unsure of which parsing keywords to use, type the examples that are listed below each field. You can always go back and change this later.

7. Enter the **Active Directory FORESTS (not DOMAINS) to search for users in** value and click on **Next**.

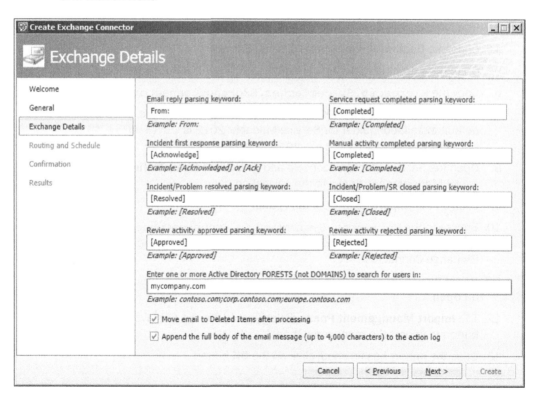

8. In the **Routing and Schedule** step you have to choose some templates to apply when creating and updating Incidents and Service Requests.

   You should create specific templates to use for the Exchange Connector, but in our example here, select the **Default Incident Template** for new Work Items and Incident updates, and select the **Default Service Request Template** for Service Request updates.

9. To complete the configuration of the Exchange Connector, click on **Next** followed by **Create** and **Close**.

How it works...

The Exchange Connector will connect to the mailbox of the workflow account using the Exchange Autodiscovery service on a configurable interval, and will then look for new e-mails. Upon receiving a new e-mail, the Exchange Connector will take a look at the subject. If the subject includes a Work Item ID in square brackets (such as [SR921]), it will try to update the action log of that Work Item with the text in the body of the e-mail.

If the subject doesn't contain a Work Item ID enclosed in square brackets, the Exchange Connector will create a new Work Item based upon the template specified when configuring the connector.

It's also possible to resolve, close, vote on review activities, and so on using the connector. This is based upon the parsing keywords specified in step 6 of the *Part 3 – Configure the Exchange Connector* section. For instance, if you would like to resolve the incident with ID IR562, you could simply send an e-mail to the mailbox of your workflow account, with the incident ID enclosed in square brackets in the subject ([IR562]) and specifying the parsing keyword for resolving an incident in the body of the e-mail ([Resolved]).

There's more...

When using the Exchange Connector, you will have to make sure that every notification template in use has the Work Item ID enclosed in square brackets in the e-mail subject. Otherwise replies to automatic notifications might result in new Incidents/Service Requests instead of updating an existing one.

Send Email task

The Exchange Connector also includes a Send Email task. The Send Email solution is used to e-mail a user directly from an Incident. This is especially useful for requesting user input for instance. Just like the Exchange Connector replaces the built-in functionality for incoming e-mail, the Send Email solution was created to replace the built-in task called Request User Input.

This function is bundled in the download package for the Exchange Connector but is stored in a separate management pack. If you want this functionality you need to import this management pack.

Instructions on how to configure the Send Email solution is not included in this book but a good set of instructions is included in the exchange connector download.

See also

▸ For more information regarding the Exchange Connector, please take a look at the following blog posts on the official Service Manager blog:

- ❑ `http://blogs.technet.com/b/servicemanager/archive/2012/04/15/exchange-connector-3-0-rc-released.aspx`

- ❑ `http://blogs.technet.com/b/servicemanager/archive/2011/02/11/how-to-notify-the-assigned-to-user-when-an-incident-is-updated-via-the-exchange-connector.aspx`

- ❑ `http://blogs.technet.com/b/servicemanager/archive/2011/02/08/tricky-way-to-handle-review-activity-approvals-with-the-exchange-connector.aspx`

Making the description field in the Incident form to auto grow

By default the description field of an Incident or a Problem only displays three rows of text. If you enter more than three rows of information into that field, you will have to scroll in order to read it all. This makes it hard to read and to get a quick overview of the actual issue. The solution to this is to change the behavior of the Description field to automatically grow with its content.

This is probably the most common form of customization for any organization using Service Manager and is a great way to start learning the Authoring Tool.

Getting ready

Make sure you have downloaded and installed the Authoring Tool. Note that the version of the Authoring Tool has to match the version of your Service Manager installed.

Download the Authoring Tool available at `http://www.microsoft.com/en-us/download/details.aspx?id=28726`.

How to do it...

In this example we will take a look at how to change the behavior of the Description field in the Incident form to auto grow with its content.

1. Start the Authoring Tool.

2. Go to the **Form Browser** and click on the **Reload Content** button.

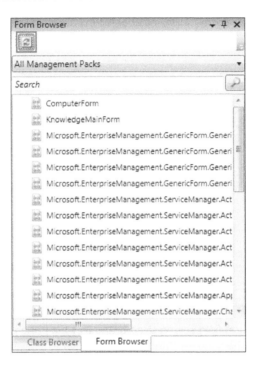

3. Enter `Incident` in the search field and locate **System.WorkItem.Incident. ConsoleForm**.

4. Now right-click on **System.WorkItem.Incident.ConsoleForm** and select **View**.

5. The Incident form should now be displayed in a read-only mode. Click on the **Customize** button that is located on the orange header just above the actual incident form.

6. You will now be prompted for a management pack to store your form customizations in.

If you have made any customizations to the Incident form previously, you must save the changes you are about to make in the same management pack. Otherwise, you should create a new management pack to store this and all future Incident form customizations.

7. Once you have browsed to your existing management pack or created a new one, make sure that it is select and click **OK**.

8. The Incident form should now be displayed in an editable mode.

9. Select the **Description** field by clicking on it.

10. With the **Description** field selected, go to the **Details** pane and locate the **Height** property. The value of **Height** should be set to **55**, and that's why there's only room for three rows of text.

11. Change the value of the **Height** property to **Auto**.

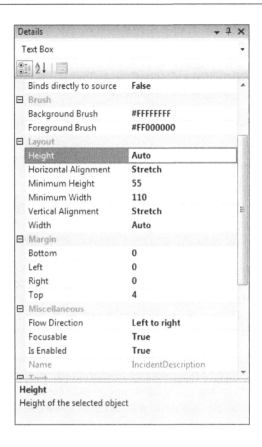

12. That's all we have to change for the **Description** field to auto grow. Save the management pack by going to the **File** menu and selecting **Save All**.

13. Next, we will have to import this management pack into Service Manager.

14. Open the Service Manager console and go to the **Administration** workspace. Then select **Management Packs** in the navigation pane.

15. Click on the **Import** task in the task pane.

16. Browse to the management pack you just created or edited, select it and click on **Open**.

17. The **Import Management Packs** dialog should now be displayed. Click on the **Import** button to import the management pack.

18. Once the import has finished, click on the **OK** button.

How it works...

Once you have imported this management pack into Service Manager, the **Description** field of new and existing Incidents should automatically grow with its content. This behavior is much more convenient and makes it much easier to read.

Note that the exact same procedure can be used to change the behavior of the **Description** field in the Problem form.

There's more...

The Authoring Tool is great for doing these kinds of customizations. It's easy and pretty straightforward. There is one thing to keep in mind when customizing forms in the Authoring Tool though, and that is you need to actually keep track of *every single change* you make to the form.

What does that mean? Well, if you first set the height of the description field to **Auto**, then change it to **100**, and then finally set it back again to **Auto**, the Authoring Tool will actually write three rows of code into the management pack for all these changes. This makes it hard to read the XML code if you ever are going to modify it "by hand". It could also affect the performance of loading the form.

To get around this, make sure that you don't play around too much when editing a form. It might be better to play around first then start all over and redo it when you are certain of which properties you want to configure. Another option is to clean the XML code in an XML editor, such as Notepad, when you are done with the customization in the Authoring Tool.

The authors recommend you seal your management pack if you have customized any forms.

See also

> ▸ For more information regarding Authoring Tool and how to use it to customize and extend Service Manager, see the *Customizing default forms* and *Sealing management packs* recipes in *Chapter 10, Extending SCSM with Advanced Personalization*

Extending the Incident class with a new property

In this recipe we will take a look at extending an existing class with a new property. This can be done when you want to keep track of something that isn't available by default. You might want to keep track of the Incident discovery date for instance. That's not a property of the Incident class by default, so if you would like to do so you will have to extend the class.

Getting ready

Make sure you have downloaded and installed the Authoring Tool. Note that the version of the Authoring Tool has to match the version of your Service Manager installed.

Download the Authoring Tool available at `http://www.microsoft.com/en-us/download/details.aspx?id=28726`.

How to do it...

1. Start the Service Manager Authoring Tool.
2. Locate **Class Browser** and click on the **Reload Content** button.

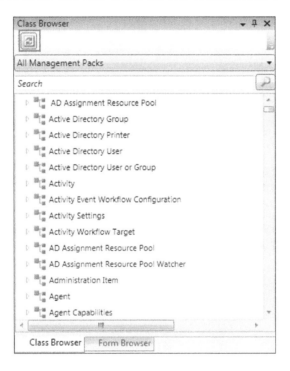

3. Enter `Incident` in the **Search** field and hit *Enter*.
4. Locate the **Incident** class, right-click on it and select **View**.

5. The Incident class should now be displayed in a read-only mode. In order to extend the Incident class, right-click on the Incident class in the **Management Pack Explorer** and select **Extend class**.

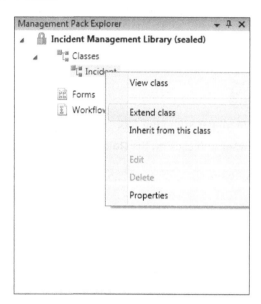

6. You will now be asked in which management pack you want to store your class extension. Click on **New...** to create a new management pack to store it within.

7. Give it a proper name and click on **Save**.

8. Make sure your new management pack is selected in the **Target Management Pack** dialog and click **Ok**.

9. To add a new property to the Incident class, click on the **Create property...** button.

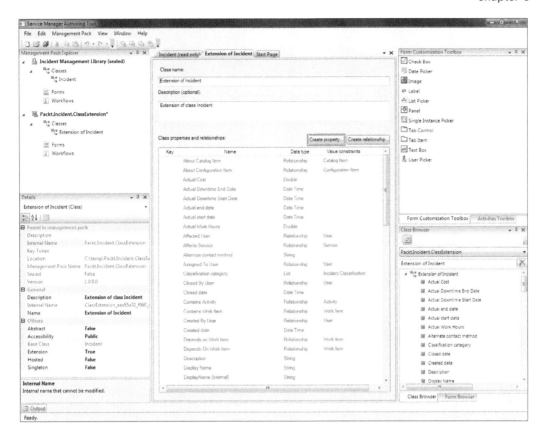

10. Change the internal name to `IncidentDiscoveryDate` (without spaces) and click on **Create**.

11. In the **Details** window, change the name to `Incident Discovery Date` (with spaces).

12. Then change the **Data Type** to **Date Time**.

13. Save your management pack by going to **File** and select **Save All**.

14. Open the Service Manager console and go to the **Administration** workspace.

15. Go to **Management Packs** and click on the **Import** task.

16. Browse to the management pack we just created and click on **Open**.

17. In the **Import Management Packs** dialog, click on **Import**.

18. For now, ignore the warning displayed and click on **OK**.

How it works...

After you have imported the management pack created in the Authoring Tool the incident class has been extended with a new property. This new property is available under the **Extension** tab in the Incident form.

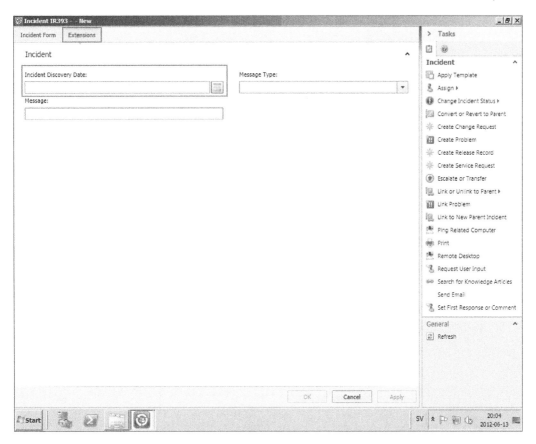

This is a simple way of extending an existing class in Service Manager with new properties that you might need. Even though you haven't modified the form, Service Manager has made it possible to enter data in this field by presenting it on the **Extension** tab. The next step would be to add a field for the new property on the actual form to avoid people forgetting to enter the information.

All management packs that include class extensions should be sealed before they are imported into Service Manager. There are a few reasons for this, some of them are as follows:

- ▶ You want to protect your management pack from being modified
- ▶ Only sealed management packs are copied to the Data Warehouse
- ▶ You are not able to reference unsealed management packs

There's more...

To get a grasp of the properties of each class, you could use the Authoring Tool to locate each class and then display it. You might be surprised that the property you want to extend your class with already exists, it's just not displayed on the form. But an even better way to get an understanding of the Service Manager class hierarchy and model, would be to take a look at the System Center Common Model for Service Manager Visio drawing. This Visio is included in the Service Manager Job Aids package that is downloadable from Microsoft available at `http://www.microsoft.com/en-us/download/details.aspx?id=27850`.

See also

- ▸ For more information about sealing a management pack, please see the *Sealing management packs* recipe in *Chapter 10, Extending SCSM with Advanced Personalization*
- ▸ For more information regarding the Authoring Tool and how to use it to customize and extend Service Manager, see the *Using the SCSM Authoring Tool* recipe in *Chapter 10, Extending SCSM with Advanced Personalization*

7

Designing Change and Release Management

In this chapter we will cover:

- ▶ Creating and configuring Change Request Templates
- ▶ Creating and managing Change Management Review Activities
- ▶ Creating Manual Activities for Change Management
- ▶ Creating and managing Dependent Activities in Change Management
- ▶ Creating and personalizing Change Management Parallel Activities
- ▶ Creating and personalizing Change Management Sequential Activities
- ▶ Creating and personalizing Change Management Activity notifications
- ▶ Creating and managing Build and Environment Release Records
- ▶ Creating and managing Release Record Templates
- ▶ Working with Change Requests and Release Records

Introduction

In this chapter we will provide recipes to configure Service Manager to your environment. Specifically, we will cover the Change and Release Management of Service Manager.

System Center 2012 Service Manager supports the "Change and Release Management" processes based on ITIL© or MOF.

In Change Management any change related to the IT infrastructure can be managed and controlled. Typical changes in IT are:

- Deploying Service Packs, hotfixes, patches, and updates
- Provisioning of new hardware components
- Updates on hardware and implementing new software on servers and clients

In SCSM 2012 different types of activities can be used relating to Change Requests or Change Request Templates. Activities can be sequential and/or parallel in order to reflect the individual process.

To deploy changes to the IT infrastructure the Release Management process in ITIL© provides the opportunity to create different releases based on builds and environments, as well as activities.

In this chapter we will provide recipes to configure the basics of Change Management, Release Management, and Activities. We will also see how Change Requests, Release Records, and Activities are related and work together.

The basic settings of Change Management and Release Management are described in *Chapter 2, Personalizing SCSM 2012 Administration* of this book.

Creating and configuring Change Request Templates

Change Request Templates can be used to pre-fill information in the Change Request form. These can be for instance a predefined Title, Description, Impact, Risk, and Priority.

This recipe will describe the steps to create a new Change Request Template.

Getting ready

In the SCSM 2012 console navigate to **Library | Templates**.

How to do it...

To create a Change Request Template, follow these steps:

1. Click on **Create Template** in the **Tasks** pane.
2. Enter a name. In this recipe we are using `Change Request Service Pack Installation Template`.

3. Enter a description. For instance, `This template can be used for Change Requests regarding deployment of Service Packs.`

4. Choose the **Change Request** class by clicking on **Browse** next to the **Class** field, and then click on **OK**.

5. Choose an existing management pack or create a new one to store the Change Request Template. (The *Creating Management Packs in the Authoring tool to save your SCSM personalization* recipe in *Chapter 2, Personalizing SCSM 2012 Administration* describes how to store your customizations in management packs as well as about best-practice naming conventions of the XML files.)

6. Click on **OK**.

7. Fill in the information in the related fields of the form. In this recipe we will pre-fill the fields **Title**, **Description**, **Reason**, **Area** (select **Software** from the drop-down box), **Priority** (select **Medium** from the drop-down box), in the **General** tab of the Change Request Template.

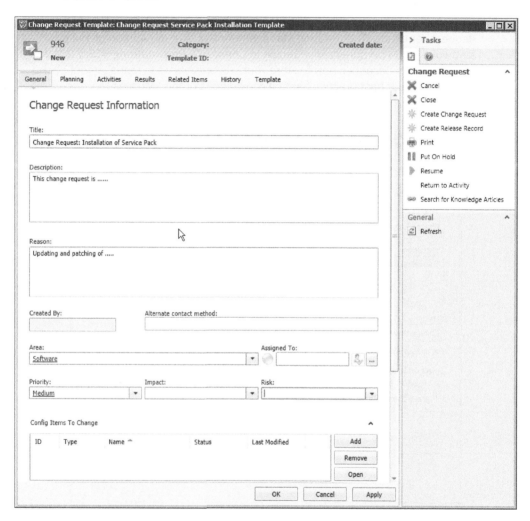

8. Pre-fill all fields you need in the **Planning** tab of the Change Request Template. In this recipe, we are using **Implementation Plan**, **Risk Assessment Plan**, **Test Plan**, and **Back out Plan**.

9. Click on **OK** to save and close the Change Request Template.

How it works...

Basically a pre-filled template in SCSM 2012 can be used to create new Work Items (for instance Incident Records, Change Requests, and Service Requests). Using templates keeps the content and information of forms consistent. Using pre-filled templates will also reduce the time each individual spends initiating the relevant Work Item

There's more...

Reporting of Change Management is important due to the visibility and tracking provided, which is key to continually improving the process.

Reporting of scheduled and actual date information

Providing the Scheduled Start and End Time of change requests is very helpful for reporting how the Change Management process is performing. These key performance indicators offer a good overview on how many change requests are completed within the planned time.

To get more information about reporting please take a look at the recipes in *Chapter 9, Reporting* of this cookbook.

See also

 ▶ Microsoft TechNet Library: Managing Changes and Activities in System Center 2012 - Service Manager: `http://technet.microsoft.com/en-us/library/hh519580`

Creating and managing Change Management Review Activities

Review Activities in SCSM 2012 are used for approval of all the following steps and activities in a Change Request. This recipe will show how the different fields of a Review Activity can be configured.

Getting ready

To create Review Activities in a Change Request Template open the SCSM 2012 console and navigate to **Library | Templates**. Open the Change Request Service Pack Installation Template we created in the previous recipe.

How to do it...

To add a Review Activity in a Change Request or Change Request Template, follow these steps:

1. Click on the **Activities** tab in the Change Request form.
2. Click on **+ Activities**.
3. Choose **Default Review Activity** in the list of templates and click on **OK**.

4. In the **Review Activity Template** we will fill in the **Title** and **Description** fields.

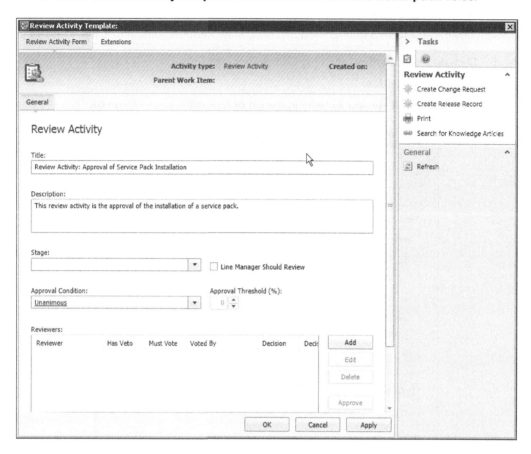

5. If the Line Manager of the requester should review, select the option **Line Manager Should Review**. If enabled, the manager of the user is discovered by the Manager attribute of the user in the CMDB (synced by the AD Connector from Active Directory).

6. Add Reviewers manually by clicking on **Add** in the **Reviewers:** section. Select the option **Has veto** or **Must vote** if needed.

7. Click on **OK**.

8. Add more reviewers manually.

9. If you add more than one reviewer you can define the approval condition.

   ❑ **Unanimous**: All reviewers have to vote

   ❑ **Automatic**: The approval is done without anyone having to vote

   ❑ **Percentage**: For example, only 50 percent (Approval Threshold (%)) of the reviewers need to vote

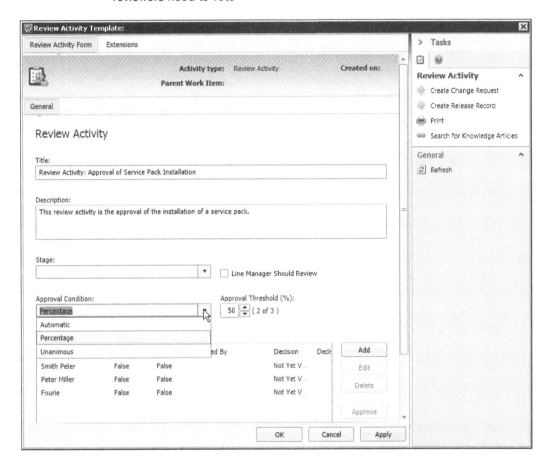

10. Click on **OK** to close the Review Activity form.

11. In the next recipe we will add more activities, so don't close the Change Request Template.

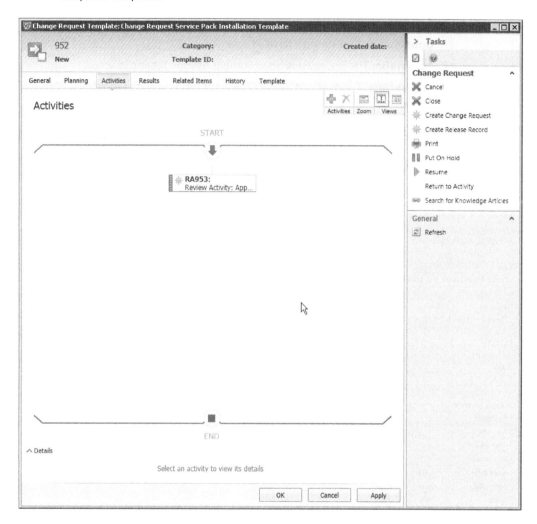

How it works...

If the Change Request Template is applied to a new Change Request, all pre-filled fields and all activities are available in the newly-created Change Request.

A SCSM 2012 workflow will set the first activity to the status **In Progress**, all other activities will be set to the status **Pending** by default. The Change Request will also get the status **In Progress**.

The Review Activity provides the option to determine the manager of the requester automatically. The manager information is synced automatically from Active Directory by the AD Connector of SCSM 2012.

Also it is possible to require a reviewer "must vote" and "has a veto".

You can configure a Review Activity so that all, or only subsets of reviewers have to review and provide approval.

There's more...

Notifying reviewers and adding additional activities are common tasks and requirements in the Change Management process.

Notification of reviewers

To see how to notify a reviewer if a Review Activity gets updated to the status **In Progress** please take a look at the *Creating and personalizing Change Management Activity notifications* recipe in this chapter.

Add more activities to a Service Request created on a template

You can add additional activities to a Change Request that was created using template during the process of working with the Change Request.

 You can add more activities as long as the last activity in the Change Request isn't completed.

See also

▸ Microsoft TechNet Library: Managing Changes and Activities in System Center 2012 - Service Manager: `http://technet.microsoft.com/en-us/library/hh519580`

Creating Manual Activities for Change Management

Manual Activities in SCSM 2012 can be used to reflect the different manual steps during the Change Management process.

This recipe will show how to configure the different properties of Manual Activities in SCSM 2012.

Getting ready

If you closed the Change Request Form in the last recipe after creating a Review Activity, open the Change Request Template we created in the recipe before by navigating to **SCSM 2012 console | Library | Templates | Change Request Service Pack Installation Template**. Click on the **Activities** tab in the Change Request form.

If the form of the Change Request Template is still open just continue with *the How to do it...* section.

How to do it...

To add a Manual Activity in a Change Request or Change Request Template, follow these steps:

1. Click on **+ Activities** and select **Default Manual Activity** from the list. Click on **OK**.

2. Fill the **Title** and **Description** field.

3. Pick a **Priority** and **Area**. We will choose **Medium** from the **Priority** drop-down box and **Software** from the **Area** drop-down box, because the Change Request Template is related to the Installation of a Service Pack.

4. Click on **OK** to close the Manual Activity Template form.

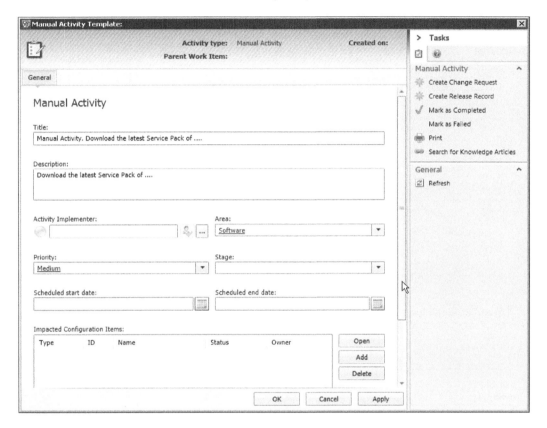

5. Click on **OK** to close the Manual Activity form.

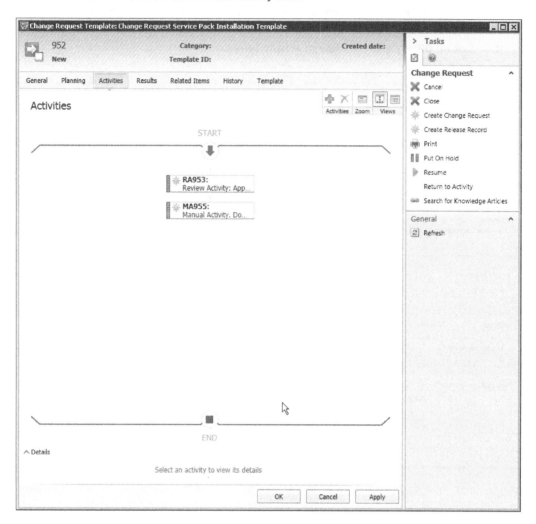

6. Click on **OK** to close the Change Request Template.

How it works...

A SCSM 2012 workflow will set the first activity to the status **In Progress**, all other activities will be set to the status **Pending**. The Change Request will also get the status **In Progress**.

The Manual Activity allows you to capture the manual steps required in your defined Change Management process.

Typically an Implementer is assigned to the Manual Activity. The Implementer is the person responsible for carrying out the manual action specified in the manual activity. Using this information you are able to send a notification to the relevant individuals when the activity status is set to **In Progress**.

Also, you can configure the **Scheduled Start** and **Scheduled End Date**. This can be key to reporting as it provides visibility on how many activities are performed and completed in the scheduled time.

There's more...

Note that the Activity Implementer helps to optimize the process. Also reporting offers a good opportunity to improve the Change Management process.

Notification of Activities Implementer

To see how to notify an implementer if a Manual Activity is updated to status **In Progress** please take a look at the *Creating and personalizing Change Management Activity notifications* recipe in this chapter.

Reporting of Scheduled and Actual Date information

Providing the Scheduled Start and End Time of Manual Activity is very helpful for reporting.

To get more information about reporting in SCSM 2012 please take a look at the recipes in *Chapter 9, Reporting* of this cookbook.

See also

 ▶ Microsoft TechNet Library: Managing Changes and Activities in System Center 2012 - Service Manager: `http://technet.microsoft.com/en-us/library/hh519580`

Creating and managing Dependent Activities in Change Management

Dependent Activities in SCSM 2012 can be used to link activities between different Change Requests and Release Records, if relationships between the management processes are needed. This recipe will show how to create Dependent Activities in a Change Request template.

Getting ready

To create a Dependent Activity in a Change Request Template open the SCSM 2012 console and navigate to **Library | Templates**. Open `Change Request Service Pack Installation Template` we created in an earlier recipe.

How to do it...

To create a Dependent Activity, follow these steps:

1. Click on the **Activities** tab in the Change Request form.

2. Click on **+ Activities**.

3. Choose **Default Dependent Activity** in the list of templates and click on **OK**.

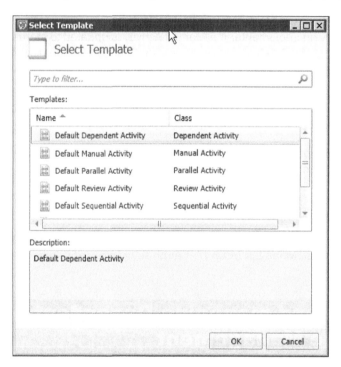

4. In the Dependent Activity Template form add the **Title** and **Description** information. If the **Owner** or **Assigned To User** is static for all Change Requests based on this Template you can add the Users in the corresponding fields. The **Owner** is responsible for the Dependent Activities related to the process; the **Assigned To User** is the user who is working on the task of the activity. For instance, the **Owner** is responsible for installing the service pack. The **Assigned To User** will install the service pack.

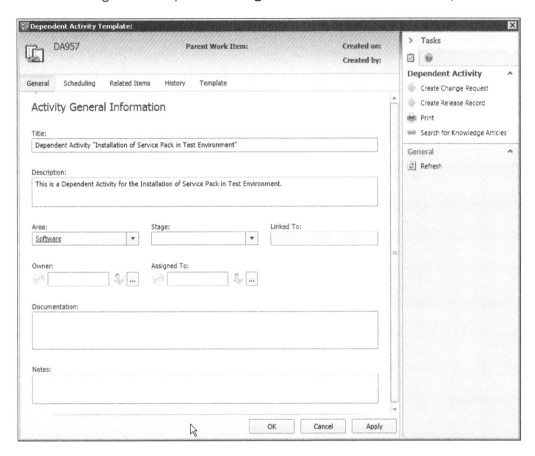

5. Click on **OK** to close the Dependent Activity Template.

6. Click on **OK** to close the Change Request Template.

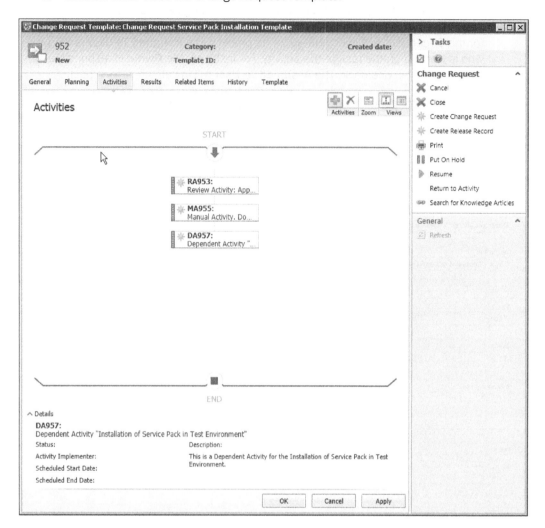

How it works...

Dependent Activities are used to relate activities in Change Request to an activity in a Release Record. This offers the option to link different process steps of Change Management to the corresponding steps in Release Management.

For instance: The Change Request for installing a Service Pack (only one Change Request) might have three Dependent Activities to three different Release Management Records (Installing the Service Packs to three different environments; Test-, Pre-Production-, Production-Environment).

There's more...

Change Management and Release Management are related. Dependent Activities are how this relationship is reflected in SCSM 2012.

Linking activities in Change Requests to activities in Release Records

The linking of Dependent Activities in Change Requests to activities in Release Records can't be done in a Change Request Template. You have to create a new Change Request based on a Change Request Template and a new Release Record before you are able to link a Dependent Activity of a Change Request to an activity in the Release Record. For more information on how to do this please take a look at the *Working with Change Requests and Release Records* recipe in this chapter.

See also

▸ Microsoft TechNet Library: Managing Changes and Activities in System Center 2012 - Service Manager: `http://technet.microsoft.com/en-us/library/hh519580`

Creating and personalizing Change Management Parallel Activities

Activities in SCSM 2012 are executed sequentially by default. To run different activities in parallel we need a Parallel Activity container.

This recipe will show how to create and work with Parallel Activities in SCSM 2012.

Getting ready

To create Parallel Activities in a Change Request Template open the SCSM 2012 console and navigate to **Library | Templates**. Open `Change Request Service Pack Installation Template` that we created in an earlier recipe.

How to do it...

The following steps describes how to create and personalize Parallel Activities:

1. Click on the **Activities** tab in the Change Request form.

2. Click on **+ Activities**.

3. Choose **Default Parallel Activity** from the list of templates and click on **OK**.

4. In the **General** tab we will fill the **Title** and **Description** field. We will select **Software** from the **Area** drop-down box.

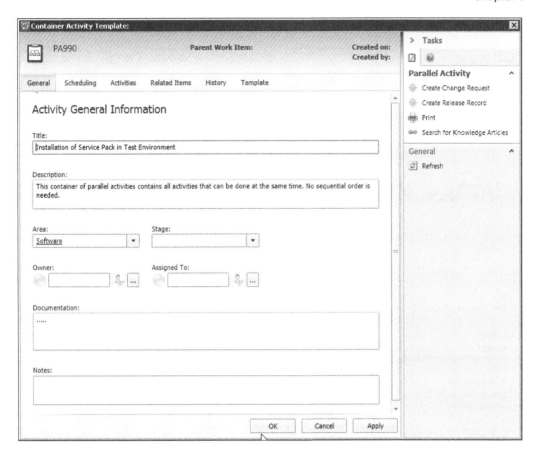

5. Click on the **Activities** tab.

6. Add Manual Activities to the Container Activity Template. In this recipe we will add the following three Manual Activities:

   ❑ Install Service Pack on x86 Clients in Test Environment

   ❑ Install Service Pack on x64 Clients in Test Environment

   ❑ Install Service Pack on Server 1 in Test Environment

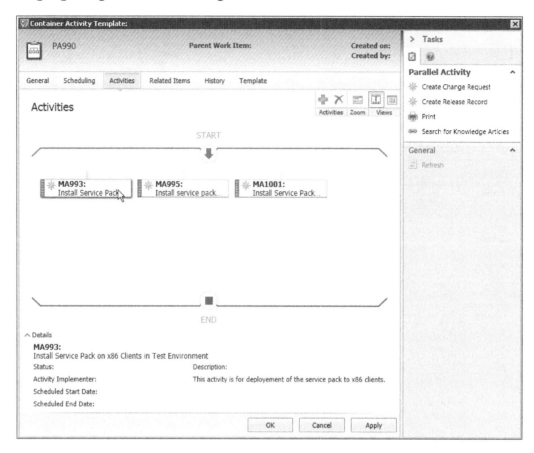

7. Click on **OK** to close the Container Activity template.

8. Click on **OK** to close the Change Request template.

How it works...

The Parallel Activity in SCSM 2012 works like a container. Each activity added to this container will get the same status update, **In Progress** if the Parallel Activity is changed from **Pending** to **In Progress**. This provides the ability to execute some Change Management process activities in parallel. For instance, if we want to perform the same activities on different systems (install Service Pack x86 version on some systems and install Service Pack x64 version on some other systems, or install the Service Pack on clients and servers in parallel). When all activities within the container are completed, the Parallel Activity will also be marked as **Completed**.

There's more...

Here is some more information about the different types of activities in SCSM 2012.

How to work with Review, Manual, and Dependent Activities

Please take a look at the following recipes to see how to work with different types of activities in SCSM 2012:

- ▶ *Creating and managing Change Management Review Activities*
- ▶ *Creating Manual Activities for Change Management*
- ▶ *Creating and managing Dependent Activities in Change Management*

How to work with Sequential Activities inside of Parallel Activities

If you need to add Serialized/Sequential Activities inside of a Parallel Activity container take a look at the next recipe of this chapter.

See also

- ▶ Microsoft TechNet Library: Managing Changes and Activities in System Center 2012 - Service Manager: `http://technet.microsoft.com/en-us/library/hh519580`

Creating and personalizing Change Management Sequential Activities

If you have configured Parallel Activities as described in the previous recipe, all activities will be set to the status **In Progress** at the same time. If you need to serialize activities inside of a Parallel Activity container you must use Sequential Activities.

This recipe will show you how to work with Sequential Activities inside of a Parallel Activity container.

Getting ready

To create Sequential Activities in a Change Request Template open the SCSM 2012 console and navigate to **Library | Templates**. Open the `Change Request Service Pack Installation Template` that we created in an earlier recipe.

How to do it...

Follow these steps to create a Sequential Activity:

1. Click on the **Activities** tab in the Change Request form.

2. Open the Parallel Activity we created in the previous recipe. (Right-click on the title of the Parallel Activity and select **Open**).

3. Click on the **Activities** tab in the Container Activity Template form.

4. Click on the **+ Activities**.

5. Choose **Default Sequential Activity** from the list of templates and click **OK**.

6. Fill the **Title**, **Description**, and **Area** fields.

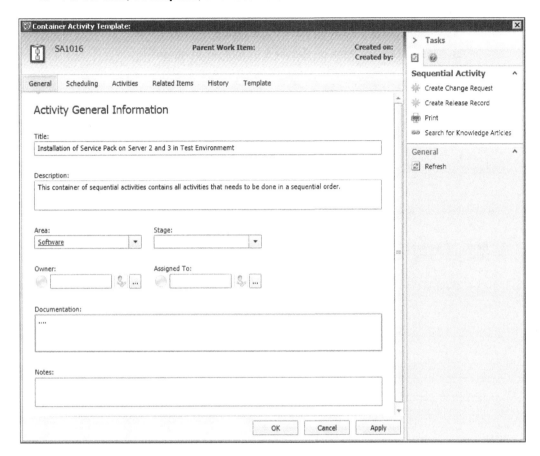

7. Click on **Activities**.

8. Add Manual Activities to the Container Activity Template. In this recipe we will add two Manual Activities:

- ❑ Install Service Pack on Server 2 in Test Environment
- ❑ Install Service Pack on Server 3 in Test Environment

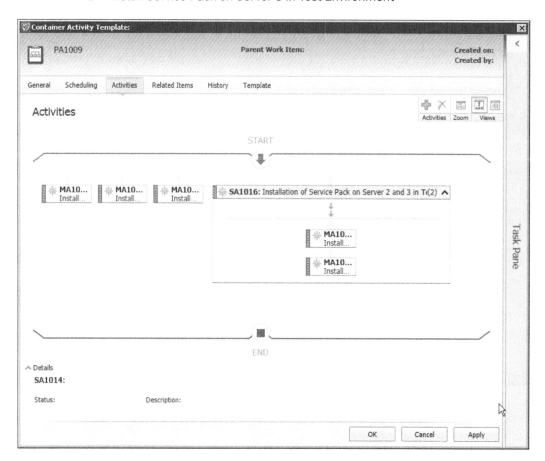

9. Click on **OK** to close the Container Activity Template.

10. Click on **OK** to close the Change Request Template.

How it works...

Sequential Activities in SCSM 2012 work like the Parallel Activities described in the previous recipe by providing a single container for one or more activities.

All activities inside a Sequential Activity container are processed in a serialized order. If the Sequential Activity changes to **In Progress**, the first activity inside it will get the same status. All other activities will be in the status of **Pending**. When the first activity moves to a status **Completed,** the next activity will change to **In Progress**, and so on. When the last activity in a Sequential Activity container is marked as **Completed** the Sequential Activity container will also be marked as **Completed**.

Sequential Activities can be used inside a Parallel Activity container if some activities need to be serialized. For instance, in this recipe we used the example of installing the Service Pack in parallel on different systems, but we need to install the Service Pack on two servers in a sequential order.

There's more...

Here is some more information on how to work with the different types of Activities in SCSM 2012.

How to work with Review, Manual, and Dependent Activities

Please take a look at the following recipes in this chapter to see how to work with different types of activities in SCSM 2012:

- ▶ *Creating and managing Change Management Review Activities*
- ▶ *Creating Manual Activities for Change Management*
- ▶ *Creating and managing Dependent Activities in Change Management*

How to work with Parallel Activities in SCSM 2012

Please take a look at the previous recipes to see how Parallel Activities work in SCSM 2012.

See also

- ▶ Microsoft TechNet Library: Managing Changes and Activities in System Center 2012 - Service Manager: `http://technet.microsoft.com/en-us/library/hh519580`

Creating and personalizing Change Management Activity notifications

In SCSM 2012 it is possible to send notifications to "Reviewers" of Review Activities and "Implementers" of Manual Activities. This is helpful because different activities in a Change Request will change their status during the Change Management process. For instance, a Manual Activity status changes from **Pending** to **In Progress** after a previous Review Activity is approved.

This recipe will show how this notification workflow can be configured.

Getting ready

There are two ways to create a notification in SCSM 2012.

The first one is to navigate to **Administration | Notification | Subscription | Create Subscription**. The wizard will lead you through the creation of the notification.

The second method is to configure a workflow by navigating to **Administration | Workflows | Configuration** and selecting the relevant process type.

We will use the second method and it is described in detail in this recipe. The major difference between these two methods is the option to apply a template to the activity with additional information.

To create an Activity Notification workflows open the SCSM 2012 console and navigate to **Administration | Workflows | Configuration**.

How to do it...

To create a new notification, follow these steps:

1. Double-click on **Activity Event Workflow Configuration**.
2. In the Select Class form select **Review Activity** and click on **OK**.

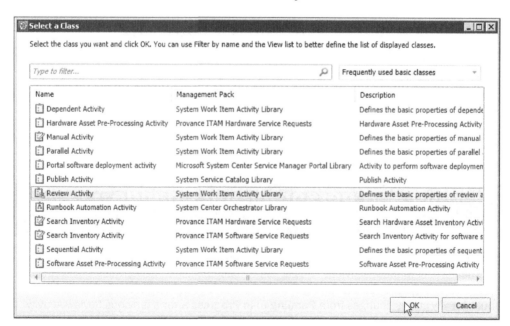

3. In the **Configure Workflows** window click on **Add**.

4. Read the instructions and information on the **Before You Begin** page.

5. Click on **Next**.

6. Fill in the **Title** (Change Request Reviewer Notification Workflow) and a **Description** (This workflow will send a notification to the reviewer if a Review Activity status changed from "Pending" to "In Progress".) fields in the **Workflow Information** page

7. Select **When an object is updated** from the **Check for events:** list.

8. Select a management pack to save the workflow in (for example, Custom. ChangeManagement.Library).

9. Click on **Next**.

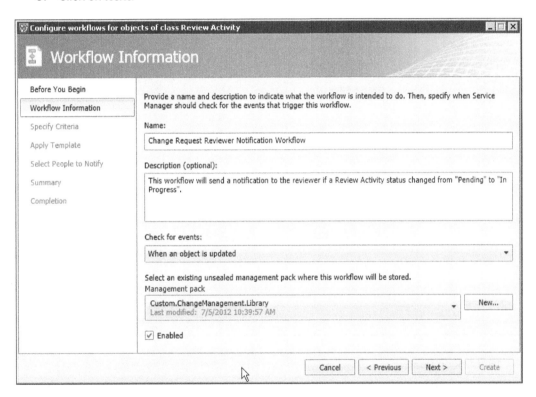

10. In the **Specify Criteria** page click on **Changed from**.

11. In the **Available Properties** list search for **Status**, select the checkbox, and click on **Add**.

12. In the **Criteria** section, besides **[Activity] Status** click on the list with conditions and select **equals**.

13. In the **Criteria** section, besides **[Activity] Status** click on the list with status and select **Pending**.

14. In the **Specify Criteria** page click on **Changed to**.

15. In the **Available Properties** list search for **Status**, select the checkbox, and click on **Add**.

16. In the **Criteria** section, besides **[Activity] Status** click on the list with conditions and select **equals**.

17. In the **Criteria** section, besides **[Activity] Status** click on the list with status and select **In Progress**.

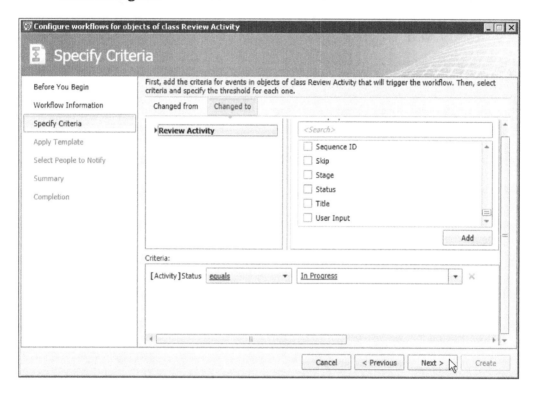

18. Click on **Next**.

19. In the **Apply Template** page do not apply any template.

20. Click on **Next**.

21. In the **Select People to Notify** page check the **Enable notification** checkbox.

22. Select **Reviewers** from the **User** drop-down box.

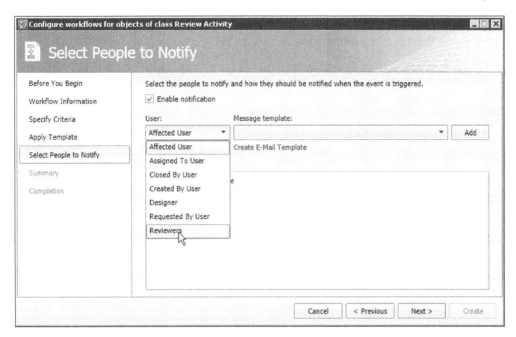

23. Select an existing message template from the list or create a new notification template by clicking on **Create E-Mail Template**.

24. Click on **Add**.

25. Click on **Next**.

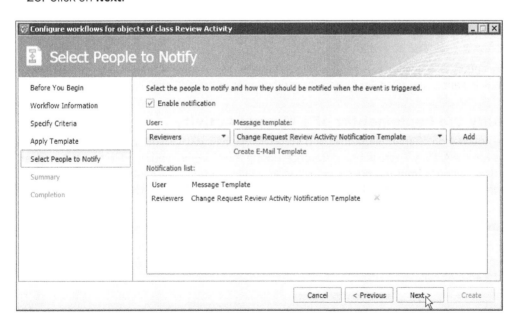

26. Verify the summary and click on **Create**.

27. In the **Configure Workflow** window click on **OK**.

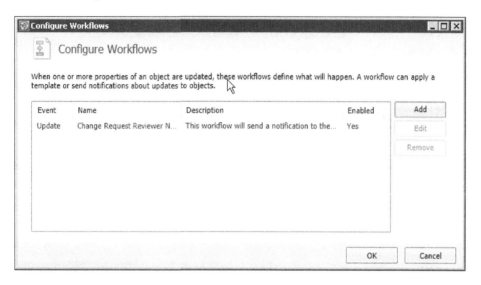

The notification workflow will be initiated when the specified condition is met. In our workflow the notification will be sent to the reviewer if the status of the review activity changes from **Pending** to **In Progress**.

There's more...

Notification on activities is a good way to automate the Change Management process. An e-mail is sent to the reviewer or activity implementer of the activity when it becomes "active".

Notify the Implementer of a Manual Activity

The notification of an implementer of a Manual Activity works similar to notifying the reviewer of a Review Activity There is one difference during the creation: you need to select **Assigned To User** because **Implementer** is not listed as a listed option. The **Assigned To User** in the list of possible recipients correlates to the **Implementer** of a Manual Activity.

Working with Notification templates

For more information on how to create and work with Notifications, please take a look at the *Creating formatted e-mail notification templates* recipe in *Chapter 2, Personalizing SCSM 2012 Administration*.

See also

> ▶ Microsoft TechNet Library: Managing Changes and Activities in System Center 2012 - Service Manager: `http://technet.microsoft.com/en-us/library/hh519580`

Creating and managing Build and Environment Release Records

In SCSM 2012 Release Management you can define different builds and environments of your IT infrastructure.

For instance, builds can be different versions of software (different versions for x86 and x64 operating systems).

An Environment can be a test, pre-production, and/or production environment in your IT infrastructure.

This recipe will show you how to create builds and environments in the Release Management process of SCSM 2012.

Getting ready

To create and manage Environments of Release Records open the SCSM 2012 console and navigate to **Configuration Items | Environments | All Environments**.

To create and manage Builds of Release Records open the SCSM 2012 console and navigate to **Configuration Items | Builds | All Builds**.

How to do it...

To create a new Environment follow these steps:

1. Click on **Create Environment** in the **Tasks** pane.
2. Fill in the information in the **Display Name**, **Title**, and **Description** fields .
3. Choose **Deployed** from the **Asset Status** drop-down box.
4. Choose **Pre-Production** from the **Category** drop-down box.

5. Click on **OK** to close the form.

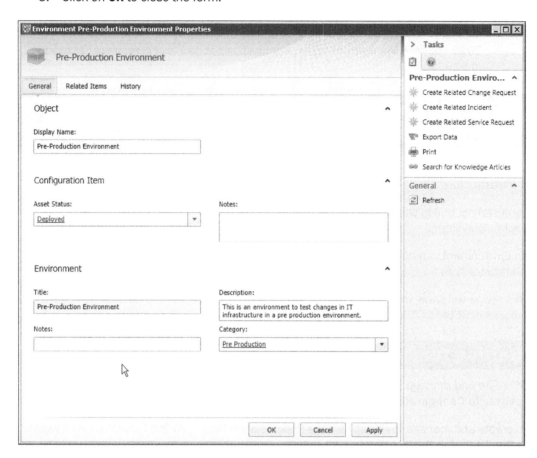

6. Create multiple environments to reflect your IT infrastructure.

To create a new Build follow these steps:

1. Click on **Create Build** in the **Tasks** pane.
2. Fill in the **Display Name**, **Title**, **Version**, **Description**, and **Source Path** fields.
3. Choose an asset status from the **Asset Status** drop-down box, for example, **Undefined**.
4. Choose a category from the **Category** drop-down box. In our recipe we have selected **Software**.

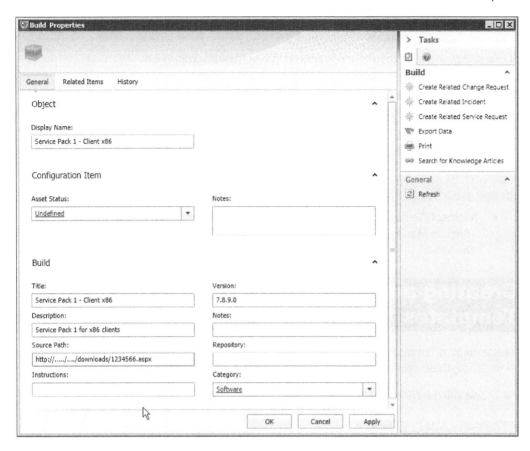

5. Click on **OK** to close the **Build** window.

6. Create new Builds for all the different versions you need:

   ❑ Service Pack 1 - Client x86

   ❑ Service Pack 1 - Client x64

   ❑ Service Pack 1 - Server x64

How it works...

Builds and Environments can be used in Release Records to relate the release of a build of software or hardware modification to a specified environment. This will also define the scope of the release.

There's more...

A build is logical and is therefore not limited to a software version only.

Builds are not only software related

A build can describe different hardware builds as well. For instance, different CPU architectures such as "Intel processor based" or "ARM processor based". Another example might be different types of servers (physically or virtual).

See also

> ► Microsoft TechNet Library: Managing Release Records in System Center 2012 - Service Manager: `http://technet.microsoft.com/en-us/library/hh495529`

Creating and managing Release Record Templates

Release Record Templates can be used to pre-fill information in the Release Record form. For instance, these can be a predefined Title, Description, Impact, Risk, and Priority.

This recipe will describe the steps required to create a new Release Record Template.

Getting ready

In the SCSM 2012 console navigate to **Library | Templates**.

How to do it...

To create a Release Record Template, follow these steps:

1. Click on **Create template** in the **Tasks** pane.
2. Enter a name in the **Name** field. In this recipe we will use `Release Record Service Pack Installation Template`.

3. Enter a description in the **Description** field. For instance, `This template can be used for Release Records regarding deployment of Service Packs.`

4. Choose the **Release Record** class by clicking on **Browse** next to the **Class** field, and then click on **OK**.

5. Choose an existing management pack or create a new one to store the Release Record Template. (The _Creating Management Packs in the Authoring tool to save your SCSM personalization_ recipe in _Chapter 2, Personalizing SCSM 2012 Administration_ describes how to store your customizations in management packs as well as best-practice naming conventions of the XML files.)

6. Click on **OK**.

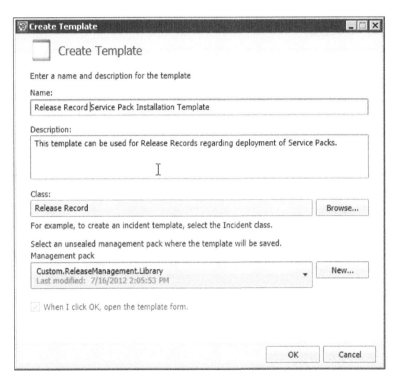

7. Fill in the information in all fields of the form. In this recipe we will pre-fill the fields **Title**, **Description**, **Type** (select **Planned** from the drop-down box), **Category** (Select **Fix** from the drop-down box), **Impact** (select **Standard** from the drop-down box), **Risk** (Select **Medium** from the drop-down box), and **Priority** (Select **Medium** from the drop-down box) fields in the **General** tab of the Release Record Template.

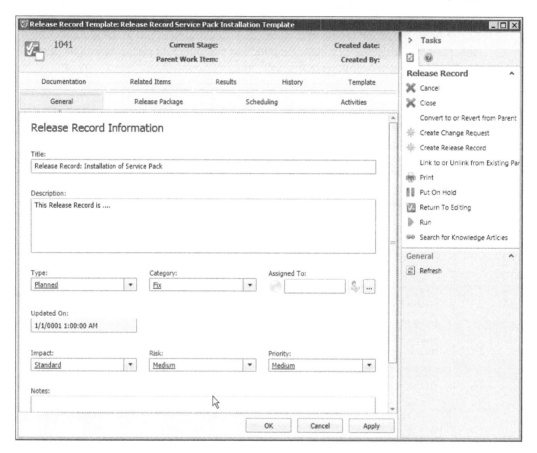

8. In the **Documentation** tab add some information regarding this Release Record Template. For instance some information on how the release is done.

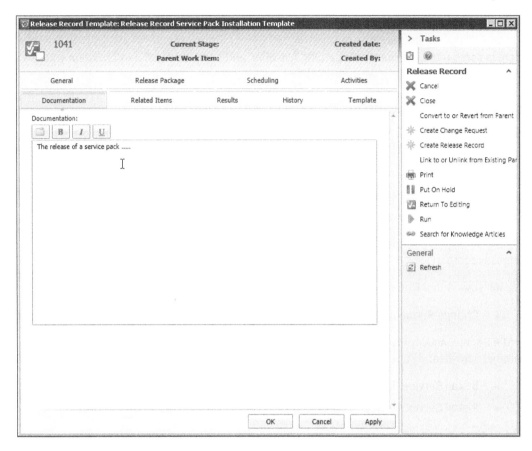

9. Click on **OK** to close the template.

How it works...

Basically a pre-filled template in SCSM 2012 can be used to create new work items (for instance Release Records, Incident Records, Change Requests, and Service Requests). Using templates keeps the content and information of forms consistent. Using pre-filled templates will also reduce the time each individual request spends initiating the relevant Work Item.

There's more...

Here is some more information regarding Activities and some additional information you can use to fill in the Release Record Template.

Working with Activities

In this recipe we will not talk about how to work with the different types of activities in a Release Record template. This topic is covered in the following recipes of this chapter:

 ▸ *Creating and managing Change Management Review Activities*

 ▸ *Creating Manual Activities for Change Management*

 ▸ *Creating and managing Dependent Activities in Change Management*

Here is an example scenario using the activities described in the previous recipes for a release record.

We will start with a Dependent Activity to link a Change Request configured as follows:

 ▸ Change Request name: Install Service Pack

Add a Parallel Activity Container named "Install Service Pack" with the following two Manual Activities:

 ▸ Install Service Pack on x86 clients

 ▸ Install Service Pack on x64 clients

We will then create a Sequential Activity container for this Change Request called:

 ▸ Install Service Pack on Servers

Containing the following Manual Activities:

 ▸ Install Service Pack on Server1

 ▸ Install Service Pack on Server2

 ▸ Install Service Pack on Server3

Add more specific information to a Release Record Template

Optionally you can add some more specific information to a Release Record Template as required and relevant to your processes:

Release Package tab:

- ▸ **Configuration Items to Modify**: Specific CIs that are related to this Release Record
- ▸ **Affected Services**: Business Services that are affected by these Release Records

Scheduling tab:

- ▸ It doesn't make sense to provide this information in a template. This tab should be filled out during the creation of a Release Record based on this template.

See also

- ▸ Microsoft TechNet Library: Managing Release Records in System Center 2012 - Service Manager: `http://technet.microsoft.com/en-us/library/hh495529`

Working with Change Requests and Release Records

After setting up the Change and Release Management in SCSM 2012 this recipe will show you how to create a new Change Request and Release Record. Also, it will show you how to add links between these two management processes.

Getting ready

To create a new Change Request in SCSM 2012 open the console and navigate to **Work Items | Change Management**.

To create a new Release Record in SCSM 2012 open the console and navigate to **Work Items | Release Management**.

How to do it...

Creating a new Change Request:

1. Click on **New Change Request** in the **Tasks** pane.
2. Choose `Change Request Service Pack Installation Template` we created in an earlier recipe in this chapter.

3. Click on **OK**.

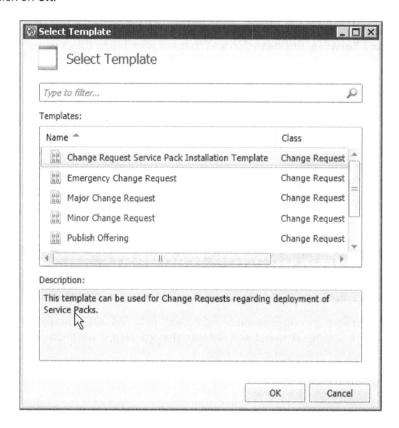

4. As we provided a lot of the information already in the Change Request Template only a few things need to be added:

   ❑ Add the related computers to **Config Items To Change**. For instance, we will add **Client1**, **Client2**, **Server1**, **Server2**, and **Server3** in this recipe. Click on **Add** and pick the computers from the list, then click on **OK**.

   ❑ Select **Standard** from the **Impact** drop-down box and **Medium** from the **Risk** drop-down box.

5. Click on **OK** to close the form and create the Change Request.

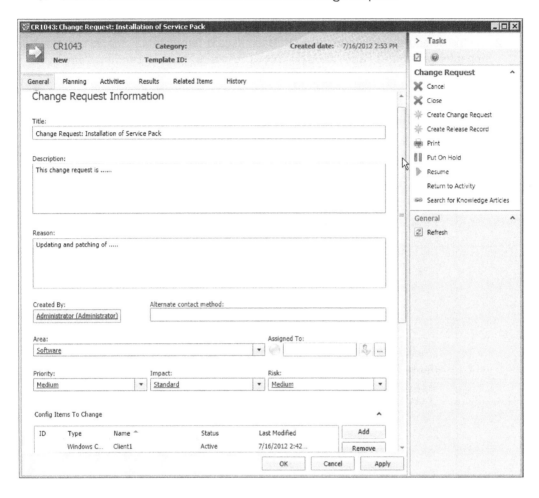

Creating a new Release Record:

1. Click on **New Release record** in the **Tasks** pane.

2. In the Select Template choose the Release Record Template we created earlier in this chapter called `Release Record Service Pack Installation Template.`

3. Click on **OK.**

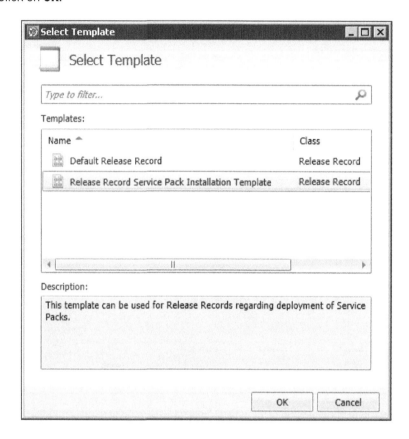

4. All the required information in the **General** tab are provided by the template.

5. Click on **Release Package** tab and add the related computers to **Configuration Items to Modify**. For instance, we will add **Client1**, **Client2**, **Server1**, **Server2**, and **Server3** in this recipe. Click on **Add** and pick the computers from the list, then click on **OK**.

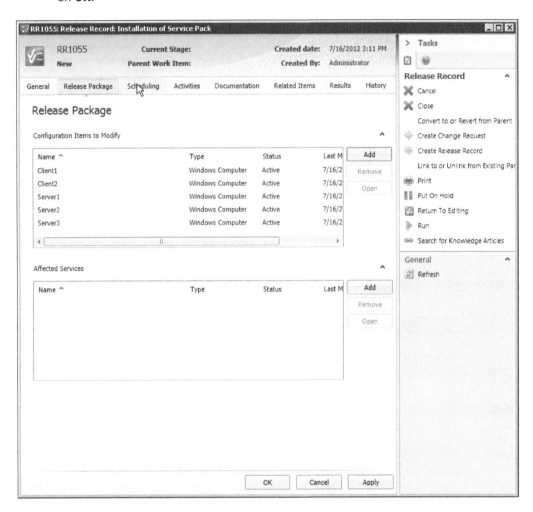

6. In the **Scheduling** tab provide the scheduled (planned) time information, planned work, and planned costs.

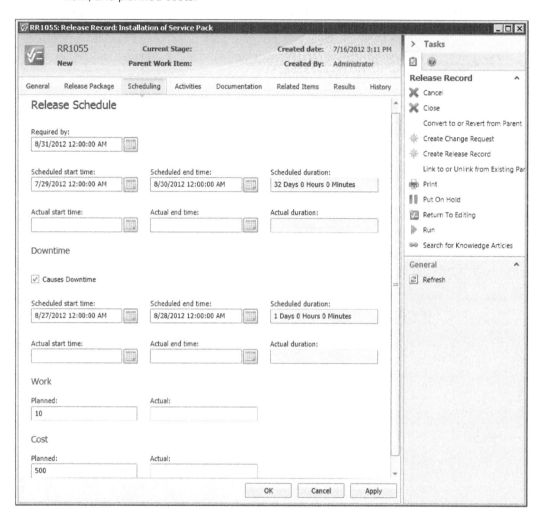

7. In the "Activities" you can use the activities we added in the previous recipe or you can build your own activities for this specific release.

   We will start with a Depended Activity to link a Change Request configured as follows:

   ❑ Change Request name: Install Service Pack

   Add a Parallel Activity Container named "Install Service Pack" with the following two Manual Activities:

   ❑ Install Service Pack on x86 clients

   ❑ Install Service Pack on x64 clients

We will then create a Sequential Activity container for this Change Request called:

❑ Install Service Pack on Servers

Containing the following Manual Activities:

❑ Install Service Pack on Server1

❑ Install Service Pack on Server2

❑ Install Service Pack on Server3

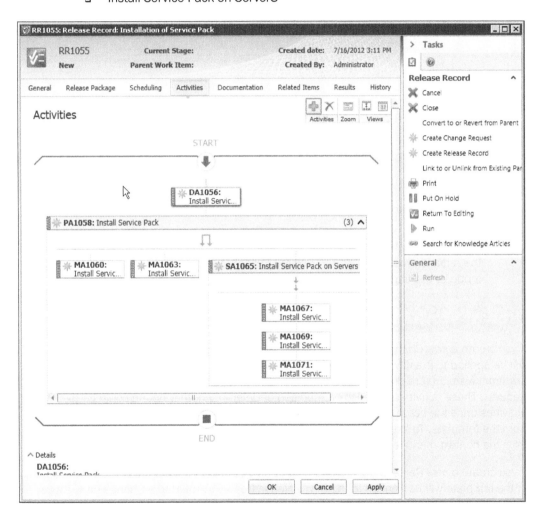

8. You can add additional specific information to each activity you added like **Impacted Configuration Items** and **Implementer**.

9. Right-click on the Dependent Activity and choose **Link to Change Request Activity**.

10. Choose the Dependent Activity from the Change Request we created earlier in this recipe and click on **OK**.

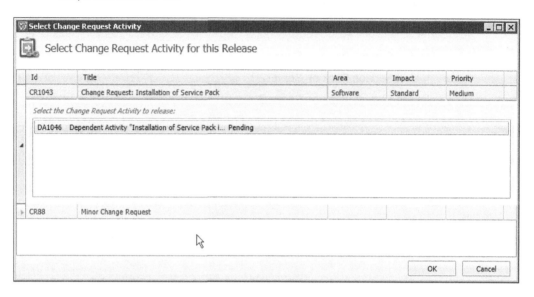

11. Click on **OK** in the Release Record form to close the form.

12. After providing all the information in the Release Record select the created Release Record we created, and click on **Run** in the **Tasks** pane and add a comment to start the release process. After the Release Record is started you can switch to the editing mode by clicking on **Return to editing** in the **Tasks** pane.

How it works...

If you create a new Change Request based on a Change Request template, all pre-filled fields will be applied to the new Change Request object. You can modify or delete the template at any time. Also, the pre-defined activities within the template are added to the new Change Request. These activities can also be modified or deleted. Another option could be to skip activities once the actual Change Request has been created instead of deleting the activities from the template. To skip an activity select the activity, right-click and choose **Skip Activity** from the context menu, enter a comment and click on **OK**.

If you create a new Release Record based on a Release Record template the predefined fields of the template will be applied to the new Release Record. Similar to a Change Request you can modify or delete the pre-filled fields of the activities of the Release Record template. As in the Change Request, the activities can be modified, deleted, or skipped. To start a Release Record process, you need to click on **Run** in the **Tasks** pane and add a comment.

To combine different configuration items you can add this to Builds. For complex and large releases it can be helpful to use Parent/Child Release records.

Using Environments and Builds

Instead of adding each individual CI, which will be affected by the release record you can add the environments and/or the builds in the **Release Package** tab.

Using Parent/Child Release Records

If a release is very complex you can use Parent/Child release records instead of creating a lot of different activities. This offers the option to split a complex release process into smaller pieces.

For instance, take a look at the following figure:

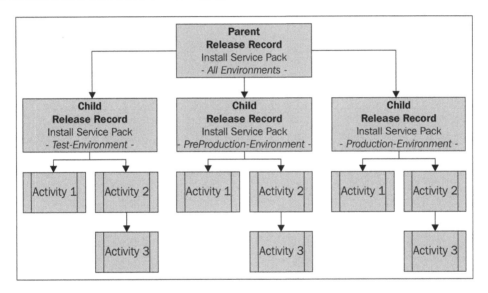

Reporting of Scheduled and Actual Date information

Providing the Scheduled Start and End Time of change requests, release records, and all the different activities and also providing the Actual Start and End Time is very helpful for reporting on how the Change Management and Release Management processes are performing. These key performance indicators offer a good overview on how many change requests, release records, and activities are completed in the planned time.

To get more information about reporting please take a look at the recipes of *Chapter 9, Reporting* of this cookbook.

See also

▶ Microsoft TechNet Library: Managing Release Records in System Center 2012
  - Service Manager: `http://technet.microsoft.com/en-us/library/hh495529`

8
Implementing Security Roles

In this chapter, we will cover:

- ▸ Viewing basic settings for Security roles
- ▸ Adding users to the End User role
- ▸ Creating and managing Service Request roles
- ▸ Creating and managing Incident Management roles
- ▸ Creating and managing Problem Management roles
- ▸ Creating and managing Change and Release Management roles
- ▸ Creating hybrid roles
- ▸ Configuring the self-service catalog security role
- ▸ Listing SCSM security role details with PowerShell

Introduction

This chapter discusses the security model used in System Center 2012 Service Manager (SCSM) and provides the configuration steps required to personalize the security model to your needs.

Security is applied across all objects you can manage in SCSM. The security model in use is commonly known as Role Based Administration (RBA). The RBA model provides a consistent method of delegating security control over what a user can interact with, and what actions they can perform. System Center 2012 Service Manager has 13 default security roles.

The 13 default roles are as follows:

- ▸ Activity Implementers
- ▸ Administrators
- ▸ Advanced Operators
- ▸ Authors
- ▸ Change Initiators
- ▸ Change Managers
- ▸ End Users
- ▸ Incident Resolvers
- ▸ Problem Analysts
- ▸ Read-Only Operators
- ▸ Release Managers
- ▸ Service Request Analysts
- ▸ Workflows

The default security roles cannot be removed and have only one editable option; you can assign users or groups to a default role. The actions and implied actions of SCSM security roles can be found in the official product administrative guide and online at `http://technet.microsoft.com/en-us/library/hh495625`.

The security settings you apply to your SCSM environment require you to plan and test your scenarios. The recipes in this chapter will provide us with the technical steps required to implement your personal security model.

Viewing basic settings for Security roles

This recipe provides the steps required to view the out of the box SCSM security roles available to you.

Getting ready

You need to have successfully installed the SCSM product, are a user in SCSM Administrators role, and have the SCSM console open.

You must be a member of the SCSM Administrators role to perform the tasks in this recipe. The default members of the SCSM Administrators role are, the user account used to install SCSM and the members of the Administrators group specified.

How to do it...

In this recipe we will review the default End Users role in the SCSM console.

1. Navigate to **Service Manager Console | Administration | Security | User Roles**.

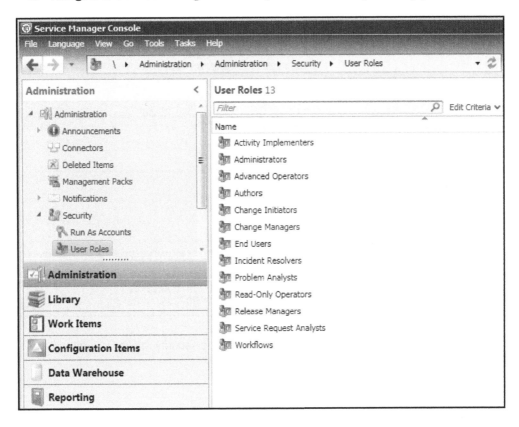

2. Select the **End Users** role in the middle pane and click on **Properties** under the task options.

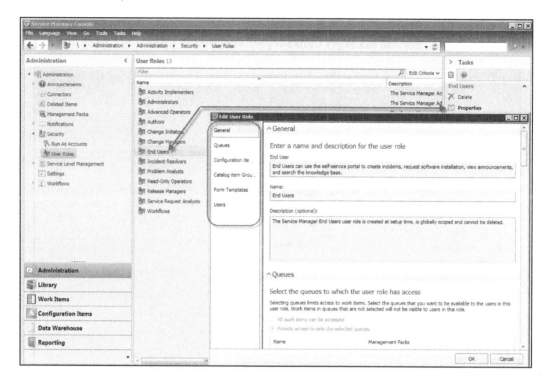

3. Review the default settings for each section of the security role to understand the scope of the security role.

How it works...

The general section of each role provides an overview of the role and the scope of access to the securable items in SCSM.

The default security roles, have all sections set to read-only (cannot be edited), except the users section. You can add or remove users to a security role to grant them rights to preconfigured permissions.

There's more...

The default roles are templates for custom roles you create, except for two special roles:

▸ **Administrators**: This role cannot be used as a template and by default, has the user account used to install SCSM, the service manager service account, and the SCSM administrators group specified during the installation as members

▸ **Workflows**: This role cannot be used as a template and by default has the account specified for the workflow as the only member

Data Warehouse User roles

There are two additional roles in a SCSM implementation where a Data Warehouse Management Server is installed and registered with an instance of SCSM. The registered Data Warehouse roles are:

▸ **Report Users**: Users in this role are granted access to the reporting node, and their SQL Reporting Service Rights determine what interaction the user can have with the published reports.

▸ **Administrators**: Users in this role are granted administrative access to the Data Warehouse node. Users added to this administrator's role do not automatically become members of the Administrators role defined under SCSM Administrator Security Roles.

To view the Report Users or the Data Warehouse Administrators role, select the **Data Warehouse | Security | User Roles**.

See also

▸ The *Configuring report permissions* recipe in *Chapter 9, Reporting* provides additional information on the Report User role

Adding users to the End User role

This recipe provides the steps required to add a user or group to a default SCSM security role. We will use the End User role to demonstrate these steps.

Getting ready

You need to have successfully installed the SCSM product, are a user in the SCSM Administrators role, and have the SCSM console open.

The default members of the SCSM Administrators role are the user account used to install SCSM, and the members of the Administrators group specified.

How to do it...

The following are the steps you need to perform to add a user to a default SCSM role:

1. Follow steps 1 and 2 of the *Viewing basic settings for Security roles* recipe to select the properties of the End Users role.

2. By default, this role has the special group authenticated Users assigned to it. Select the **Users** section in the **End User Role** window and click on **Add**. Type the name of the user or group and click on **Check Names...** to validate the user or group. Click on **OK**.

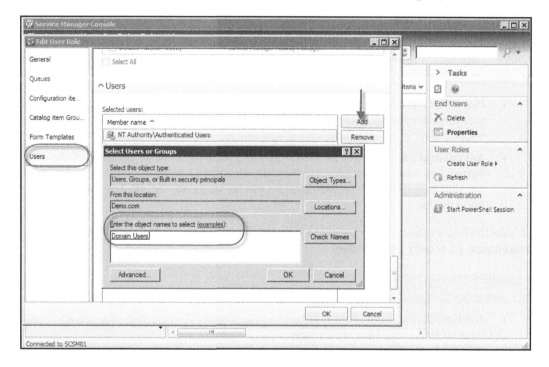

3. Repeat the previous steps for all users or groups you want to add to the role. Note that you can add multiple accounts in one step by separating your selection with a semicolon.

How it works...

The user(s) or members of the groups you add to a default SCSM security role will be granted the rights associated with the role.

A user can be a member of more than one role. The rights of a user in multiple roles are cumulative (for example, a user assigned the End User and Activity Implementer roles will have the combined rights of both roles).

There's more...

Here are some additional real-world tips to consider.

Beware of the Authenticated users

The End Users and Report Users roles have the NT\Authenticated users automatically assigned. Plan to remove this default setting and replace it with your specific users. The default setting adds additional implied permissions (for example, a read-only operator will be able to create incidents because NT\Authenticated users is part of the End Users role which has the rights to create a work item).

Creating and managing Service Request roles

This recipe provides the steps required to complete the creation of a Service Request role.

Getting ready

You must meet the following prerequisites before you complete this task:

▶ **Planning**: Agree the support group analysts and categories for Service Requests (For example, use a table to capture the planning information). Plan for views and queues for security scope filtering. We will use a Service Request support team called Service Desk in this recipe.

Process	Process role	SCSM Security role (template)	AD Group	Categories (Classification)
Service Request Fulfillment	Service Desk	Service Request Analysts	SCSM – SR Service Desk	User account password resets, printer consumables

▶ **Installation and Authorization**: You need to have successfully installed the SCSM product, are a user in SCSM Administrators role, and have the SCSM console open.

▶ **Console Tasks**: Create custom Service Request queues and views to reflect the organization process for managing service request fulfillment.

In this recipe we assume you have configured the following:

▶ A queue called Custom SR – Service Desk (scoped to the Service Request Class | Criteria support group = SR – Service Desk). See *Chapter 3, Configuring Service Level Agreements (SLAs)* for detailed steps on how to create SCSM queues.

▶ A View called Custom SR – All Service Desk Requests (Criteria support group = SR – Service Desk).

How to do it...

Follow these steps to create and manage a Service Request security role:

1. Navigate to **Service Manager Console | Administration | Security | User Roles**.

2. Select **User Roles | Create User Role | Service Request Analyst** from the **Tasks** menu.

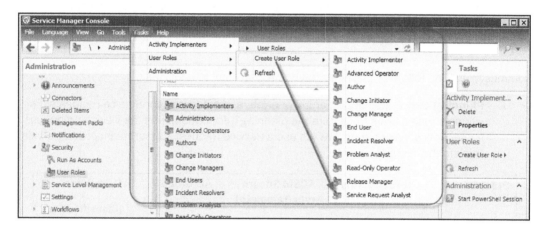

3. Click on **Next** in the **Before You Begin** wizard page.

4. On the **General wizard** page type the following mandatory and optional information:

   ❑ **Name:** SR - Service Desk Team

   ❑ **Description (optional):** Service Request Role scoped for the Service Desk support group

5. In the **Management Packs** wizard page select only management packs related to Service Requests. (Include custom management packs used to store Service Request configurations.)

6. In the **Queues** wizard page select **Provide access to only the selected queues**. Select the custom queue for the role (for example, **Custom SR – Service Desk**). Click on **Next**.

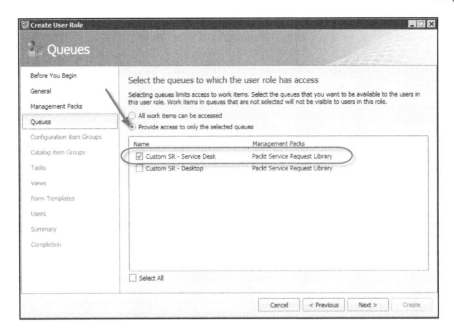

7. Click on **Next** in the **Configuration items Group** and **Catalog items Group** wizard pages.

8. In the **Tasks** wizard page select **Provide access to only the selected tasks**. Select the specific tasks relevant to the role (for example, we will not select **Configure Workflow Rules** for this analyst role). Click on **Next**.

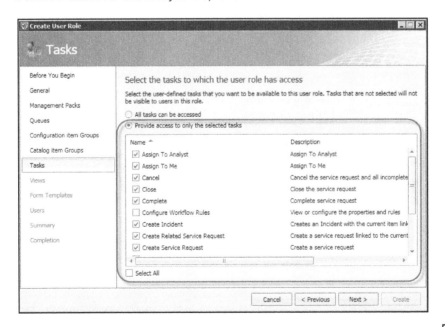

9. In the **Views** wizard page select **Provide access to only the selected views**. Select the specific views relevant to the role and click on **Next**.

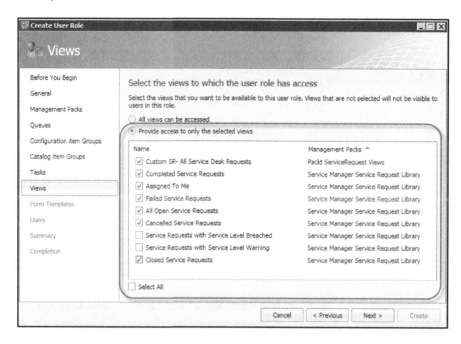

10. In the **Forms Templates** wizard page select **Provide access to only the selected forms**. Select the specific forms relevant to the role and click on **Next**.

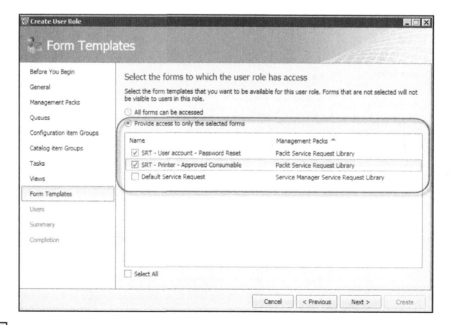

11. In the **Users** wizard page follow the **Adding Users to the End User Role** task steps to select the Active Directory group for the role (as discussed in the *Getting ready* section of this recipe). Click on **Next**.

12. Review the **Summary** page; click on **Previous** to correct any configurations in previous wizard pages. Then, click on **Create** to complete the role creation.

13. Click on **Close** on the Completion wizard page.

How it works...

Role-based security configuration and management is similar to computer file access security. Compare SCSM security delegation to granting access to files stored in a particular network location. You need to plan for the following:

Computer files Access Network Share	SCSM console or portal
Folders structures grouped by file type, department, or content	SCSM Access Categories: Administration, library, Work Items, and Configuration Items
Create shares to represent a logical view and abstract the physical structure	SCSM Queues and Views
Grant action permissions on the content of the folders	SCSM Create, Delete, Edit, and category specific actions
Grant permissions for actions on the host machine of the shares	SCSM Infrastructure Administrative Settings
Local Security Groups (for example, Power Users)	SCSM built-in roles which you copy to create custom roles
Grant access permission by user or groups	Active directory users or groups
Windows Explorer and other file access tools including file processing applications	SCSM console and portal

The following figure presents a graphical illustration of how role-based security works in SCSM:

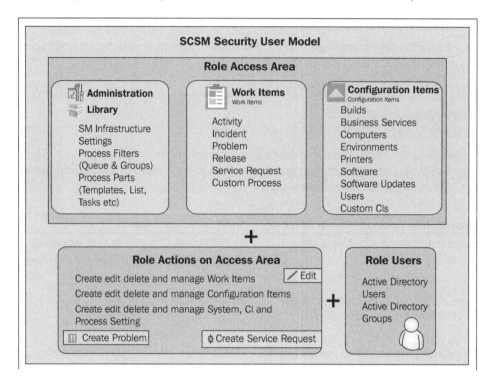

The principles of file access delegation apply to SCSM; in both cases you must plan for roles to support the processes. In this recipe, we focused on Service Request fulfillment as a process and created a role with access to perform actions on the process objects in the scope of management. The following table is a breakdown of the wizard selection categories:

SCSM wizard page	Description and notes
Management packs	This provides the means to filter what you select in subsequent wizard pages when you are creating a role. This is a major benefit of organizing your configuration in specific management packs.
Queues	Queues are similar to the principle of a fair ground ticket. By default, all work items can be accessed based on the SCSM security role template (get in line for all rides). You use a queue to grant access to a subset of work items (get in line for these specific rides).
Configuration Item Groups	Similar to queues but applicable to configuration items. For example, you can create a group for all workstation class computers and grant access to only those groups for the role.

SCSM wizard page	Description and notes
Catalog Item Groups	These groups are specific to the service catalog and grants the role access to specific categories accessed by using the Self-Service Portal
Tasks	The actions you can perform relevant to the process category and infrastructure settings. For example, you may be able to create and modify service requests but not be able to cancel a service request
Views	The views selected here control what is displayed in the SCSM console for the specific role. By default this would be the built-in system views. You must configure custom views before you create the role if you want to assign the views at the role creation stage. Views created after the security role wizard completion can be granted by editing the role.
Forms Template	The process templates a role user can select when creating objects in a specific process. For example, you can create a new service request using a pre-configured template. You are only presented with templates assigned to the role. The default option grants access to all process specific templates.
Users	This is where you associate the SCSM specific role with the console or portal users.

Plan and create roles for the process instead of creating roles for specific people within a team.

There's more...

There is a hidden but very important security configuration for SCSM security roles and full implication for members of the security roles. The hidden configuration is better known as implied and inherited security.

Implied permissions

Review the product documentation for the inherited and implied permissions when you select the role template.

See also

▶ *Appendix B, Useful Websites and Community Resources* provides links to useful resources on complex security models for SCSM and official online product documentation

Creating and managing Incident Management roles

This recipe provides the steps required to complete the creation of an Incident Management role.

Getting ready

You must meet the following prerequisites before you complete this task:

 ▸ **Planning:** Agree the support group analysts and categories for Incident Management (for example, use a table to capture the planning information). Plan for views and queues for security scope filtering. We will use an Incident Management team called Desktop Support in this recipe.

Process	Process role	SCSM Security role (template)	AD Group	Categories (classification)
Incident Management	Desktop Support	Incident Resolvers	SCSM – IM Desktop Support	Hardware\Clients, Software\Client Application

 ▸ **Installation and Authorization**: You need to ensure you have successfully installed the SCSM product, are a user in SCSM Administrators role, and have the SCSM console open.

 ▸ **Console Tasks**: Create custom Incident Management queues and views to reflect the organization process for Incident Management.

In this recipe we assume you have configured the following:

 ▸ A queue called Custom IM – Desktop Support (scoped to the Incident Class | Criteria support group = IM – Desktop Support). See *Chapter 3, Configuring Service Level Agreements (SLAs)* for detailed steps on how to create SCSM queues.

 ▸ Two Views called Custom - IM All Desktop Support Incidents (Criteria support group = IM – Desktop Support and all the states of an IM except closed) and Custom IM All Unassigned Desktop Support Incidents (Criteria support group = IM – Desktop Support, all the status of an Incident except closed and Assigned User is Null).

How to do it...

Follow these steps to create and manage incident class related security roles:

1. Navigate to **Service Manager Console | Administration | Security | User Roles**.

2. Select **User Roles | Create User Role | Incident Resolvers** from the **Tasks** menu.

3. Click on **Next** in the **Before You Begin** wizard page.

4. In the **General** wizard page type the following mandatory and optional information:

   ❑ **Name**: IM - Desktop Support Team

   ❑ **Description (optional)**: Incident Management Role scoped for the Desktop support group

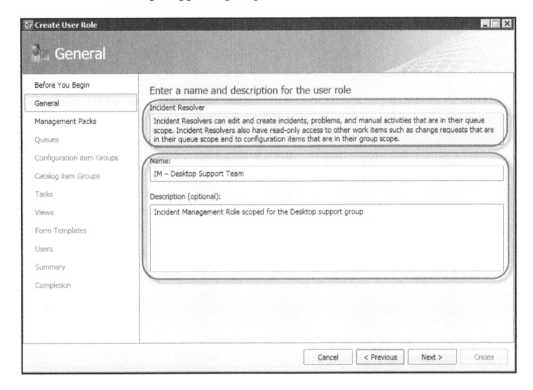

5. In the **Management Packs** wizard page select only management packs related to Incident Management (include custom management packs used to store Incident Management configurations).

6. In the **Queues** wizard page select **Provide access to only the selected queues**. Select the custom queue for the role (for example, **Custom – IM Desktop Support**). Click on **Next**.

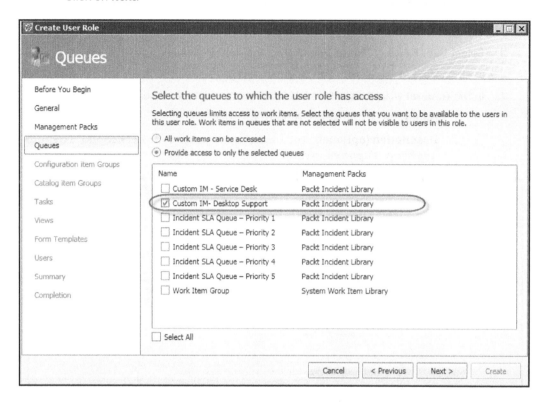

7. Click on **Next** in the **Configuration items Group** and **Catalog items Group** wizard pages.

8. In the **Tasks** wizard page select **Provide access to only the selected tasks**. Select the specific tasks relevant to the role (for example, we will not select **Configure Workflow Rules** for this Incident Management role). Click on **Next**.

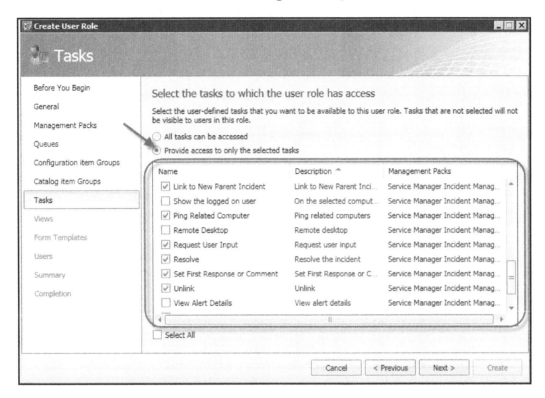

9. In the **Views** wizard page select **Provide access to only the selected views**. Select the specific views relevant to the role and click on **Next**.

10. In the **Form Templates** wizard page select **Provide access to only the selected forms**. Select the specific forms relevant to the role and click on **Next**.

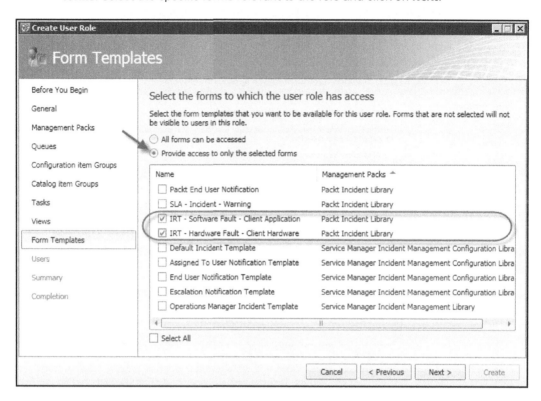

11. In the **Users** wizard page follow the *Adding users to the End User role* recipe steps to select the Active Directory group for the role as discussed in the planning information for the role creation. Click on **Next**.

12. Review the **Summary** page; click on **Previous** to correct any configuration in the previous wizard pages. Click on **Create** to complete the role creation.

13. Click on **Close** in the **Completion wizard** page.

How it works...

The *How it works...* section discussed in the *Creating and managing Service Request roles* recipe in this chapter is applicable to this recipe. You must plan specifically for the Incident Management process.

There's more...

SCSM in some cases has inconsistencies with the naming of list items and how they appear in forms. Here is a real-world common setting example that can be confusing to the SCSM console user.

Support Group alias (Incident Tier Queue)

The support group field referenced in the queue and views for Incident Management has a specific name in the Library, Incident Tier Queue.

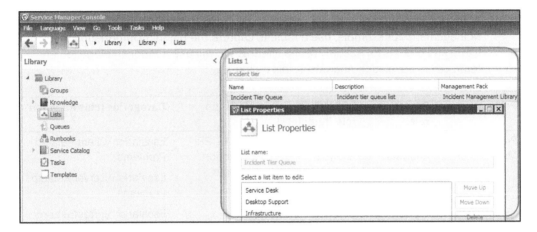

This support group is not shared with the Service Request process though they appear as the same list name in the respective forms of the processes.

See also

> ▸ *Appendix B, Useful Websites and Community Resources* provides links to useful resources on complex security models for SCSM and official online product documentation

Creating and managing Problem Management roles

This recipe provides the steps required to complete the creation of a Problem Management role.

Getting ready

You must meet the following prerequisites before you complete this task:

▶ **Planning**: Agree the logical support group analysts and categories for Problem Management (for example, use a table to capture the planning information). Plan for views and queues for security scope filtering. We will use a Problem Management team called Escalation Analysts in this recipe.

Process	Process role	SCSM Security role (template)	AD Group	Categories (classification)
Problem Management	Escalation Analysts	Problem Analysts	SCSM – PR Escalation Analysts	Escalation\Client Related Problems, Escalation\Server Related Problems, Escalation\Infrastructure Related Problems

▶ **Installation and Authorization**: You need to have successfully installed the SCSM product, are a user in SCSM Administrators role, and have the SCSM console open.

▶ **Console Tasks**: Create custom Problem Management queues and views to reflect the organization process for Problem Management.

In this recipe we assume you have configured the following:

▶ A queue called Custom PR – Escalation Analysts (scoped to the Problem Class | Criteria Classification = Escalation\Client Related Problems OR Escalation\Server Related Problems OR Escalation\Infrastructure Related Problems). See *Chapter 3, Configuring Service Level Agreements (SLAs)* for detailed steps on how to create SCSM queues.

▶ Three Views called Custom – PR Client Related Escalations, Custom – PR Server Related Escalations and Custom – PR Infrastructure Related Escalations (Criteria is the problem classification category related to the respective escalation).

How to do it...

Here are the steps to create and manage a Problem Management class security role:

1. Navigate to **Service Manager Console | Administration | Security | User Roles**.

2. Select **User Roles | Create User Role | Problem Analysts** from the **Tasks** menu.

3. Click on **Next** in the **Before You Begin** wizard page.

4. In the **General** wizard page type the following mandatory and optional information:

   ❑ **Name**: PR - Escalation Analysts

   ❑ **Description (optional)**: Problem Management Role scoped for the Escalation Analysts group

5. In the **Management Packs** wizard page select only management packs related to Problem Management (include custom management packs used to store Problem Management configurations).

6. In the **Queues** wizard page select **Provide access to only the selected queues**. Select the custom queue for the role (for example **Custom – PR – Escalation Analysts**) and click on **Next**.

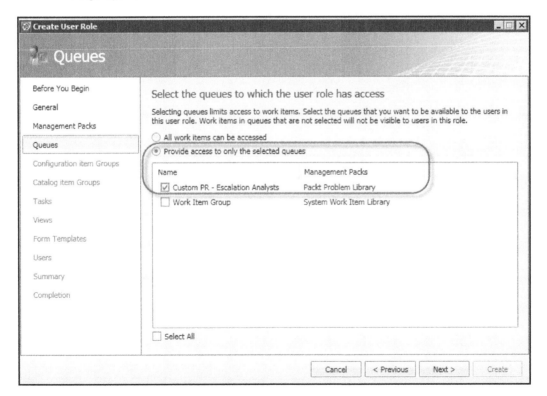

7. Click on **Next** in the **Configuration items Group** and **Catalog items Group** wizard pages.

8. In the **Tasks** wizard page select **Provide access to only the selected tasks**. Select the specific tasks relevant to the role (for example, we will not select the **Close** task for this Problem Management role). Click on **Next**.

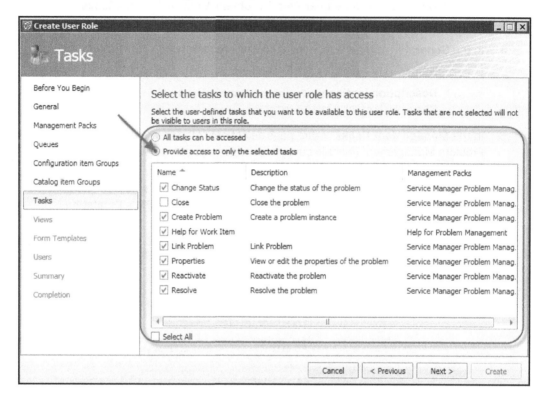

9. On the **Views** wizard page select **Provide access to only the selected views**. Select the specific views relevant to the role and click on **Next**.

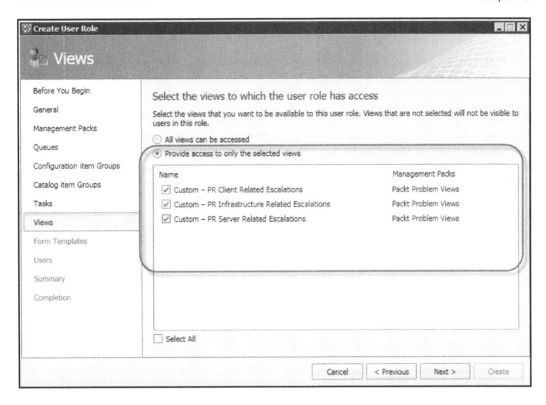

10. In the **Forms Templates** wizard page select **Provide access to only the selected forms**. Select the specific forms relevant to the role and click on **Next**.

11. In the **Users** wizard page follow the *Adding users to the End User role* recipe steps to select the Active Directory group for the role as discussed in the *Getting ready* section of this recipe. Click on **Next**.

12. Review the **Summary** page; click on **Previous** to correct any configuration in the previous wizard pages. Click on **Create** to complete the role creation.

13. Click on **Close** in the **Completion** wizard page.

How it works...

The *How it works...* section, discussed in the *Creating and managing Service Request roles* recipe earlier in this chapter, is applicable to this recipe. You must plan specifically for the Problem Management process. The Problem Management process does not have a support group configuration option in SCSM.

This recipe demonstrates the difference in approach to role creation based on a process. The approach for Problem Management requires you to use a different category for organizing and managing the role. The recipe example is organized using the classification category. A similar approach is used for the views, which allows us to structure the Problem Management role creation and management.

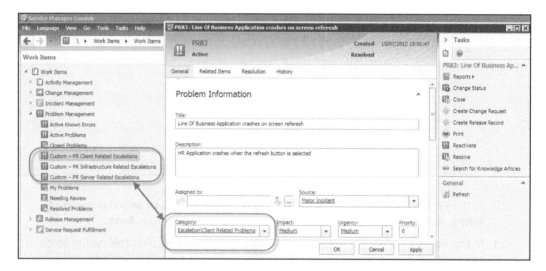

See also

- *Appendix B, Useful Websites and Community Resources* provides links to useful resources on complex security models for SCSM and official online product documentation

Creating and managing Change and Release Management roles

This recipe provides the details on creating and managing the roles required for Change and Release Management using SCSM.

Getting ready

You must plan to meet the following prerequisites before you complete this task:

▸ **Planning**: Agree the Change and Release Management categories and roles (for example, use a table to capture the planning information). Plan for groups and queues for security scope filtering.

Process	Process role	SCSM Security role (template)	AD Group	Categories (area)
Change Management	Change Initiators	Change Initiator	SCSM – CR Change Analysts	Standard - Infrastructure
Change Management	Change Owners	Change Managers	SCSM – CR Change Managers	All Change Management Categories
Release Management	Release Owners	Release Managers	SCSM – RR Release Managers Analysts	All Release Management Categories

▸ **Installation and Authorization**: You need to have successfully installed the SCSM product, are a user in SCSM Administrators role, and have the SCSM console open.

How to do it...

Follow these steps to create Change and Release management class security roles:

1. Create SCSM Groups for Configuration Items in scope of Change Management. Use the steps in the *Creating a configuration item group* recipe in *Chapter 4, Building the Configuration Management Database (CMDB)*.

2. Create SCSM views by using Change and Release category.

3. Follow the steps detailed in the *Creating and managing Service Request roles* recipe to create the Change and Release management roles based on Change Initiators, Change Managers, and Release Managers. Use the groups and views you create for the Change and Release management process to limit the scope of authority.

How it works...

The *How it works...* section discussed in the *Creating and managing Service Request roles* recipe is applicable to this recipe. You must plan specifically for the Change and Release management process.

There are two typical scenarios for Change and Release Management process roles organizations:

▸ Virtual roles of the Incident Management team

▸ Dedicated Change and Release Management team

In the first scenario plan to use the AD groups created for the Incident Management roles as the assigned users of the Change and Release Management role. The authors recommend best practice of creating dedicated groups by processing and adding the same users as members.

In the second scenario plan the Change and Release Management roles using the **RACI (Responsible, Accountable, Consulted, and Informed)** model as a guide. Use the agreed role plan to implement the SCSM role model.

There's more...

Built-in security roles which you can use as templates are great for testing as they have implied and inherited permissions over all objects by default.

Using the built-in roles

The built-in roles provide a means to delegate SCSM security roles to the specific process areas. Plan to use custom roles to avoid granting unnecessary access to SCSM. The built-in roles are assigned global scope access to all work and configuration items. You must limit the scope of access using groups and views to avoid unplanned access to SCSM process areas.

Creating hybrid roles

This recipe discusses the steps required to create hybrid roles in SCSM. Hybrid roles members require delegation across multiple SCSM processes.

Getting ready

You need to have successfully installed the SCSM product, are a user in SCSM Administrators role, and have the SCSM console open.

Review and document the role areas required for the hybrid roles.

How to do it...

Follow these steps to create hybrid roles (roles that are combined of two or more classes):

1. Document the hybrid process role (for example, users of the hybrid role need to have access to the following: Service Request, Incident Management, and Problem Management).

Process	Process role	SCSM Security role (template)	AD Group
Service Request Fulfillment	Service Desk	Service Request Analysts	SCSM – SR Service Desk
Incident Management	Desktop Support	Incident Resolvers	SCSM – IM Desktop Support
Problem Management	Escalation Analysts	Problem Analysts	SCSM – PR Escalation Analysts

2. In the SCSM console validate the users or groups assigned to each role in scope. In the console navigate to the **Administrators | Security | User Roles** and select a role. Select **Properties** under the **Tasks** pane and click on **Users**. Add the hybrid role users to the group assigned to the role.

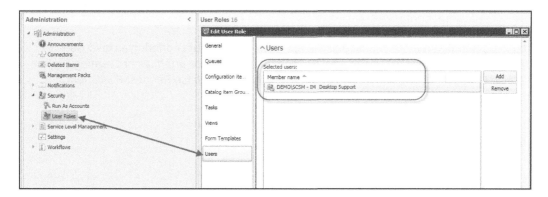

3. Repeat step 2 for all roles in scope of the hybrid role.

How it works...

SCSM implements its role-based model by class of process and objects. The notion of a hybrid role for a standard installation requires you to add users to the specific roles dedicated to each process.

The security and rights delegated to a single user across multiple roles is cumulative.

There's more...

SCSM as a product is highly customizable, and as a result you may have an environment which has different classes or extensions to the existing classes discussed in this chapter.

Advance extensions

You can extend the SCSM product to create a hybrid class to support a hybrid delegation model. The extension of SCSM is discussed in *Chapter 11, Automating Service Manager 2012*. In case you have extended SCSM, follow the steps for role security creation in general. Plan to tailor the queues and views to the extended configuration or work items.

Configuring the self-service catalog security role

System Center 2012 Service Manager has a role-based security model for its self-service portal. This recipe discusses the security delegation configuration required to implement this model for an organization.

Getting ready

You need to have successfully installed the SCSM product, are a user in SCSM Administrators role, and have the SCSM console open.

You need to have created at least one Service offering or Request offering as discussed by following the task steps in the *Creating Service Catalog Service offerings* or *Creating Service Catalog Request offerings* recipes in *Chapter 5, Deploying Service Request Fulfillment*.

How to do it...

Here are the steps to create a self-service catalog security role:

1. In the SCSM console navigate to **Library | Groups**.

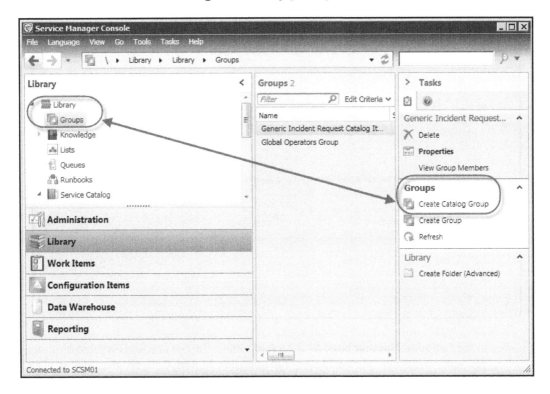

2. Under **Tasks** select **Create Catalog Group**.
3. Read the **Before You Begin** information and click on **Next**.

4. In the **General** page fill in the mandatory group name and optionally provide a description for the group. Select a management pack and click on **Next**.

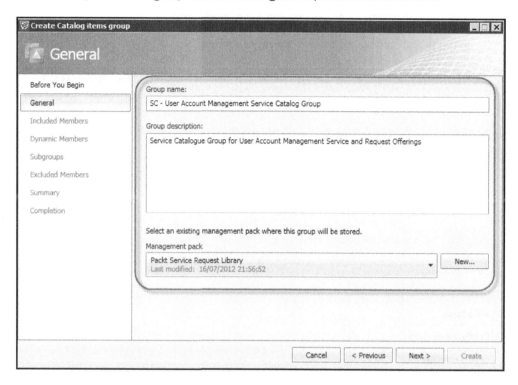

5. In the **Included Member** page click on **Add**. Select the Service and Request offering you want to include in the catalog group and click on **Add**. Click on **OK** and then click on **Next**.

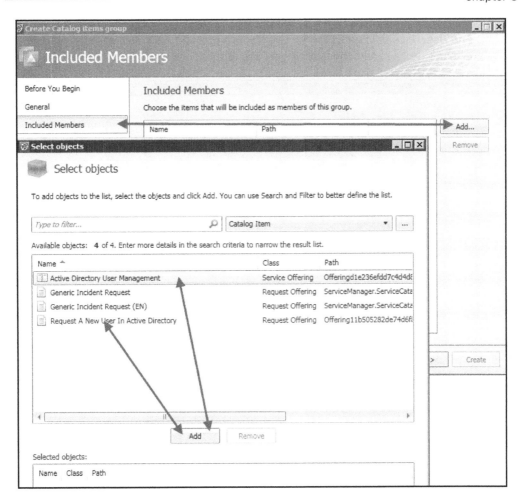

6. Click on **Next** in the **Dynamic Members**, **Subgroups**, and **Excluded Members** pages.

7. Review the **Summary** page and click on **Create** to complete the group creation.

8. Navigate to **Administration | Security | User Roles**. Select **Create User Role | End User**. Provide a name for the role (for example, SC - Account Management Portal Role) and optionally type a description for the role. Click on **Next**.

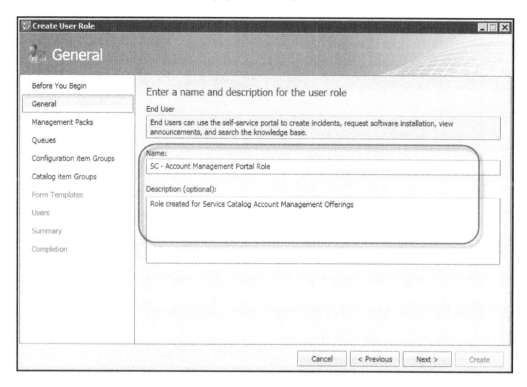

9. In the **Management Pack** page select the management pack the catalog group is saved in and click on **Next**.

10. Leave the default selections for **Queues** and **Configuration Groups** and click on **Next**.

11. In the **Catalog items Groups** page select the catalog group we created and click on **Next**.

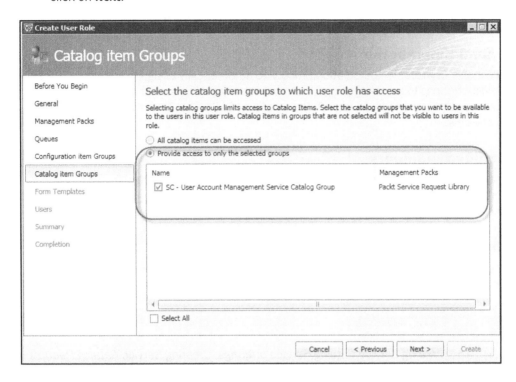

12. Leave the default option in the **Forms Templates** page and click on **Next**.

13. In the **Users** page click on **Add** to select the users or groups you want to assign the role to, and then click on **Next**.

14. Review the **Summary** page and click on **Next** to complete the role creation.

How it works...

Service catalog groups are used to implement role-based security on the self-service portal. You must assign Service and Request offerings to a Catalog group and assign the Catalog group to a user role. Only administrators can access a published self-service offering if a catalog group with the offerings are not assigned to a user role.

The continual management of the self-service is performed by assigning active directory users and groups to the user roles.

A real-world scenario is to assign the User Account Management offerings to only the Human resources department. We achieve this objective by creating an SCSM role as discussed in this recipe and allocate an Active directory group for the Human Resources department.

There's more...

Here are some additional real-world tips and tricks on creating and managing security roles.

Dynamic membership

You can use keywords in the creation process to automatically assign Service offerings and Request offerings to a catalog group. You must specify criteria similar to the process used to create views (discussed in *Chapter 2, Personalizing SCSM 2012 Administration*) to achieve this objective.

Excluded members

Dynamic groups are great, but we may want to protect specific offerings (for example, offerings tied to automated approved processes). During the catalog group creation process select the offerings you want to exclude in the **Excluded Members** page.

Editing the catalog group

You can maintain and edit the catalog groups by viewing the properties and editing the relevant wizard pages.

See also

▶ The *Creating Service Catalog Service offerings*, *Creating Service Catalog Request offerings*, and *Publishing Service offerings and Request offerings* recipes in *Chapter 5, Deploying Service Request Fulfillment* provide steps for creating and publishing Service and Request Offerings associated with the Catalog groups

Listing SCSM security role details with PowerShell

SCSM security role delegation can be managed using PowerShell commands. In this recipe we discuss and provide steps to list the typical settings for all configured SCSM Security User role using the SCSM PowerShell commands.

Getting ready

You need to ensure you have successfully installed the SCSM product, are a user in SCSM Administrators role, and have the SCSM console open.

You must download and install the SCSM PowerShell Cmdlets found at `http://smlets.codeplex.com/` (see the *Downloading and installing SMLets* recipe in *Chapter 11, Automating Service Manager 2012*).

How to do it...

Here are the steps you must follow to list the configuration of security roles using PowerShell commands:

1. Copy the following code into a notepad or a plain text editor:

```
Import-Module SMLets

$Roles = Get-SCSMUserRole
ForEach ($Role in $Roles)
{
    Write-Output "===============================================
=="
    Write-Output $Role.DisplayName "(" $Role.ProfileDisplayName
")"
    Write-Output $Role.Description
    Write-Output "===============================================
=="
    Write-Output "USERS"
    ForEach ($User in $Role.Users)
    {
        Write-Output "   " $User
    }
    Write-Output " "
    Write-Output "VIEWS"
    ForEach ($View in $Role.Views)
    {
        Write-Output "   " $View.DisplayName
    }

    Write-Output " "
    Write-Output "OBJECT SCOPES"
    ForEach ($Object in $Role.Objects)
    {
        Write-Output "   " $Object.DisplayName
    }

    Write-Output " "
    Write-Output "TEMPLATES"
    ForEach ($Template in $Role.Templates)
    {
        Write-Output "   " $Template.DisplayName
    }
```

```
        Write-Output " "
        Write-Output "CLASSES"
        ForEach ($Class in $Role.Classes)
        {
            Write-Output "  " $Class.DisplayName
        }

        Write-Output " "
        Write-Output "CONSOLE TASKS"
        ForEach ($CredentialTask in $Role.CredentialTasks)
        {
            $T = Get-SCSMConsoleTask $CredentialTask.First
            Write-Output " " $T.DisplayName
        }
    }
```

2. Save the file as a PowerShell file with a `.PS1` extension to a filesystem location (for example, `C:\AllSCSMUserRoles.ps1`).

3. Start a PowerShell command prompt as an Administrator.

4. Run the following command:

   `Set-ExecutionPolicy RemoteSigned`

5. Press the *Y* and *Enter* keys.

6. In the PowerShell command window navigate to the location of the script. Type `C:\AllSCSMUserRoles.ps1`.

7. Press the *Enter* key.

8. A list of all the default SCSM roles and any custom roles you have created is presented.

```
Administrator: Windows PowerShell
================================================
IM - Desktop Support Team ( Incident Resolver )
Incident Management Role scoped for the Desktop support group
================================================
USERS
    DEMO\SCSM - IM  Desktop Support

VIEWS


    Custom - IM All Unassigned Desktop Support Incidents


OBJECT SCOPES
    Global Settings
    Star Rating
    Configuration Item
    Data Warehouse SDK Resource Store (internal)
    Catalog Item
    Custom IM- Desktop Support

TEMPLATES
    IRT - Hardware Fault - Client Hardware
    IRT - Software Fault - Client Application

CLASSES

CONSOLE TASKS
================================================
Release Managers ( Release Manager )
The Service Manager Release Managers user role is created at setup time, is globally scoped and cannot be deleted.
================================================
USERS

VIEWS


OBJECT SCOPES

TEMPLATES

CLASSES

CONSOLE TASKS
```

How it works...

The script is an example of using the SMLets commands to get information from SCSM. Using PowerShell you can perform many of the console actions including managing SCSM Security roles. You can find additional examples and usage options at `http://technet.microsoft.com/en-us/library/hh316214`.

There's more...

Running a script and seeing the output is great but you may want to save the results of the script.

Piping the script output to a text file

You can save the output of the PowerShell script to a text file by following these steps:

1. In the PowerShell command window navigate to the location of the script. Type `C:\AllSCSMUserRoles.ps1 >> C:\<yourfilename.txt>`.

2. Press the *Enter* key.

See also

▸ *Using SMLets to delete a Work Item* and *Autoclose resolved Incidents with SMLets and a custom workflow* recipes in *Chapter 11, Automating Service Manager 2012* for additional SCSM management examples using PowerShell commands

9
Reporting

In this chapter we will walk you through the various options of using the Service Manager Data Warehouse to gain insight into the data stored in the Service Manager database. We will specifically cover using reporting and advanced analytics with the following tasks:

- ▶ Viewing SCSM reports
- ▶ Creating Favorite and Linked reports
- ▶ Creating reports with Report Builder
- ▶ Configuring report permissions
- ▶ Delivering reports automatically using report subscriptions
- ▶ Analyzing data with Microsoft Excel
- ▶ Using the Analysis Library to publish Excel reports
- ▶ Using SharePoint for advanced dashboards

Introduction

Service Manager periodically transfers data that is stored in the operational database to the Service Manager Data Warehouse databases through a process called **Extract Transform and Load** (**ETL**). The processes required for keeping the data in the Data Warehouse in sync with the operational database are controlled by the Service Manager Data Warehouse Management Server role.

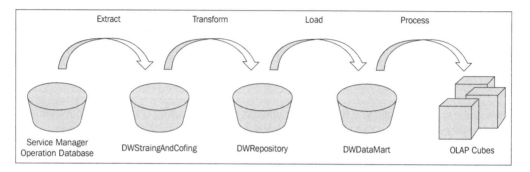

The ETL process is started on a scheduled interval. The first step is the extract workflow that reads new data from the operational database and writes it to the **DWStagingAndConfig** database. The raw data is then picked up by the transform workflow that does the required reformatting for bringing the data into the final format optimized for reporting prior to storing it in the **DWRepository** database. The load workflow then transfers the data to the **DWDataMart** database where it can be used for reporting.

The reasons for transferring data to the databases of the Service Manager Data Warehouse are to:

▸ Offload data from the Service Manager operational database to improve performance

▸ Provide a long-term storage of historical data stored in Service Manager

▸ Optimize and provide data for reporting

The **DWDataMart** database is the database used for all reporting needs. In addition, Service Manager comes with a set of pre-defined OLAP cubes to facilitate advanced analysis of data. An **OLAP cube** is a multi-dimensional data structure that is optimized for aggregating and analyzing large amount of data, while also allowing access to the most granular information. The SCSM Data Warehouse leverages Microsoft SQL Server Analysis Services to provide OLAP cubes to end users.

With both the **DWDataMart** database and the OLAP cubes, Service Manager provides powerful means for creating simple reports as well as gaining advanced insight into the data by analyzing it from multiple perspectives.

In this chapter we will provide recipes to work with common reporting tools that allow you to access and analyze the data stored in the **DWDataMart** database and the OLAP cubes.

Viewing SCSM reports

In this recipe we will show you how to navigate through the reporting section of the Service Manager console and how to work with the built-in reports which are shipped out-of-the-box with Service Manager.

Getting ready

Before you can work with reports, it is required that you have already installed a Service Manager Data Warehouse Management Server and that it has been registered with the Service Manager server installation. Also, you need to ensure that the initial synchronization of the Management Packs is complete and the ETL jobs have run. Information on how to complete these two tasks can be found in the TechNet library at the following URL:

```
http://technet.microsoft.com/en-us/library/hh519643
```

This process normally takes several hours to complete from the time the Data Warehouse Management Server is registered.

How to do it...

We will now walk you through the steps required for viewing SCSM reports through the Service Manager console.

1. Navigate to the **Reporting** section of the **Service Manager** console.

2. Under the **Reports** node, you will see a couple of folders that contain predefined reports for different types of work items and configuration items. Click on the **Incident Management** folder.

3. You will see the built-in reports for incident management listed in the view. In this example, we want to retrieve a list of all incidents concerning hardware problems. Click on the **List of Incidents** report and then click on **Run Report** from the tasks bar.

4. In the parameter section of the report window, under **Classification Category**, unselect the **(All)** option and check the **Hardware Problems** option.

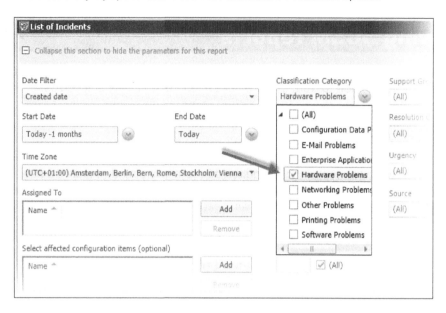

5. Click on the **Run Report** option from the task bar to generate and view the report in the console.

6. Click on the floppy disk icon and choose the desired format to export the report.

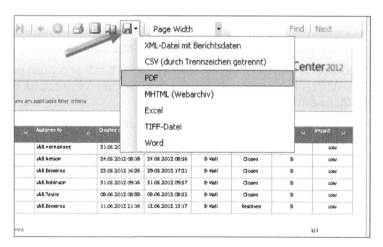

How it works...

Service Manager uses SQL Server Reporting Services to provide its reporting capabilities. The folders and reports that are listed under the **Reporting** section of the **Service Manager** console represent the way how the reports are organized in SQL Server Reporting Services.

When a report is opened in the console, Service Manager loads the report definition and displays its parameters to allow for filtering data in the report. The options and controls available for filtering data can be defined by using management packs.

There's more...

In this section we will show you how you can access reports from a web browser, which is particularly interesting for users that do not have access to the SCSM console.

Accessing reports from a browser

The **Reporting** section in the **Service Manager** console is a very comfortable way of accessing reports quickly from within the console. However, a common scenario is to allow the users that do not work with the Service Manager console to access reports. For instance, you might want to run incident statistics by your users' departments and hand out a report to each department head.

Creating such a report using the Service Manager console, exporting it to a suitable format, and sending it to each department head is quite cumbersome. Instead, you can grant your department heads access to the reports through the web browser.

Open your web browser and navigate to the following URL:

```
http://[SCSMDWSQL]/Reports
```

Replace [SCSMDWSQL] with the fully qualified domain name of the SQL server, which is used for reporting. If SQL Server Reporting Service is running as a named instance, the syntax of the URL will be the following:

```
http://[SCSMDWSQL]/Reports_[InstanceName]
```

When you click on the **SystemCenter** folder and then click on the **ServiceManager** folder, you will see the same folder structure that was previously displayed in the **Service Manager** console. You might want to switch to **Tile View** to get a better overview of the folder and file structure.

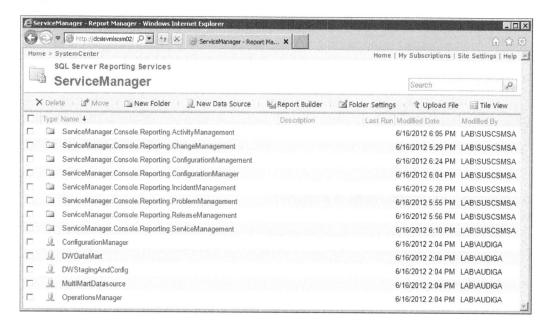

You will notice that the folder and file names, as well as the controls used for defining your report parameters are much less comprehensive than when the reports are consumed through the Service Manager console. If you use the web browser to navigate the reports, SQL Server Reporting Services represents the actual file and folder names and also renders the default controls for the report parameters. This behavior can be overridden when accessing reports through the **Service Manager** console by using corresponding directives in management packs.

If you want to provide reports to users through the web browser, we recommend that you create custom reports for your end users that do not make use of advanced management pack features but are comprehensively consumable through the web browser instead. You can create your own folder and report file structure in SQL Server Reporting Services and limit access to only the folders you want your users to see.

See also

Refer to the following recipes for more information on how to manage report permissions and folder structures:

▸ *Creating simple reports* recipe later in this chapter

▸ *Configuring report permissions* recipe later in this chapter

Creating Favorite and Linked Reports

Service Manager 2012 allows you to save the selections you make in the parameters section of the report window for future use. You can either save your settings for just yourself or create a Linked Report that will also be available to other users.

Getting ready

It is recommended that you follow the instructions from the previous recipe *Viewing SCSM reports* to get familiar with how to open reports using the **Service Manager** console.

How to do it...

The selections that you make in the parameter section of the report window can be stored as a **Favorite Report**, allowing you to access the report with the same selections at a later point in time. Favorite Reports are personal and cannot be accessed by other users.

1. Open the report of your choice in the **Service Manager** console.

2. Make the desired selections in the parameters section of the report window. For example, follow the instructions in the *Viewing SCSM reports* recipe to create a list of incidents about hardware-related problems.

3. In the task pane on the right-hand side, click on **Save as Favorite**, enter a name for the report, and then click on **OK**.

4. The **Favorite Report** will now appear under the **Favorite Reports** folder in the **Reporting** section of the **Service Manager** console.

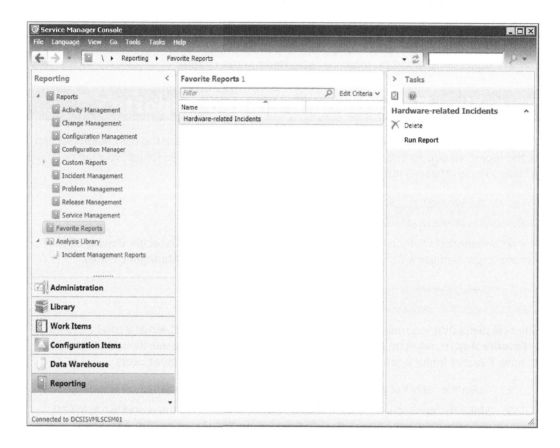

A **Linked Report** is a Favorite Report that can be accessed by other users. You can create Linked Reports only from reports that were imported through Management Packs. Follow these instructions to create a Linked Report:

1. Open the report of your choice in the **Service Manager** console.

2. Make the desired selections in the parameters section of the report window. For example, follow the instructions in the *Viewing SCSM reports* recipe to create a list of incidents about hardware-related problems.

3. In the task pane on the right-hand side, click on **Save as Linked Report**.

4. Enter a name for the report, and choose the management pack where you would like to save the Linked Report definition to.

5. Under **Select Folder**, choose the folder where you would like your report to show up under. Click on **OK**.

6. All the users with access to Service Manager reports and to the destination folder can now access the Linked Report by navigating to the respective location in the **Reporting Section** of the Service Manager console.

 You require Publisher or Content Manager permissions in SQL Server Reporting Services to be able to create Linked Reports.

How it works...

Favorite Reports are stored directly in the Service Manager database, whereas Linked Reports are actually a feature of SQL Server Reporting Services, which allows users to create a view on the underlying report with predefined selections for its parameters.

See also

Refer to the following recipes for more information on how to view reports and manage report permissions:

▶ The *Viewing SCSM reports* recipe in this chapter

▶ The *Configuring report permissions* recipe later in this chapter

Creating reports with Report Builder

This recipe will walk you through the steps of using Report Builder 3.0 to create new reports for Service Manager. We will also show you how to create a custom folder structure in SQL Server Reporting Services to store your reports in.

Getting ready

Although Report Builder offers a visual wizard for creating the queries that will be used for retrieving data from the Service Manager Data Warehouse database, it is hardly possible to work with reporting effectively without at least knowing the basics of the **Structured Query Language** (**SQL**) used for querying relational databases.

Furthermore, you will need to get familiar with the database model of the **DWDataMart** database. The database model is well-documented and is part of the SM Job Aids, which can be downloaded from the Microsoft website:

`http://www.microsoft.com/en-us/download/details.aspx?id=27850`

Also, you must install Microsoft .NET Framework 3.5 on all computers you intend to run Report Builder from.

How to do it...

First, we will create a custom folder structure in SQL Server Reporting Services to store our reports.

1. Open your web browser and navigate to the following URL: `http://[SCSMDWSQL]/Reports`.

2. Replace `[SCSMDWSQL]` with the fully qualified domain name of the SQL server that is used for reporting. If SQL Server Reporting Service is running as a named instance, the syntax of the URL will be the following: `http://[SCSMDWSQL]/Reports_[InstanceName]`.

3. Click on the **SystemCenter** folder, then click on the **ServiceManager** folder.

4. Click on **New Folder**, enter a name for the folder, such as **Custom Reports**, and optionally enter a description. Click on **OK**.

5. Click on the newly created folder and then click on **New Folder** to create a new subfolder. Enter a name for the folder—**Incident Management**, and optionally enter a description. Click on **OK**.

6. Click on the newly created subfolder.

Note that the permissions applied to the newly created folders will be inherited from the parent **ServiceManager** folder. You can break inheritance and apply custom permissions to your folders. Instructions on how to manage report permissions can be found later in this chapter.

With the folder structure created, we are now going to create the report:

1. Click on the **Report Builder** button from the toolbar. Report Builder will be streamed to your computer.

   If you see the error message **To use Report Builder, you must install .Net Framework 3.5 on this computer** and you made sure .NET Framework has already been installed, you will need to run Internet Explorer in IE8 mode (you can switch mode by using the Developer Tools (F12)), or install Report Builder on your computer (see the following *There's more...* section).

2. If you see a security warning, click on **Run** to start the application.

3. Once Report Builder has started, on the **Getting Started** window, choose **New Report | Table or Matrix Wizard**.

4. In the **Choose a dataset** dialog, select **Create a dataset**, and then click on **Next**.

5. In the **Choose a connection to a data source** dialog, select the **DWDataMart** data source. If it is not displayed in the list, click on **Browse**, navigate to the **SystemCenter\ServiceManager** folder, choose **DWDataMart**. Click on **Open**. Finally click on **Next** to proceed.

6. The **Enter Data Source Credentials** dialog will be displayed because Report Builder needs credentials to access the database. If the user account that you are using to run Report Builder has access to the DWDataMart database, you can choose the **Use the current Windows user** option and click on **OK**. Otherwise, you will need to provide the password of the Service Manager Reporting Account.

7. The **Design a query** dialog will open.

8. In the **Relationships** section, create the following relationships:

Left Table	Join Type	Right Table	Join Fields
IncidentDimvw	Inner	WorkItemDimvw	EntityDimKey = EntityDimKey
WorkItemDimvw	Left Outer	WorkItem AffectedUser Factvw	WorkItemDimKey = WorkItemDimKey
WorkItem AffectedUser Factvw	Left Outer	UserDimvw	WorkItemAffectedUser_ UserDimKey = UserDimKey
IncidentDimvw	Left Outer	Incident Classificationvw	Classification_ IncidentClassificationId = IncidentClassificationId
IncidentClassificationvw	Left Outer	DisplayString Dimvw	EnumTypeId = BaseManagedEntityId

9. On the left-hand side of the Design a query wizard, expand **dbo\Views** which is under the Database view:

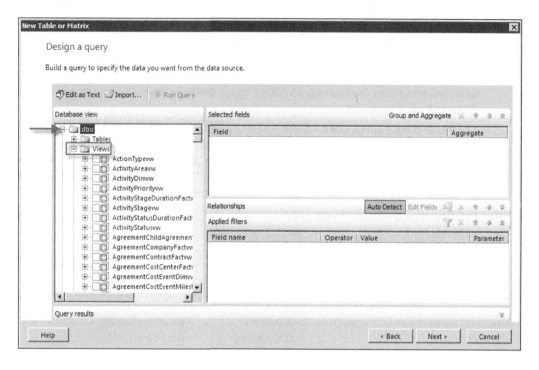

10. In the middle pane navigate to the **Relationships** section (you may have to expand the **Relationship** pane). Click on **AutoDetect** to activate the relationship button:

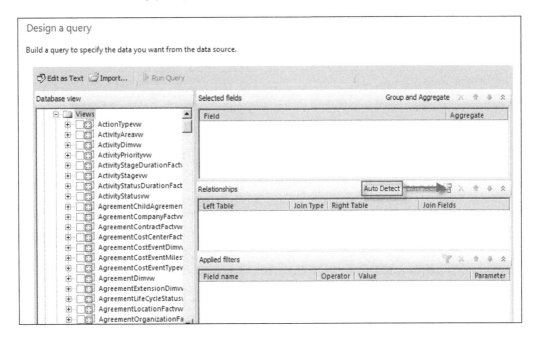

11. Click on the icon for adding relationship as indicated in previous the screen picture. An empty relationship entry is added to the relationship section.

12. Click on the left part of the relationship. A new window is presented showing the dataset schema. Navigate to and expand **dbo\views**. Select the table on the left-hand side view for instance `IncidentDimvw`.

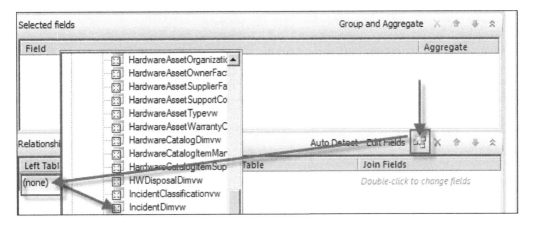

13. Click on the right part of the relationship. A new window is presented showing the dataset schema. Navigate to and expand **dbo\views**. Select the right table view for instance `WorkItemDimvw`.

14. To select the join field, double click the space below the join field and click on the Add Field Icon. Use the relationship tale to select the left and right join fields.

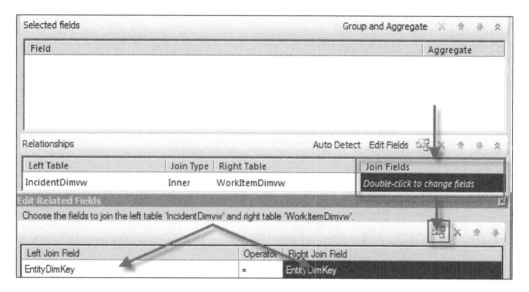

15. Repeat the previous steps to complete the relationship table ensure you change the join operator and views where specified in the table.

The following screenshot shows the required configuration of the **Relationships** section:

1. From the **Database view** section, select the following fields from the **dbo\Views** folder to add them to the **Selected fields** section, and configure the fields as follows:

Field	Aggregate
IncidentDimvw.Id	Count Distinct
DisplayStringDimvw.DisplayName	Grouped by
UserDimvw.DisplayName	Grouped by

2. In the **Applied filters** section, add the following filters:

Field name	Operator	Value
WorkItemAffectedUserFactvw.DeletedDate	is	(null)
DisplayStringDimvw.LanguageCode	is	ENU

Please see the following screenshot that shows all the required settings for designing the query:

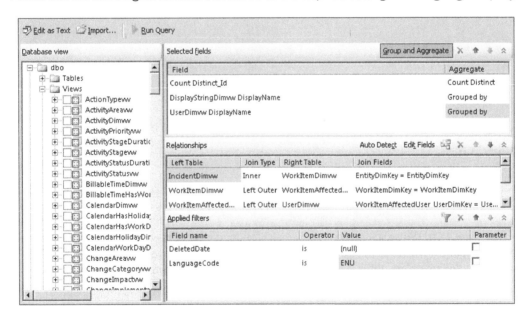

1. Click on **Next** to proceed to the **Arrange fields** dialog.

2. Drag the **DisplayStringDimvw_DisplayName** field to the **Column groups** area.

3. Drag the **UserDimvw_DisplayName** field to the **Row groups** area.

4. Drag the **Count_Distinct_Id** field to the **Values** area. Click on the arrow next to the fieldname and choose **Sum**. Click on **Next**.

5. In the **Choose the layout** dialog, make sure **Show subtotals and grand totals is selected**, and then click on **Next**.

6. In the **Choose a style dialog**, choose a style of your choice, and then click **Finish**. The wizard is now finished and you will see the report in the design view of Report Builder.

7. Replace the text **Click to add title** with a title such as **Incidents by Affected User**.

8. Replace the top-left column heading with **Affected User**.

9. Now it's time to test our report. Click **Run** from the Report Builder toolbar.

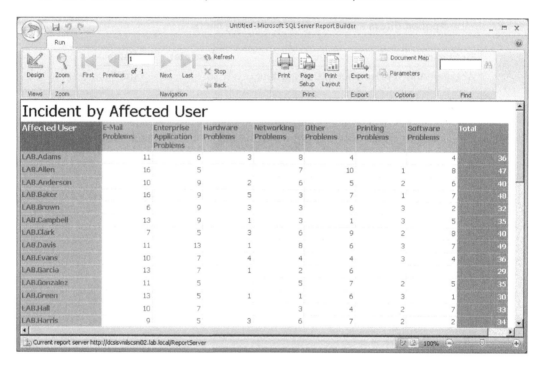

Incident by Affected User

Affected User	E-Mail Problems	Enterprise Application Problems	Hardware Problems	Networking Problems	Other Problems	Printing Problems	Software Problems	Total
LAB.Adams	11	6	3	8	4		4	36
LAB.Allen	16	5		7	10	1	8	47
LAB.Anderson	10	9	2	6	5	2	6	40
LAB.Baker	16	9	5	3	7	1	7	48
LAB.Brown	6	9	3	3	6	3	2	32
LAB.Campbell	13	9	1	3	1	3	5	35
LAB.Clark	7	5	3	6	9	2	8	40
LAB.Davis	11	13	1	8	6	3	7	49
LAB.Evans	10	7	4	4	4	3	4	36
LAB.Garcia	13	7	1	2	6			29
LAB.Gonzalez	11	5		5	7	2	5	35
LAB.Green	13	5	1	1	6	3	1	30
LAB.Hall	10	7		3	4	2	7	33
LAB.Harris	9	5	3	6	7	2	2	34

Current report server http://dcsisvmlscsm02.lab.local/ReportServer

10. Press *Ctrl+S* or click on the floppy disk icon to save your report. In the **Save As Report** dialog, navigate to the newly created folder in the SQL Server Reporting Services folder structure, enter a name such as **Incident by Affected User**, then click **Save**.

11. Open the **Service Manager** console. If it was already started, you might need to restart the console for the newly created folders and reports to show up.

12. Navigate to the **Reporting** section of the **Service Manager** console.

13. Under the **Reports** node, you will see the newly created folders, and the report will show under the folder you saved it to.

As you can see, the report that you created can now be opened either through the **Service Manager** console or by accessing SQL Server Reporting Services directly through your browser.

If you would like to edit the report, navigate to the folder where it is stored using your browser, hover over the report file, and click the arrow next to the report, then click on **Edit in Report Builder**.

How it works...

Service Manager leverages SQL Server Reporting Services for providing rich reporting functionalities to the end users. As an administrator, you can create your own reports that access the DWDataMart database provided by the Service Manager Data Warehouse server.

SQL Server 2008 R2 Report Builder 3.0 is a powerful tool that you can use to design your reports and save them to SQL Server Reporting Services. Using folders and security settings, you can establish a custom reporting structure with permissions that correspond to your organization's needs. All reports can be accessed either through the web browser, or you can use the **Service Manager** console to browse and consume your reports.

There's more...

If you are authoring reports often, you might prefer to install Report Builder to your local computer. In this section, we will show you how to do this. We will also walk you through the process of editing SQL queries for your reports and copying existing reports.

Installing Report Builder 3.0 on your computer

Report Builder 3.0 ships with SQL Server 2008 R2. As you have seen in the *How to do it* section of this recipe, Report Builder can be streamed to your computer by clicking on the **Report Builder** button on the SQL Server Reporting Service web page. This allows you to manage your reports from virtually anywhere without the need to comply with any software requirements on the computer that you are working with.

However, if you use mostly the same computer to work with reports, you might want to install Report Builder 3.0, eliminating the need to stream the software to the computer every time you launch it.

You can download SQL Server 2008 R2 Report Builder 3.0 from the following URL:

```
http://www.microsoft.com/en-us/download/details.aspx?id=6116
```

During the installation procedure, the setup will ask you for the default target server URL. Enter the following URL if you are running SQL Server Reporting Services as a default instance:

```
http://[SCSMDWSQL]/reportserver
```

Replace [SCSMDWSQL] with the fully qualified domain name of the SQL server that is used for reporting. If SQL Server Reporting Service is running as a named instance, the syntax of the URL will be the following:

```
http://[SCSMDWSQL]/reportserver_[InstanceName]
```

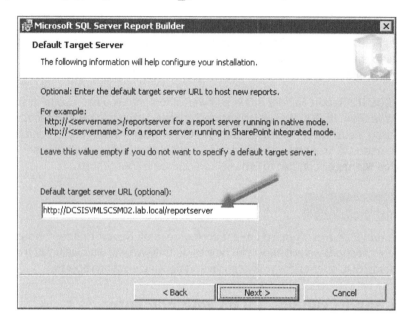

Writing SQL queries for your reports

When you are familiar with SQL, you might be faster to write the queries directly in SQL Server Management Studio. Use this query instead of walking through the wizard as described in this recipe. Click on the **Edit as Text** option in the **Design a query** dialog and paste the query directly in the editor. The following is the query that was used for the example in this recipe:

```
SELECT
COUNT(DISTINCT IncidentDimvw.Id) AS [Count Distinct_Id]
,DisplayStringDimvw.DisplayName AS [DisplayStringDimvwDisplayName]
,UserDimvw.DisplayName AS [UserDimvwDisplayName]
FROM
IncidentDimvw
  INNER JOIN WorkItemDimvw
    ON IncidentDimvw.EntityDimKey = WorkItemDimvw.EntityDimKey
  LEFT OUTER JOIN WorkItemAffectedUserFactvw
    ON WorkItemDimvw.WorkItemDimKey = WorkItemAffectedUserFactvw.
WorkItemDimKey
  LEFT OUTER JOIN UserDimvw
```

```
    ON WorkItemAffectedUserFactvw.WorkItemAffectedUser_UserDimKey
= UserDimvw.UserDimKey
   LEFT OUTER JOIN IncidentClassificationvw
    ON IncidentDimvw.Classification_IncidentClassificationId =
IncidentClassificationvw.IncidentClassificationId
   LEFT OUTER JOIN DisplayStringDimvw
    ON IncidentClassificationvw.EnumTypeId = DisplayStringDimvw.
BaseManagedEntityId
WHERE
WorkItemAffectedUserFactvw.DeletedDate IS NULL
   AND DisplayStringDimvw.LanguageCode = N'ENU'
GROUP BY
DisplayStringDimvw.DisplayName
,UserDimvw.DisplayName
```

Copying existing reports

Designing reports can be a very time consuming process. Once you have established and designed a report, you might want to copy the report instead of starting from scratch. This allows you to maintain the layout of the reporting controls and other settings that you made in your report definition.

1. Open the report in Report Builder.

2. Click on the **Report Builder** on the top-left and click on **Save As** to save the report under a new name at the desired location.

3. In the **Report Data** section, under **Datasets**, delete any existing datasets.

4. Add new dataset by right-clicking the **Datasets** folder and clicking on **Add Dataset**.

5. Give it a name and choose the option **Use a dataset embedded in my report**.

6. Select the **DWDataMart** data source. Then either copy and paste the SQL query into the **Query** textbox or launch the wizard by clicking on **Query Designer**.

7. Once you have created your dataset, make sure that all the reporting controls point to the newly created dataset. For a table report, right-click the top-left corner and choose **Tablix Properties**. Change the **Dataset name** to the new dataset.

8. Add new columns to the table and make sure you delete any columns that still reference fields from the old dataset.

See also

Refer to the following recipe for more information on how to manage report permissions:

> ▸ The *Configuring report permissions* recipe in this chapter

Configuring report permissions

A common issue when working with reporting is that some users cannot see the report folders and files in the **Reporting** section of the **Service Manager** console. It is important to know that access to the reports is controlled by the permissions configured in SQL Server Reporting Services.

When you first install the Service Manager Data Warehouse Management Server, the setup will automatically add the Service Manager Service Account as well as the Management Group Administrators group or user as Content Managers to SQL Server Reporting Services. Any other users that work with Service Manager need to be granted access to the reports manually.

Getting ready

Before you can configure report permissions, it is important to have a concept of how you would like your reports to be organized and structured in folders, and whom you will need to grant the access to.

How to do it...

In this example, we will grant a user or a group Read access to all the reports of Service Manager.

1. Open your web browser and navigate to the following URL: `http://[SCSMDWSQL]/Reports`.

2. Replace `[SCSMDWSQL]` with the fully qualified domain name of the SQL server which is used for reporting. If SQL Server Reporting Service is running as a named instance, the syntax of the URL will be the following: `http://[SCSMDWSQL]/Reports_[InstanceName]`.

3. Navigate to **Folder Settings | Security | New Role Assignment**.

4. In the **Group or user name** box, type the domain and name of the group or the user you would like to grant access to in the format `[Domain]\[User/Group]`. Check the **Browser** option and then click **OK**.

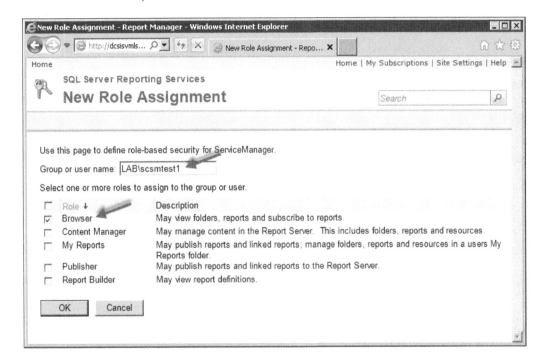

5. In the menu to the top-right, click on **Home** to get back to the root folder view. Click the on **SystemCenter** folder. Then click on the **ServiceManager** folder.

6. Repeat the procedures described in *steps 2* and *3* to grant the same permissions to the **ServiceManager** folder.

The user or the members of the group that you configured will now be able to access the Service Manager reports through both the **Service Manager** console as well as the web browser. Please note that the users will have to restart the **Service Manager** console to be able to see the folders and reports.

How it works...

The way how permissions are configured in SQL Server Reporting Services is very similar to what you might know about configuring permissions in an NTFS file system. You can work with permissions on folders that are inherited to subfolder and files, and also, break inheritance where needed. This allows you to control which folders and reports are made available to your end users.

There's more...

When working with permissions in SQL Server Reporting Services, you should know about the basic concepts of security roles and the inheritance of permissions. We will cover these two topics in this section.

Security roles

Configuring permissions for reports requires deciding which actions the users are allowed to perform on the corresponding permission level. These actions can be configured by the use of security roles.

The following three security roles are important to know about when working with SQL Server Reporting Services security settings:

▶ The **Browser security role** allows the members to view folders, reports, and subscribe to reports.

▶ The **Publisher security role** allows the members to publish reports and linked reports.

▶ The **Content Manager security role** allows the members to manage content in the report server. This includes folder, reports, and other resources such as data sources, data sets, and so on.

Security settings inheritance

If you thoroughly plan and configure report permissions for Service Manager, and provided that the instance of SQL Server Reporting Services is not used for other purposes than Service Manager, you can revert the security settings on the **ServiceManager** folder back to parent security. You will, then, only configure permissions on the root folder, and you will have the ability to apply less restrictive permissions on any subfolder you want by breaking inheritance from the parent.

To revert the security settings of a folder back to its parent, proceed as follows:

1. On the SQL Server Reporting Services website, open the folder for which you would like to change the security settings.

2. Click on **Folder Settings | Security**.

3. Click on **Revert to Parent Security**.

4. A warning message will appear. Confirm by clicking on **OK**.

To break inheritance of the security settings of a folder's parent folder, proceed as follows:

1. On the SQL Server Reporting Services website, open the folder for which you would like to change the security settings.

2. Click on **Folder Settings | Security**.

3. Click on **Edit Item Security**.

4. A warning message will appear. Confirm with **OK**.

Delivering reports automatically using report subscriptions

SQL Server Reporting Services allow your users to subscribe to reports. Using report subscriptions, you can deliver reports to your end users' mailbox in the desired format on a scheduled interval.

Getting ready

Before you can make use of reports subscriptions, e-mail delivery options need to be configured for SQL Server Reporting Services.

1. Log on to the server that hosts SQL Server Reporting Services with an account that has administrative privileges on both the local computer and SQL Server.

2. Start Reporting Services Configuration Manager. This program can be found under **Start | All Programs | Microsoft SQL Server 2008 R2 | Configuration Tools**.

3. Check the **Server Name** and **Report Server Instance** to make sure that you are connecting to the correct instance of SQL Server Reporting Services. Click on **Connect**.

4. Under **E-mail Settings**, enter the e-mail address that you want to use as the sender address for report delivery.

5. Enter the SMTP Server host name or IP address, then click on **Apply**. Click on **Exit** to close the Reporting Services Configuration Manager window.

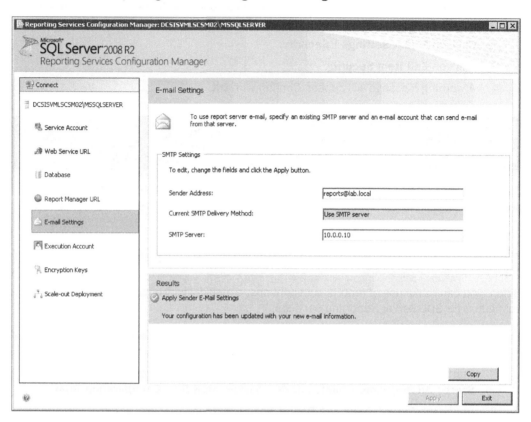

 For e-mail delivery to work, the SMTP server you entered in the Reporting Services Configuration Manager must be configured to allow relaying from the IP address of the computer SQL Server Reporting Services is running on.

SQL Server Reporting Services uses SQL Server Agent to schedule and run the report subscriptions. For this to work, SQL Server Agent needs to be configured to start automatically when the operating system starts.

1. Log on to the server that hosts SQL Server Reporting Services with an account that has administrative privileges on both the local computer and SQL Server.

2. Start SQL Servicer Configuration Manager. This program can be found under **Start | All Programs | Microsoft SQL Server 2008 R2 | Configuration Tools**.

3. Under **SQL Server Services**, double-click on **SQL Server Agent**.

4. Under the **Service** tab, choose **Automatic** as the **Start Mode**. Click on **OK**.

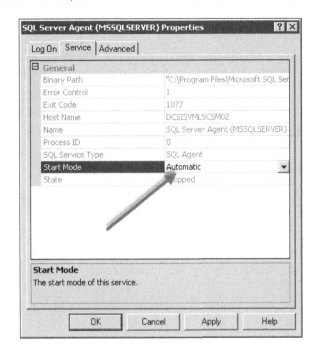

5. Right-click on **SQL Server Agent** and click on **Start**.

How to do it...

Next, we will walk you through the steps required for creating and managing report subscriptions in SQL Server Reporting Services.

1. Open your web browser and navigate to the following URL:
   `http://[SCSMDWSQL]/Reports`.

2. Replace `[SCSMDWSQL]` with the fully qualified domain name of the SQL server which is used for reporting. If SQL Server Reporting Service is running as a named instance, the syntax of the URL will be the following:
   `http://[SCSMDWSQL]/Reports_[InstanceName]`.

3. Navigate to the report that you would like to create a subscription for. In this example, we are creating a subscription for the report we created in the *Creating reports with Report Builder* recipe. Navigate to the **SystemCenter** | **ServiceManager** | **Custom Reports** | **Incident Management** folder.

4. Hover over the report file and click on the arrow next to the report; then click on **Subscribe**.

5. Enter the e-mail address you would like the report to be delivered to. Optionally, enter e-mail addresses in the **Cc** and **Bcc** fields. You can also enter a custom **Reply-To** address, if replies from users should be sent to a different e-mail address from the sender address.

6. If you want the report to be attached to the e-mail, check the **Include Report** option and choose the desired render format. We are going to choose **PDF** in this example.

7. Optionally, check the **Include Link** option, if you would like a URL to be added to the e-mail that allows the recipient to navigate directly to the report using a web browser.

8. Click **Select Schedule** and define the delivery frequency for this subscription. Click on **OK**.

9. Click **OK** to save and activate the subscription.

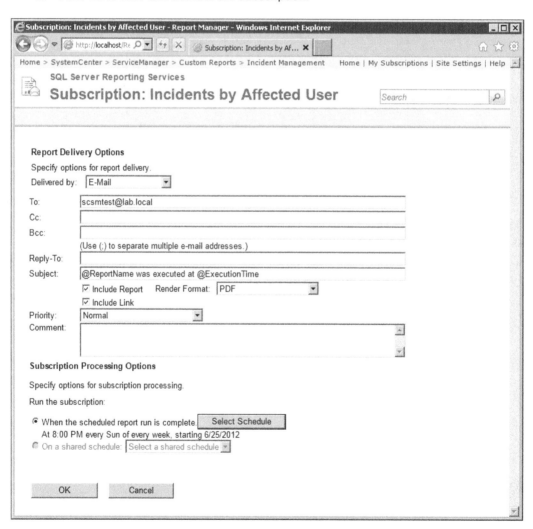

To manage your subscriptions, click on the **My Subscriptions** link from the top-right menu bar of the SQL Server Reporting Services web page. From here you can edit and delete the existing report subscriptions.

How it works...

SQL Server Reporting Services uses SQL Server Agent for scheduling and running report subscriptions. Each subscription creates a job for SQL Server Agent with a random GUID as the job name. When subscription jobs are executed, SQL Server reads the configuration of the subscription from the ReportServer database, calls SQL Server Reporting Services to run the report, and then sends the result to the recipients using the SMTP server configured for SQL Server Reporting Services.

There's more...

A common request when working with report subscriptions is to offer the ability to send reports to user-defined recipients. This section walks you through the steps required to fulfill this request.

Allowing non-Content Managers to define e-mail addresses

When users that are not a member of the Content Manager security role create subscriptions, the recipient name in the To: field is self-addressed using the domain user account of the person creating the subscription.

If you are using an SMTP server or forwarder that uses e-mail accounts that are different from the domain user account, the report delivery will fail when the SMTP server tries to deliver the report to that user.

To work around this issue, you can modify configuration settings that allow users to enter a name in the To: field:

1. Open `RSReportServer.config` with a text editor. The file can be found on the server hosting SQL Server Reporting Services in the SQL Server installation directory under the `MSRS10_50.[InstanceName]\Reporting Services\ReportServer` sub-folder.

2. Set `SendEmailToUserAlias` to `False`.

3. Set `DefaultHostName` to the **Domain Name System** (**DNS**) name or IP address of the SMTP server or forwarder.

4. Save the file.

Analyzing data with Microsoft Excel

Online Analytical Processing (OLAP) cubes are a new feature in SCSM 2012 that leverages the Service Manager Data Warehouse infrastructure to provide self-service Business Intelligence capabilities to the end user.

An OLAP Cube is a data structure that overcomes limitations of relational databases by providing rapid analysis of data. Cubes can display and sum up large amounts of data while also providing users access to the most granular of data. These cubes are stored in SQL Server Analysis Services databases. Self-service BI tools such as Excel and SQL Server Reporting Services can target these cubes and allow the user to analyze the data from multiple perspectives.

In this recipe, we are going to show you how you can use Microsoft Excel to allow your users to quickly and easily create simple reports by directly accessing OLAP cubes from Service Manager.

Getting ready

Before you can work with OLAP cubes, it is a requirement that you have already installed a Service Manager Data Warehouse Management Server and that it has been registered with the Service Manager server installation. You also need to ensure that the initial synchronization of the Management Packs is complete and the ETL jobs have run. In addition, you need to make sure that the cubes that are defined in the Management packs have been created and fully processed. This normally takes several hours to complete from the time the Data Warehouse Management Server was registered.

How to do it...

In this example, we are going to create a report in Microsoft Excel which displays the number of incidents by affected user and incident classification. The output will be the same as from the report we created using Report Builder in the Creating reports with Report Builder recipe.

1. Open the **Service Manager** console and navigate to **Cubes** in the **Data Warehouse** section.

2. Click on the **Service Manager WorkItems Cube**. Ensure that the **Status** indicates **Processed**. Then click on **Analyze Cube In Excel** from the task pane on the right-hand side.

   Microsoft Excel will start and automatically establish a connection to the respective cube in SQL Server Analysis Services.

3. The list of measures and dimensions in the **PivotTable Field List** can be overwhelming. Hence we can reduce the size of it by selecting the measure group **IncidentDim** from the **Show Fields** related to dropdown.

4. Now select the following fields from the list:

   ❏ **- IncidentDim\IncidentDimCount**

   ❏ **- AffectedUserDim\Display Name**

   ❏ **- IncidentDim_IncidentClassification\More fields\
   IncidentClassificationValue**

5. Move the **IncidentClassificationValue** field from the **Row Labels** area to the **Column** Labels area.

With only these few mouse clicks, we have created a report with the same content like the one created with Report Builder in the recipe *Creating reports with Report Builder*.

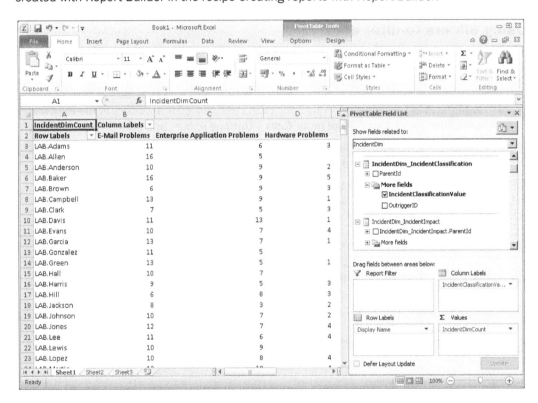

You can now use regular Microsoft Excel features to further customize your report. In order to refresh the data in your report, simply right-click anywhere in the PivotTable and click on **Refresh**.

How it works...

Microsoft Excel uses an active connection in the background to connect to the OLAP cube in SQL Services Analysis Services. By making your selections using the PivotTable feature, Excel dynamically creates **MultiDimensional eXpression (MDX)** queries in the background that are sent to SQL Server Analysis Services. The results returned are then displayed in the PivotTable.

There's more...

Excel comes with many more features for reporting than we could cover in this book. Next, we are going to show you one example of using Slicers to filter your data.

Using Slicers to filter data

Slicers are easy-to-use filtering components that allow you to filter the data in the PivotTable with a set of buttons. For instance, you can create a slicer for filtering the PivotTable we created earlier by the status of the incident.

1. With the PivotTable report in Microsoft Excel still open, click anywhere in the PivotTable area, then switch to the **PivotTable Tools | Options** ribbon, and click on **Insert Slicer**.

2. Select the **IncidentDim_IncidentStatus\More fields\IncidentDim_IncidentStatus. IncidentStatusValue** field and click on **OK**. The **Slicer** appears in Excel.

3. Now you can click on the buttons to filter data. For instance, click on the **Resolved** button to show only resolved incidents in the PivotTable.

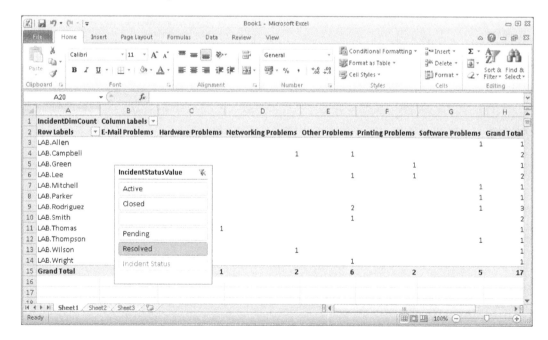

Refer to the following recipe to see how reports created in Microsoft Excel can be made available to other users from within the **Service Manager** console:

▸ *Using the Analysis Library to publish Excel reports* later in this chapter

Using the Analysis Library to publish Excel reports

Service Manager 2012 introduces Analysis Libraries that allow you to make reports created in Microsoft Excel available to other users from within the Reporting workspace in the **Service Manager** console.

Getting ready

Before you can save reports to the Analysis Library, you must create at least one storage area and map it to an Analysis Library. You might want to create many Analysis Library folders for different departments or ITSM processes.

In this example, we are using a file share on the Service Manager Management Server to serve as an Analysis Library.

1. Log on to the Service Manager management server with an account that has administrative privileges on the local computer.

2. Open Windows Explorer and create a new folder such as `C:\AnalysisLibraries`.

3. Create a new subfolder named `IncidentManagement` under the newly created folder.

4. Right-click on the `IncidentManagement` folder, click on **Properties**, and then click on the **Security** tab.

5. Ensure that all the users you would like to be able to read reports have **Read and Execute** permissions. Change the security settings if required.

6. Ensure that all the users you would like to be able to save new reports or modify existing reports have **Read** and **Execute**, and **Write** and **Modify** permissions. Change the security settings if required.

7. Change to the **Sharing** tab and click on **Advanced Sharing**.

8. Check **Share** this folder, click on **Permissions**, select **Everyone,** and make sure that both **Change** and **Read** are selected in the **Allow** column.

9. Click on **OK** to close the **Permissions** dialog. Click on **OK** to close the **Advanced Sharing** dialog, and then click on **Close**.

10. Open the **Service Manager** console with an account that has administrative rights in the Service Manager Data Warehouse. Navigate to the **Analysis Libraries** folder in the Data Warehouse workspace.

11. Click on **Add Library Folder** from the task pane on the right-hand side.

12. Enter a name, such as **Incident Management Reports**, and a description for the Analysis Library.

13. In the **UNC Path** field, enter \\[ServerName]\IncidentManagement, replacing [ServerName] with the name of your Service Manager management Server.

14. Click on **OK** to create the Analysis Library.

How to do it...

Now we are going to show you how you can save reports that were created in Microsoft Excel to an Analysis Library.

1. Follow the procedures in the **Analyzing data with Microsoft Excel** recipe to create an Excel report.

2. In Microsoft Excel, click on **File | Save As**.

3. In the **File name** textbox, enter \\[ServerName]\IncidentManagement, replacing [ServerName] with the name of your Service Manager management Server. Press *Enter* to navigate to the network share.

4. In the **File name** textbox, enter a filename for the Excel report, and then click on **Save**.

5. Close Microsoft Excel.

This report has now been saved to the Analysis Library and other users can access it directly from the **Service Manager** console.

1. Open the **Service Manager** console and navigate to the **Reporting** workspace.

2. Under **Analysis Library** you will see that the Analysis Library that we created.

3. When you select the **Analysis Library**, the Excel report is displayed in the list view of the **Service Manager** console.

4. Select the report, and then click on **Open Excel File** from the task pane on the right-hand side.

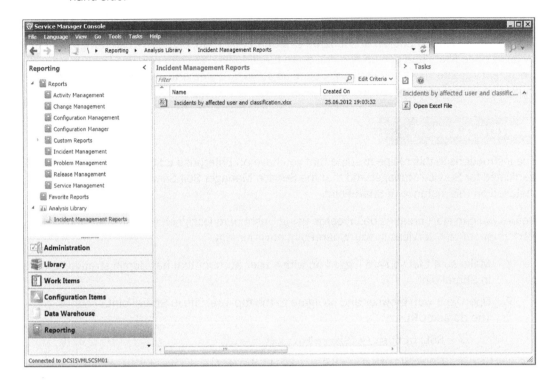

How it works...

An **Analysis Library** is effectively a file share on the network that is used to save Excel files to. You can create many network shares for different users, departments, ITSM processes, and so on, to best reflect your reporting requirements. Also, the network shares can be created on any computer, such as a file server, provided the security is configured properly so that your users can access the files on the network.

See also

Refer to the following recipe to see how reports can be created by using Microsoft Excel:

▸ The *Analyzing data with Microsoft Excel* recipe previously mentioned in this chapter

Using SharePoint for advanced dashboards

PerformancePoint Services, a feature available in the Enterprise edition of SharePoint 2010, allows you to create compelling dashboards with live data from the Service Manager data warehouse. When you publish dashboards to a SharePoint site, end users can navigate them by using page filters and drill-up and drill-down functionality. You can also use Dashboard Designer to create views and elements, such as scorecard elements, KPIs, data sources, indicators, and reports for use in dashboards.

Getting ready

The instructions in this recipe assume that you have an Enterprise Edition of SharePoint 2010 dedicated for Service Manager and that the Service Manager Self-Service Portal has been installed on this instance of SharePoint.

Before you can start creating dashboards using Dashboard Designer, you must activate PerformancePoint Services in your SharePoint environment.

1. Make sure that you are logged on with a user account that has administrative rights in SharePoint.

2. Open your web browser and navigate to the top-level site in SharePoint. The default URL is:

    ❑   SSL: `https://[SharePointServer]`

    ❑   Non-SSL: `http://[SharePointServer]`

3. Replace `[SharePointServer]` with the name of your SharePoint server.

4. Go to **Site Actions | Site Settings**.

5. Under **Site Collection Administration**, click on **Site** collection features. On the **Features** page, click on **Activate** next to **SharePoint Server Publishing Infrastructure and PerformancePoint Services Site Collection Features**.

6. Next, open the SharePoint 2010 Central Administration page. The link can be found under **Start | All Programs | Microsoft SharePoint 2010 Products**.

7. Under **Application Management**, click on **Manage service applications**. Click on **PerformancePoint Service Application**, and then click on **PerformancePoint Service Application Settings**.

8. In the **Secure Store and Unattended Service Account** area, type the credentials of a service account that has the necessary permissions on all data sources you intend to use, such as the Service Manager service account, and then click on **OK**.

9. If an error message appears that says **The Unattended Service Account cannot be set for the service application**, you can resolve this problem by doing the following:

❑ Navigate to the SharePoint 2012 Central Administration page, and then under **Application Management**, click on **Manage service applications**

❑ Click on **Secure Store Service**, and then click on **Generate New Key**

❑ Type a pass phrase, and then click on **OK**

10. Close the SharePoint 2010 Central Administration page and go back to the top-level site in SharePoint.

11. Go to **Site Actions | Site Settings**.

12. Under **Site Actions**, click on **Manage site features**. Click on **Activate** next to **SharePoint Server Publishing and PerformancePoint Services Site Features**.

13. Click on **Site Actions**, and then click on **New Site**. Enter **Service Manager Dashboards** as the title of the page, and type SMDashboards as the URL.

14. Select the **Business Intelligence Center** site template from the **Enterprise** tab, and then click on **Create**.

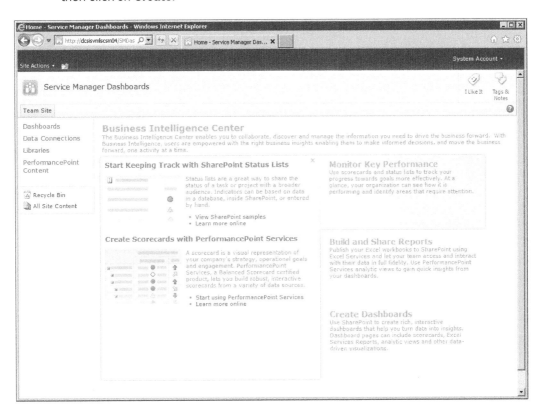

How to do it...

We are now going to show you how to create a simple dashboard in SharePoint using Dashboard Designer.

1. Navigate to the Business Intelligence Center at the following URL:

   ❑ SSL: `https://[SharePointServer]/SMDashboards`

   ❑ Non-SSL: `http://[SharePointServer]/SMDashboards`

2. Replace `[SharePointServer]` with the name of your SharePoint server.

3. On the home screen, hover over **Monitor Key Performance**, and then click on **Start using PerformancePoint Services**.

4. If an error message appears that says **An error occurred during the processing of <FolderPath>/<PageName>.aspx. Code blocks are not allowed in this file**, you can resolve this problem by inserting the following information into the `Web.config` file between the `PageParserPaths` tags of your SharePoint site:

   ```
   <PageParserPaths>
   <PageParserPathVirtualPath=<FolderPath>/<PageName>.aspx
   CompilationMode=Always AllowServerSideScript=true/>
   </PageParserPaths>
   ```

5. Click on **Run Dashboard Designer**. If you see a security warning, click on **Run to start the application**. Later, you can start Dashboard Designer from the **Start** menu.

6. In Workspace Browser, click on **Data Connections**, and then click on **Data Source from the Create menu in Dashboard Designer**. In the **Select a Data Source Template** dialog box, select **Analysis Services**, and then click on **OK**.

7. Make sure that the **Editor** tab is selected, and then type the name of the SQL Server Analysis Services server that hosts the Service Manager cubes in the **Server** textbox. Choose the **DWASDataBase** database and select **the Service Manager WorkItems Cube**.

8. Change to the **Properties** tab and change **Name** property to **SM WorkItems**. Right-click on the **SM WorkItems Data Connection in the Workspace Browser** section and click on **Save**.

9. In the **Home** tab of Dashboard Designer, click on **Add Lists**. Choose **PerformancePoint Content from the Service Manager Dashboards site**. Click on **OK**.

10. Right-click **PerformancePoint Content in the Workspace Browser**, point to **New**, and then click on **Scorecard**.

11. In the **Select a Scorecard Template** window, in the **Category** section, ensure that **Microsoft** is selected. In the **Template** section, select **Analysis Services**, and then click on **OK**.

12. On the **Select a data source** window, select the **SM WorkItems** data connection, and then click on **Next**.

13. In the **Select a KPI Source** window, select **Create KPIs from SQL Server Analysis Services** measures, and then click on **Next**.

14. In the Select **KPIs to Import** windows, click on **Add KPI**. Allow Dashboard Designer to finish loading the measures. Type **Resolved Incidents KPI** in the **Name** column, select **Incidents Resolved Count from the Actual** column, select **Increasing is Better as the Band Method**, select **Incidents Opened in the Targets** column, and then click on **Next**.

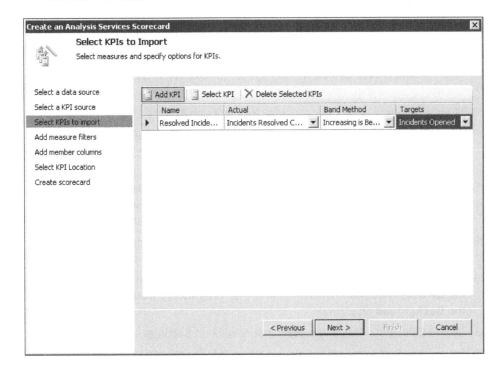

15. Click on **Next** twice to skip the Add **Measure Filters** and Add **Member Columns** windows. Click on **Finish** to create the KPI.

16. Modify the name of the new scorecard to **Resolved Incidents Scorecard**.

17. Click the **Resolved Incidents KPI from the Workspace Browser**, click on the **Target** row, and then under **Thresholds set Best to 100%, Threshold 2 to 90%**, and **Threshold 1 to 50%**.

18. Right-click **Resolved Incidents KPI**, and then click on **Save**.

19. In the Workspace Browser, select the **Resolved Incidents Scorecard** scorecard. To refresh the scorecard with the updated KPI definition, on the **Edit** ribbon tab, inside the **View** group, click on **Update**.

20. To add the **Incident Classification** hierarchy to the scorecard, in the **Details** pane, expand **Dimensions**, expand the **IncidentDim_IncidentClassification** dimension, and then drag **IncidentClassificationValue** onto the **Incident** scorecard cell.

21. In the **Select Members** dialog box, expand the **All member** list, select all the values other than the empty value, and then click on **OK**.

22. To refresh the scorecard, on the **Edit** ribbon tab, inside the **View** group, and click on **Update**. Right-click the **Resolved Incidents Scorecard** and click on **Save**.

23. Right-click on **PerformancePoint Content** in the Workspace Browser, point to **New**, and then click on **Report**.

24. In the **Select a Report Template** window, select **Analytic Grid**, and then click on **OK**.

25. In the **Select a data source** window, select the **SM WorkItems** data connection, and then click on **Finish**.

26. Modify the name of the new report to **Incidents by Affected User**.

27. To configure the report, in the **Details** pane, expand **Dimensions**, expand the **AffectedUserDim** dimension, and then drag the **User Name** attribute into the **Rows** drop zone.

28. Click the down arrow to the right-hand side of the **AffectedUserDim** hierarchy in the **Rows** drop zone. In the **Select Members** dialog box, right-click on **All**, point to **Autoselect Members**, click on **Select User Name**, and then click on **OK**.

29. In the **Details** pane, expand **Measures**, and then drag the **IncidentDimCount** measures into the **Columns** drop zone.

30. In the **Details** pane, expand **Dimensions**, expand the **IncidentDim_IncidentClassification** dimension, and then drag **IncidentClassificationValue** into the **Background** drop zone.

31. On the **Edit** ribbon tab, in the **View** group, click on **Settings**.

32. In the **View** Settings window, click on **Show Information Bar**, and then click on **OK**.

33. In the Workspace Browser, right-click on the **Incidents by Affected User** report, and then click on **Save**.

34. Right-click **PerformancePoint Content** in the Workspace Browser, point to **New**, and then click on **Dashboard**.

35. Select the two-columns template, and then click on **OK**.

36. Modify the name of the new dashboard to **Incident Dashboard**.

37. From the **Details** pane, drag the **Resolved Incidents Scorecard** scorecard and drop it in the **Left Column** zone.

38. From the **Details** pane, drag the **Incidents by Affected User** report and drop it in the **Right Column** zone.

39. Click on the **Incidents by Affected User** in the **Right Column** zone, and then click on **Create Connection** from the **Edit** ribbon menu.

40. In the **Connection** dialog, in the **Get values from list**, select **Left Column | (1) Resolved Incidents Scorecard**.

41. Click on the **Values** tab, and in **Connect To**, select the **IncidentDim_ IncidentClassificationIncidentClassificationValue** hierarchy. Select **Member Row: Member Unique Name** under **Source value**. Click on **OK**.

42. In the Workspace Browser, right-click on the **Incident Dashboard** dashboard, and then click on **Save**.

43. Click on the **File** button on the top-left of Dashboard Designer, click on **Save Workspace As**, and save the file to a location where you can find it again later.

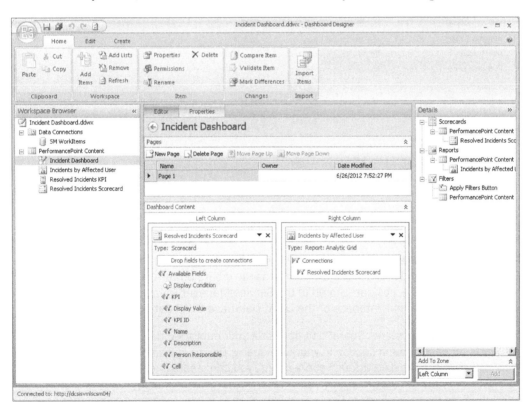

44. Right-click on the **Incident Dashboard** dashboard in the **Workspace Browser** section, and then click on **Publish to SharePoint**.

45. In the **Deploy To** dialog, select **Dashboards** under the **SharePoint** site; under **Master Page** select **minimal**, and then click on **OK**.

Once the dashboard has been published to SharePoint, Dashboard Designer will open your browser to show you the newly created Dashboard.

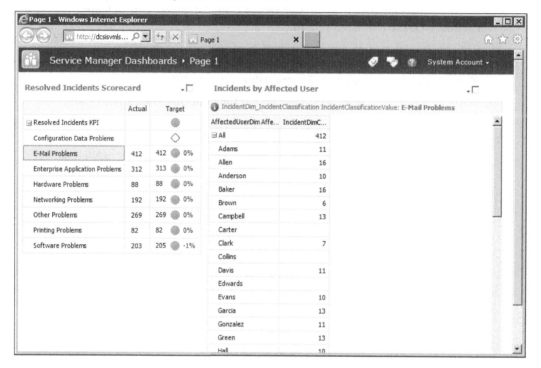

How it works...

PerformancePoint Dashboard Designer, which is included in the Enterprise Edition of SharePoint Server 2010, is a tool that you can use to create powerful dashboards in your organization that accesses data stored in the Service Manager Data Warehouse—in either the **DWDatanMart** relational database or the DWASDataBase OLAP database.

Dashboard Designer creates SharePoint pages for your published dashboards, containing WebParts for each content section in your workspace. Due to its ability of allowing different WebParts to exchange data through connections, you can create interactive dashboards that connect to various data sources, such as System Center Service Manager for information on your ITSM processes, System Center Configuration Manager for extended inventory information, as well as System Center Operations Manager for information about the health state of your systems.

10

Extending SCSM with Advanced Personalization

In this chapter we will walk you through the use of the System Center 2012 Service Manager Authoring Tool and advanced management pack authoring techniques for extending, customizing and personalizing your installation of Service Manager.
In particular, we will be covering the following tasks:

- ▶ Using the SCSM Authoring Tool
- ▶ Extending Service Manager classes
- ▶ Sealing Management Packs
- ▶ Creating new classes
- ▶ Customizing default forms
- ▶ Creating your own forms
- ▶ Using an XML editor to modify Management Packs

Introduction

Service Manager uses Management Pack files that contain definitions for the various features in the product. The features available in Service Manager as well as the behavior of the product can be customized by modify or adding management packs.

Chapter 2, Personalizing SCSM 2012 Administration, walked you through the basic concepts of management packs. Service Manager comes with a set of predefined management packs that contain the initial settings for the product. These management packs can be modified to accommodate your specific needs, and you can create new management packs that hold additional settings and customizations for the product.

There are three methods that you can use to customize Service Manager. While all the three methods result in changes to a management pack file, they differ in scope and in the complexity of the customization that they provide:

 ▸ Using the Service Manager console
 ▸ Using the Service Manager Authoring Tool
 ▸ Directly editing the Management Pack XML

The most basic and the most commonly required settings and customizations can be performed by using the Service Manager console. The customization that can be done using the console can be found in the Administration and Library workspaces. These customizations include the following:

 ▸ Administration workspace
 ▸ Notification Subscriptions
 ▸ Notification Templates
 ▸ Service Level Objectives
 ▸ Workflows
 ▸ Library workspace
 ▸ Groups
 ▸ Lists
 ▸ Queues
 ▸ Service Offerings
 ▸ Request Offerings
 ▸ Tasks
 ▸ Templates

You have performed a lot of customization to Service Manager using the Service Manager Console by following the recipes in the previous chapters of this book.

While using the Service Manager Console is sufficient for most customization requirements, there are certain limitations that require you to use the Service Manager Authoring Tool. The Service Manager Authoring Tool allows for the following kinds of advanced customizations, such as follows:

- ▸ Extending Service Manager classes
- ▸ Creating new classes
- ▸ Customizing Service Manager forms
- ▸ Creating new forms
- ▸ Creating advanced workflows

The recipes in this and the next chapter will walk you through all of these advanced personalization scenarios.

For extensive or complex customizations and for customizations that require coding, you have to edit the XML file of the management pack directly. Working directly with management pack files requires in-depth knowledge in several areas, such as the System Center Common Schema and the structure of management packs. Also, manual editing is prone to errors.

We will dedicate one recipe in this chapter to walk you through an example that requires direct editing of a Service Manager management pack.

Using the SCSM Authoring Tool

In this recipe we will introduce you to the System Center 2012 Service Manager Authoring Tool, which we will use for subsequent recipes in this chapter.

Getting ready

The System Center 2012 Service Manager Authoring Tool is a separate product that is part of the System Center 2012 Service Manager Component Add-ons and Extensions. The Authoring Tool can be obtained as a free download from the following URL:

```
http://www.microsoft.com/en-us/download/details.aspx?id=28726
```

You can install the Authoring Tool on Windows Vista (with the latest Service Pack) and Windows 7, or on Windows Server 2008 (with the latest Service Pack) and Windows Server 2008 R2. As a prerequisite, the Authoring Tool requires the .NET Framework 3.5, which you can download from the Microsoft Download Center, and the Visual Studio 2008 Shell, which can be installed from the Prerequisites page of the Authoring Tool setup wizard.

Follow these steps to install the Authoring Tool:

1. Download the System Center 2012 Service Manager Authoring Tool binaries from the URL mentioned earlier.

2. Run `SCSM2012_AuthoringTool_RTM.exe` to extract the files to a destination of your choice.

3. Navigate to the directory you extracted the files to, change to the `CDImage` folder, then double-click on `Setup.exe`.

4. Follow the on-screen instructions until you are on the **Prerequisites** page.

5. On the **Prerequisites** page, if any prerequisite test fails, you must update your computer to ensure that each prerequisite is met. If Microsoft Visual Studio 2008 Shell is not installed, click on **Install Microsoft Visual Studio Shell 2008** to install the application. Click on **Check prerequisites** again and fix any other problems until all prerequisite tests pass.

6. Click on **Next** and follow the on-screen instructions to install the Authoring Tool on your computer.

7. To start the Authoring Tool, click on the newly created shortcut in the **Start** menu under **Programs | Microsoft System Center | Service Manager 2012 Authoring**.

How to do it...

To understand and work with the Authoring Tool, we will now walk you through the different areas of the user interface.

The user interface is made up of various areas that you will use while authoring your management packs. Please note that you can rearrange and group the areas within the user interface by using the drag-and-drop feature. This allows you to tailor the user interface to your personal preferences. The following screenshot shows a typical layout of the Authoring Tool user interface.

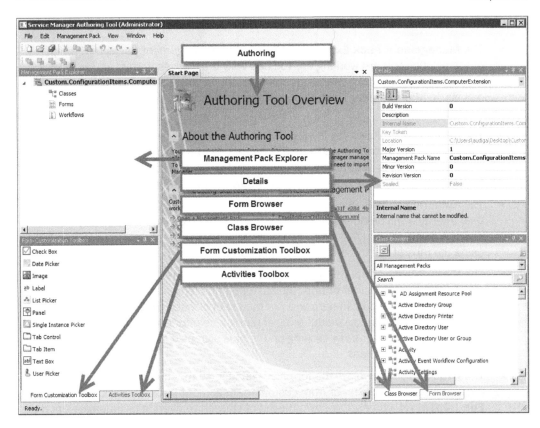

The Authoring Tool is made up of the following panes:

- ► Management Pack Explorer
- ► Details
- ► Authoring
- ► Class Browser
- ► Form Browser
- ► Form Customization Toolbox
- ► Activities Toolbox

The following is a detailed explanation of all the panes:

▸ The **Management Pack Explorer** displays all the management packs that are part of the solution you are working on. You can view the classes, forms, and workflows that are included in each management pack. When you click on an object, such as a class, in **Management Pack Explorer**, you can view and edit its properties in the **Details** pane.

▸ The **Details** pane allows you to view the properties of the selected object. Also, you can use the **Details** pane to modify properties of the currently selected object. The **Details** pane is updated every time you select an object in **Management Pack Explorer**, the **Authoring** pane, **Class Browser**, or **Form Browser** pane.

▸ The **Authoring** pane is the work area where you perform your customizations. The user interface will be different based on the type of object you are working with: classes, forms, or workflows. You can open several objects and switch between them using the tabs at the top of the **Authoring** pane.

▸ The **Class Browser** displays the classes available in all the management packs that are in the `Library` folder or from the custom management packs that you opened using **File | Open**. You can narrow down the list of classes by filtering by management pack (using the pull-down menu) or by entering a search term in the **Search** field. When you expand a class by clicking on the plus sign next to it, you will be able to see all properties of the class.

▸ The **Form Browser** displays the forms available in all the management packs that are in the `Library` folder or from custom management packs that you opened using **File | Open**. You can narrow down the list of classes by filtering by management pack (using the pull-down menu), or by entering a search term in the Search field. The **Form Browser** is your starting point for form customizations.

▸ The **Form Customization Toolbox** contains all controls that are available for being added to form extensions or newly created forms. Controls can be added to the form in the **Authoring** pane by using the drag-and-drop feature.

▸ The **Activities Toolbox** contains all out-of-the-box activities that you can use in custom workflows that you build using the Authoring Tool. The **Activities Toolbox** can be extended by custom **Activities** that you create using the Windows Workflow Foundation, which is part of the .NET Framework.

How it works...

The System Center 2012 Service Manager Authoring Tool is built on the Visual Studio integrated development environment framework. Service Manager leverages core functionalities of the .NET Framework, such as the **Windows Presentation Foundation (WPF) Framework** and the Windows **Workflow Foundation (WF) Framework** to allow for extensive customizations to the product.

Any customizations that you perform using the Authoring Tool are stored in a management pack XML file. You can then import the XML file into Service Manager to apply the customization to your Service Manager environment.

See also

Refer to the following section for more information on how to work with management packs:

- ▶ The *Creating Management Packs in the Authoring tool to save your SCSM personalization* recipe in *Chapter 2, Personalizing SCSM 2012 Administration*

Creating workflows with the System Center 2012 Service Manager Authoring Tool is covered in two recipes of *Chapter 11, Automating Service Manager 2012*:

- ▶ *Creating a custom workflow in the Authoring Tool – Export your unsealed Management Packs*
- ▶ *Autoclose resolved Incidents with SMLets and a custom workflow*

Extending Service Manager classes

Service Manager 2012 includes a very flexible class model that allows you to extend existing classes and create new classes. There are two main types of classes in Service Manager— Configuration Items and Work Items.

Configuration Items are items stored in your CMDB, such as Windows Computers, Users, Printers, and so on. These items are normally viewed in the **Configuration Items** section of the **Service Manager** console. Please refer to *Chapter 4, Building the Configuration Management Database (CMDB)*, for more information about the CMDB in Service Manager.

Work Items are classes that are used to support your ITSM processes, such as Incident, Service Request, Change Request, and so on. Work Items are typically viewed in the Work Items section of the Service Manager Console. More information about ITSM processes covered by SCSM can be found in *Chapter 1, Chapter 5, Chapter 6*, and *Chapter 7*.

In this recipe, we will walk you through the process of adding additional properties to an existing Service Manager class.

Getting ready

It is recommended that you follow the instructions in the first recipe Using the SCSM Authoring Tool to get familiar with the user interface of the System Center 2012 Service Manager Authoring Tool. Also, you will need to be familiar with the process of sealing management packs, as explained in the next recipe.

Working with SCSM classes requires knowledge of the Service Manager class concepts, model and hierarchies. Each object in Service Manager is an instance of a particular base class. All instances of a base class have a common set of properties. Properties are used to represent the details of the actual object, that is, the instance of the class. Each property has a predefined data type which defines the type of values that it can hold. There are data types for text values, numeric values and dates, among others.

Every class in Service Manager must specify a base class that identifies an existing class that the new class will specialize. The new class will inherit all properties defined in the base class, and also all properties that are defined in all parent classes of the base class.

To give you a better understanding of the concept of class inheritance, we will look at the following sample class diagram of the `System.Domain.User` class.

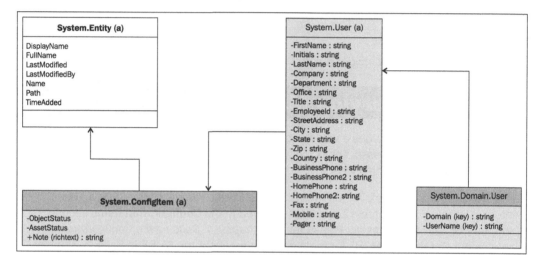

The `System.Domain.User` (the display name of which is Domain User or Group) only contains two properties names `Domain` and `UserName`. However, when you look at the class instances in the **Users** view of the **Configuration Items** section in the **Service Manager** console, you will notice that there are many more properties displayed. Through the concept of inheritance, the `System.Domain.User` class inherits all the properties of its base class— `System.User`. `System.User` which also inherits from `System.ConfigItem`, which in turn inherits from `System.Entity`. As a result, the `System.Domain.User` class includes all properties of the parent classes in the entire hierarchy. The `System.Entity` class is the topmost class in Service Manager, which all the other classes inherit from. The **(a)** denotes that the class is an abstract class. Abstract classes have no instances and exist only to act as a base class for other classes.

How to do it...

Now that you have a basic understanding of Service Manager class concepts, we are going to extend one of the existing classes using the Authoring Tool.

Our head of server infrastructure has requested the ability to store special reboot instructions as well as the technical person responsible for all servers. Service Manager uses the Windows Computer class to store computer objects, such as client computers and servers, so we are going to extend this class by two additional properties.

The special reboot instructions need to be defined as a text property, allowing the users to enter free text in the field. The field that will hold the technical person responsible, however, is a special property called a relationship. A **relationship** allows the property to hold a relationship to one instance of a predefined target class (Domain User or Group in our example).

1. Open the Authoring Tool, go to **File | New**, and create a new management pack named `Custom.ConfigurationItems.ComputerExtension.xml`.

2. Click on the management pack in **Management Pack Explorer**, then, in the **Details** pane, change the **Management Pack Name** property to **Custom Configuration Items Computer Extension**.

3. In the **Class Browser**, select **All Management Packs** from the pull-down menu. Find the **Windows Computer** class in the list of available classes.

4. Right-click on the **Windows Computer** class and click on **View**.

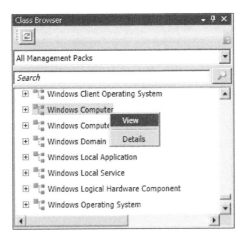

5. The Management Pack that includes the Windows Computer class will now be loaded by the Authoring Tool and displayed in the Management pack Explorer.

6. In **Management Pack Explorer**, right-click on the Windows Computer class and select **Extend** class.

7. In the **Target Management Pack** pop-up windows, make sure that the newly created management pack is selected, and then click on **OK**.

8. You will now see that a new class has been added to your management pack, and the class will also be displayed in the **Authoring** pane.

9. In the **Authoring** pane, change the class name to **Custom Windows Computer Extension** and the description to **Extension of class Windows Computer to hold server reboot instructions and technical responsible**.

10. To create the property to hold the special reboot instructions, click on **Create property...** in the **Authoring** pane, enter **RebootInstructions** as the internal name, and click on **Create**.

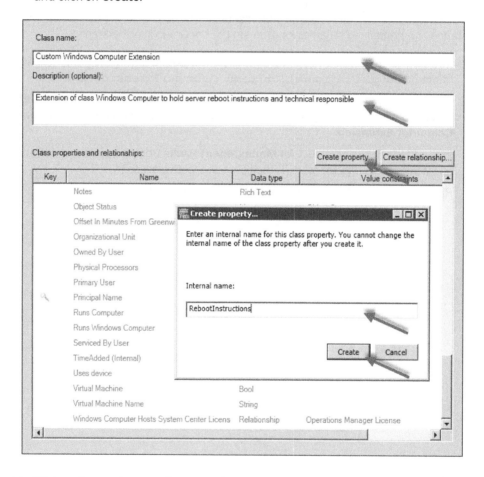

11. Click on the newly created property from the list of available properties in the **Authoring** pane. In the **Details** pane, change the **Name** property to **Reboot Instructions**.

12. To create the technical responsible person relationship, click on **Create relationship…** in the **Authoring** pane. Enter **TechnicalResponsible** as the **Internal name** and click on **Create**.

13. Click on the newly created relationship from the list of available properties in the **Authoring** pane. In the **Details** pane, change the **Name** property to **Technical Responsible**.

14. In the **Details** pane, under the Value Contraints (target) section, change the **Target Class** property to **Domain User or Group**.

15. Save the management pack using the **Save All** option from the **File** menu.

16. Seal the management pack. For more information on how to seal a management pack, please refer to the next recipe *Sealing Management Packs*.

17. Open the **Service Manager** console and navigate to the **Management Packs** view in the **Administration** section.

18. In the task pane, click on **Import**, browse to the location where you stored your management pack, and click on the **Custom.ConfigurationItems. ComputerExtension.mp** file. Click on **Open**, and then click on **Import**. If you have not sealed the management pack, when the import process is finished, Service Manager will display a warning message that unsealed management packs should not contain type definitions. We are going to cover sealing management packs in the next chapter, so you can safely ignore this message and click on **OK**.

19. Go to the **Configuration Items** section, open the **All Windows Computers** view, and double-click on any of the listed computers.

20. When you switch to the **Extensions** tab, you will see the newly created **Reboot Instructions** field as a textbox allowing you to enter special reboot instructions for your instances of Windows Computer. However, the technical responsible relationship is missing because Service Manager does not dynamically add relationship properties to forms. This will be covered later in this chapter, when we customize forms using the Authoring Tool.

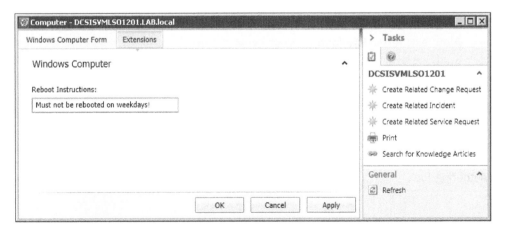

How it works...

When Service Manager detects properties that were added to existing classes using class extensions, it will display the Extensions tab on the corresponding form. Each property will be added to the Extensions area using a default control that is based on the property's data type.

Please note that Service Manager does not support dynamically displaying relationship properties in the **Extensions** tab. You will have to customize the form using the Authoring Tool to accomplish this task. Furthermore, you can define the layout and the arrangement of the controls used for your extended properties by extending the base forms contained in Service Manager. We will cover this scenario later in this chapter.

There's more...

An important choice to make when defining class properties is the correct data type. In the following section, you can find information about the data types available in Service Manager, as well as instructions on how you can use enumerations as data types.

Lists aka enumeration types

The data type of each property can be defined in the **Details** pane of the Authoring Tool. The available data types are as follows:

 ▸ **Integer**: Signed integer (-2,147,483,648 to 2,147,483,647)

 ▸ **Decimal**: Precise fractional or integral type ($\pm 1.0 \times 10e{-}28$ to $\pm 7.9 \times 10e28$)

 ▸ **Double**: Double-precision floating point type ($-1.79769313486232e308$ to $1.79769313486232e308$)

 ▸ **String**: Text type

 ▸ **Date Time**: Date/Time type

 ▸ **GUID**: Global Unique Identifier

 ▸ **Bool**: true/false

 ▸ **Rich Text**: Text in RTF form

 ▸ **Binary**: Binary data such as files

 ▸ **List**: Enumeration type

The List data type can be used to create a property that will allow the user to select a value from one of the lists available in Service Manager, such as the Incident Classification property of the Incident class. Lists are special data types named **Enumeration Types**. You can target any existing list from any management pack in Service Manager, or create your own list using the Authoring Tool.

1. In the Authoring Tool, select the property you would like to be defined as a List type, and then, in the **Details** pane, change the **Data Type** property to **List**.

2. In the **Select** a list dialog, either select an existing list, or create your own list using the **Create List...** option.

3. Save your management pack and import it into Service Manager.

4. If you have created your own list, you can define the available values under Lists in the **Library** section of the **Service Manager** console.

See also

Refer to the following recipe for more information on how to customize the form to display controls for your newly created properties:

▸ *Customizing default forms*

Sealing management packs

When planning your customizations in Service Manager, one of the most important decisions to make when designing your management packs is whether to seal management packs.

As explained in *Chapter 2, Personalizing SCSM 2012 Administration*, a sealed management pack is a read-only management pack, which cannot be written to once it has been imported into Service Manager. Furthermore, sealing a management pack enables it to be referenced from within other management packs. Some examples of what is required when referencing a management pack are mentioned here:

▸ Creating an extension of a class: In this scenario, you create a reference to the management pack that holds the base class (actually, the Authoring Tool automatically created such a reference in the background when we created a class extension in the previous recipe).

▸ Customizing a form: This involves creating a reference to the management pack which defines the base form.

▸ Creating a view: Normally, you would want to create your view through the console, which means you are going to save it in an unsealed management pack. This means that the class you are referencing in your view must be part of a sealed management pack.

Sealing management packs also ensures upgradeability. When you import a later version of a sealed management pack into Service Manager, Service Manager checks whether an upgrade is possible or not, and will reject non-upgradeable changes. If, for instance, you have a sealed management pack defining a user defined class and you have already instances stored in Service Manager. If you have to add a new property to the class, you can do this by modifying the management pack XML, increasing the version, sealing, and importing it into Service Manager again. Following this procedure, the instances that are already stored in Service Manager will remain in the database. However, if you were to apply the changes that are not upgradeable (such as removing a property), Service Manager will not be able to import the management pack. You would have to delete the existing management pack first, which obviously would result in losing the already existing instance of your class.

As a general rule, we recommend the management packs that contain the following resources, and are always sealed:

- Classes
- Class extensions
- Forms
- Form extensions

Getting ready

To seal a management pack, you need a **Strong Name Key** (**SNK**) file. You use the sn.exe tool to create a SNK file. This tool is part of the Windows **Software Development Kit** (**SDK**) and can be downloaded from the following URL:

http://www.microsoft.com/en-us/download/details.aspx?id=8279

To create your own strong name key file, first check on your computer for the existence of the sn.exe tool.

1. Click on **Start**, type cmd, press *Enter*.
2. Type cd\ and press *Enter*.

3. Type `dir sn.exe /s` and press _Enter_. This process will take a while and should output all locations where the `sn.exe` tool has been found. You can cancel the process with _Ctrl-C_ once you find the tool. Write down the location of the `sn.exe` tool. Normally, the tool should be located in the `Program Files` directory, under `Microsoft SDKs\Windows\vX.XX\Bin`.

If you were unable to find the `sn.exe` tool, download the Windows Software Development Kit from the link provided above, install it, and perform the search process again.

To create the SNK file:

1. Click on **Start**, type `cmd`, right-click on `cmd.exe`. Click on **Run as administrator**. Click on **Yes**.

2. Type the following and press _Enter_.

3. cd [Full Path to SNK file].

4. Type `sn -k <myfilename>.snk` and press _Enter_, where <myfilename> is a name you give the file.

5. Browse to the location and copy the SNK file to the directory where you store your Service Manager customizations.

How to do it...

Now that you know the concept of sealed management packs and have created your strong name key file, we are going to show you how you can seal management packs using the Authoring Tool.

1. Open the Authoring Tool, go to **File | Open**, and open the management pack that you created in the previous recipe (`Custom.ConfigurationItems.ComputerExtension.xml`).

2. Right-click on the management pack in **Management Pack Explorer** and click on **Seal Management Pack**.

3. Change the **Output Directory** to the location where the Authoring Tool should write the sealed management pack to. Then, specify your SNK file and type the company name.

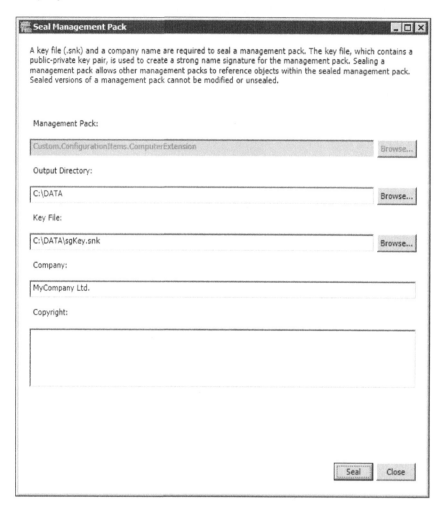

4. Click on **Seal**, wait until the message **Seal succeeded** is displayed, and then click on **Close**.

5. Open the **Service Manager** console and navigate to the Management Packs view in the Administration section.

6. If you have walked through the previous recipe and imported the unsealed version of the management pack, find the Custom Configuration Items Computer Extension management pack and delete it using the **Delete tasks** in the task pane.

7. In the task pane, click on **Import**, and browse to the location where you stored your sealed management pack. On the lower-right, change **MP files(*.xml)** to **MP files(*. mp)**, click on the `Custom.ConfigurationItems.ComputerExtension.mp` file, click on **Open**, and then click on **Import**. When the import process is finished, click on **OK**.

You have now imported the sealed management pack. Please note that the Authoring Tool automatically increases the version of the management pack every time you seal it.

There's more...

If you have to seal management packs often, we recommend you use `FastSeal.exe`. Instructions on how to use this tool can be found below.

FastSeal.exe

Instead of using the System Center 2012 Service Manager Authoring Tool for sealing your management packs, you can also use the `FastSeal.exe` command line utility. This tool is very convenient if you need to seal management packs in bulk or if you want to automate the seal process.

You can download the `FastSeal.exe` utility from the following URL:

`http://blogs.technet.com/b/servicemanager/archive/2009/12/25/sealing-management-packs.aspx`

See also

Refer to the following recipe for more information on how to work with management packs:

▶ The *Creating Management Packs in the Authoring tool to save your SCSM personalization* recipe in *Chapter 2, Personalizing SCSM 2012 Administration*

Creating new classes

Sooner or later you are likely to come into the situation where you want to store data in your CMDB for which you are unable to find a class. Examples include monitors, mobile phones, racks, buildings, locations, cost centers, and so on.

The Service Manager 2012 class model not only allows for classes to be extended, but also offers the capability to add new classes to the class model.

In this recipe, we will walk you through the steps required to create your custom class using the Authoring Tool.

Getting ready

It is recommended that you follow the instructions in the recipe Using the SCSM Authoring Tool to get familiar with the user interface of the System Center 2012 Service Manager Authoring Tool. Also, you will need to be familiar with the process of sealing management packs, as explained in the recipe Sealing Management Packs earlier in this chapter.

You will need a basic understanding of the class concepts in Service Manager. It is therefore recommended that you read through the *Getting ready* section of the previous recipe *Extending Service Manager classes*.

How to do it...

We will now use the Authoring Tool to create a new generic class named Peripheral Device to store data about monitors, scanners, and locally attached printers.

When you create a new class in Service Manager, you have to define primary key properties. The primary key properties uniquely identify each instance of the class. In other words the value of the unique key property, or the combination of values if you define more than one unique key property respectively, must be unique and cannot occur in any other instance of the class. As an example, the unique key property for the Windows Computer class is the `PrincipalName` property, which holds the **Fully Qualified Domain Name** (**FQDN**) of the computer. The Domain User or Group class defines both the `UserName` and `Domain` properties as the primary key.

In our example, we will name the primary key property `PeripheralDeviceID`. We will also define properties for the device name, a description, the serial number, and the asset number of the device.

In order to distinguish between monitors, scanners and printers, we will create an enumeration type property which is bound to a custom list that holds the available types of peripheral devices: monitor, scanner, and printer.

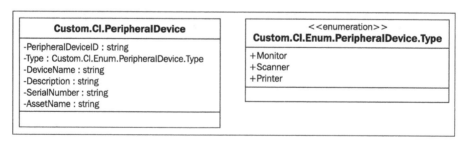

1. Open the Authoring Tool, go to **File** | **New**, and create a new management pack named `Custom.ConfigurationItems.PeripheralDevice.Class.xml`.

2. Click on the management pack in Management Pack Explorer. In the **Details** pane, change the **Management Pack Name** property to **Custom Configuration Items Peripheral Device Class**.

3. Right-click on the **Classes** node in **Management Pack Explorer** and click on **Create Configuration Item Class...**. Enter **Custom.CI.PeripheralDevice** as the **Internal name**, and then click on **OK**.

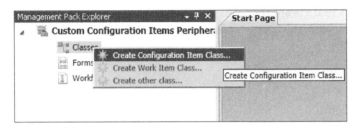

4. You will now see that a new class has been added to your management pack and the class will also be displayed in the **Authoring** pane.

5. In the **Authoring** pane, change the class name to **Peripheral Device**, and clear the description field.

6. Scroll to the bottom of the properties list in the **Authoring** pane. You will see an automatically created property named **Property_X** defined as the key property of your class. Click on the red cross next to it in order to delete the property.

7. A warning message will appear that tells you that there is no key property available for your class. We are now going to create our custom key property, so you can ignore this message and click on **OK**.

8. Click on **Create property...** in the **Authoring** pane, enter **PeripheralDeviceID** as the **Internal name**, and click on **Create**. Ignore the warning message and click on **OK**.

9. Click on the newly created property from the list of available properties in the **Authoring** pane, and then, in the **Details** pane, change the **Key** property to **True**, and change the **Required** property to **True**.

10. In the **Details** pane, change the **Auto Increment** property to **True**, and then change the **Default Value** property to **PD{0}**. This will tell Service Manager that it should automatically assign values to this property, and a prefix of PD will be used.

11. In the **Details** pane, change the **Name** property to **ID**.

12. Click on **Create property...**, enter **Type** as the **Internal name**, then click on **Create**.

13. In the **Details** pane, change the **Data Type** property to **List**.

14. In the **Select** a list dialog window, click on **Create List...**, enter **Custom.CI.Enum. PeripheralDevice.Type** as the **Internal name**, and **Peripheral Device Type** as the **Display name**. Click on Create and then click on **OK**.

15. Click on **Create property...**, enter **DeviceName** as the **Internal name**, then click on **Create**. Change the **Name** property to **Device Name**.

16. Click on **Create property...**, enter **Description** as the **Internal name**, and click on **Create**. Change the **Maximum Length** property to **4000**.

17. Click on **Create property...**, enter **SerialNumber** as the **Internal name**, and click on **Create**. Change the **Name** property to **Serial Number**.

18. Click on **Create property...**, enter **AssetNumber** as the **Internal name**, and click on **Create**. Change the **Name** property to **Asset Number**.

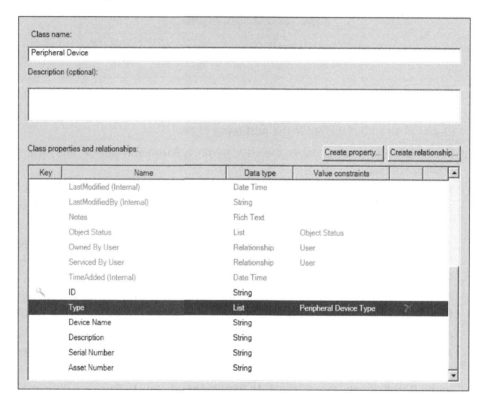

19. Save the management pack using the **Save All** option from the **File** menu.

20. Seal the management pack. For more information on how to seal a management pack, please refer to the previous recipe *Sealing management packs*.

21. Open the **Service Manager** console and navigate to the Management Packs view in the Administration section.

22. In the task pane, click on **Import**, and browse to the location where you stored your sealed management pack. On the lower-right, change **MP files(*.xml)** to **MP files(*. mp)**, click on the **Custom.ConfigurationItems.PeripheralDevice.Class.mp** file, click on **Open**, and then click on **Import**. When the import process is finished, click on **OK**.

23. Navigate to the **Library** section and click on **Lists**.

24. Double-click on **Peripheral Device Type** list and add the following values—**Monitor, Scanner**, and **Printer**. Note that you will have to specify a management pack where you want to store the list values in, because we sealed the management pack that holds the definition of the list.

Your newly created class is now ready to be used for storing data in Service Manager. However, you might wonder how you will be able to manage your peripheral devices, as there are no corresponding views available in the **Service Manager** console. Instead, you have to create at least one view yourself.

1. In the **Service Manager** console, in the **Configuration Items** section, right-click on the **Configuration Items** folder, and click on **Create Folder**.

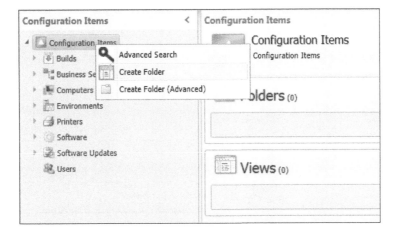

2. Enter `Peripheral Devices` as the **Folder** name. Select any of your custom management packs that you use for storing configuration management views. Alternatively, you can select the built-in management pack **Service Manager Configuration Management Configuration Library**. Click on **OK**.

3. Right-click on the newly create folder **Peripheral Devices** and click on **Create View**.

4. In the **Create View** dialog, under **General**, enter **All Peripheral Devices** as the **Name**.

5. Under **Criteria**, click on **Browse**. In the pull-down menu, select **All basic classes**. Find the **Peripheral Device** class, and then click on **OK**.

6. Under **Display**, unselect all the columns and select the following columns—**ID, Type, Device Name, Serial Number, Asset Number**.

7. Click on **OK** to save the view.

8. Click on the newly created view, and then, in the task pane, click on **Create Peripheral Device**.

9. Service Manager will load a generic form for the **Peripheral Device** class that allows you to enter data about your peripheral devices. Notice how the **ID** field is automatically populate according to our definition when we created the property in the Authoring Tool.

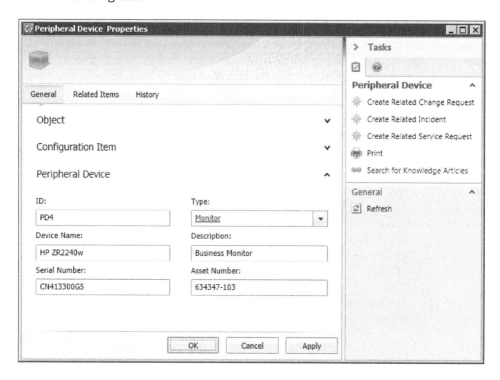

How it works...

Whenever Service Manager has to open a form for a class for which no class-specific form exists, it will open a generic form that lists all available properties for the corresponding class. Service Manager uses default controls that are based on the data type of each individual property. As with class extensions, the generic form will not display any controls for relationship properties.

You might have noticed that the generic form also includes properties that are inherited from parent classes. In the previous example, you see properties under the **Object and Configuration Item** headers. If you will be using the **Service Manager** console often for working with instances of your user-defined classes, it is recommended that you also create a user-defined form for your custom class that accommodates your individual requirements and thus improves the usability over the generic form. We will cover the creation of new forms later in this chapter.

There's more...

Instead of creating new classes with all new properties, Service Manager also allows you to inherit the properties of an existing class. The next section explains the process of inheriting from an existing class, and talk about the System Center Common Model.

Inheriting from a different class

When you create a new Configuration Item or Work Item class using the right-click on option on the classes node in the **Management Pack Explorer** of the Authoring Tool, your custom class will always have `System.ConfigItem` or `System.WorkItem` as its base class. However, you might want your custom class to inherit from a class further below in the class hierarchy. As an example, you might want to create a special type of Incident class which is used for incidents raised by your monitoring system. These incidents should include all fields of the built-in Incident class, but also have some additional properties to hold the details of the monitoring alert. Instead of extending the `Incident` class with these properties (which would then be available to all kinds of incidents), you can create a new class which inherits from the `Incident` class.

1. In the **Class Browser** of the Authoring Tool, select **All Management Packs** from the pull-down menu, and find the class you want to inherit from.

2. Right-click on the class and click on **View**.

3. The Management Pack that includes the class will now be loaded by the Authoring Tool and displayed in the **Management pack Explorer**.

4. In **Management Pack Explorer**, right-click on the class and select **Inherit from this class**.

5. In the **Target Management Pack** pop-up window, make sure that the management pack you would like to use to store your class is selected, and then click on OK.

System Center Common Model

When creating new classes in Service Manager, you might find it difficult to identify an appropriate base class that your custom class could inherit from. The most commonly used classes in Service Manager are documented in Visio UML class diagram named the **System Center Common Model** as implemented in System Center Service Manager. This document is part of the SCSM Job Aids, which can be downloaded from the following URL:

`http://go.microsoft.com/fwlink/p/?LinkID=232378`

See also

Refer to the following recipe for more information on how to create a custom form for your newly created class:

▶ *Creating your own forms*

Customizing default forms

In the previous recipes, we have learned how to extend classes and create new classes in Service Manager 2012. Obviously, when you customize the classes available in Service Manager, you would want to be able to create and edit instance of you custom classes through the console.

Although Service Manager 2012 includes a generic form for unknown classes and the Extensions tab for unknown class extensions, you might want to have control over how the forms look like in order to improve the usability of the console.

The System Center 2012 Service Manager Authoring Tools allows you to customize existing forms and also create new forms for your custom classes.

In this recipe, we will walk you through the process of adding controls to the existing Windows Computer form. We will use the class extension we created in recipe *Extending Service Manager classes* earlier in this chapter.

Getting ready

It is recommended that you follow the instructions in the first recipe Using *the SCSM Authoring Tool* to get familiar with the user interface of the System Center 2012 Service Manager Authoring Tool. Also, you will need to be familiar with the process of sealing management packs, and you will have to walk through the recipe *Extending Service Manager classes* before continuing with this recipe.

Working with forms requires knowledge about the forms infrastructure of Service Manager. Whenever you open an object in the **Service Manager** console (using the **Edit** or **Properties** task, or by double-clicking on a class instance) or whenever you create a new object (using the **Create** task), Service Manager evaluates which form to load. During this evaluation, the class type of the object is evaluated. If a form is assigned to this class type, the form is loaded. If not, Service Manager retrieves the parent class (base class) of the object, and checks if a form is bound to this class. This process is repeated until a form is found.

The following diagram illustrates the Service Manager process of form evaluation in more detail:

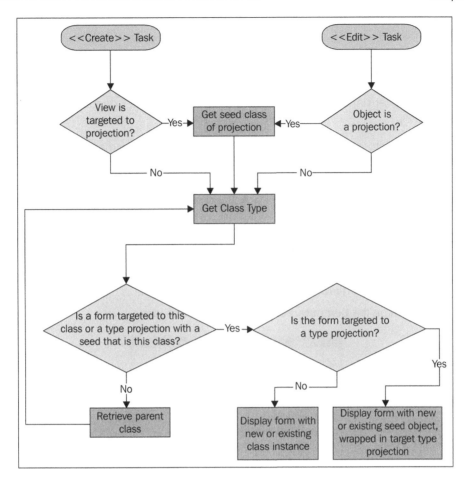

As you have noticed in the previous recipe when we created the class for peripheral devices, Service Manager will also load a form of "no form exists" up the class hierarchy. The reason for this is that Service Manager has a so called **Generic Forms**. One generic form is bound to the `System.Entity` class, which ultimately all the classes inherit from. Furthermore, generic forms exists for type projections with seed class `System.ConfigItem` and `System.WorkItem`.

How to do it...

Now that you have a basic understanding of Service Manager form concepts, we are going to extend one of the existing forms using the Authoring Tool. We will add the special reboot instructions and technical responsible properties from the Custom Configuration Items Computer Extension management pack we created in recipe Extending Service Manager classes.

1. Open the Authoring Tool, go to **File | New**, and create a new management pack named `Custom.ConfigurationItems.ComputerFormExtension.xml`.

2. Click on the management pack in **Management Pack Explorer**, then, in the **Details** pane, change the **Management Pack Name** property to **Custom Configuration Items Computer Form Extension**.

3. Go to **File | Open**, and open the sealed version of the management pack that holds the class extension (`Custom.ConfigurationItems.ComputerExtension.mp`).

4. In the **Form Browser**, select **All Management Packs** from the pull-down menu, then find the **ComputerForm** form in the list of available forms.

5. Right-click on the **ComputerForm** form and click on **View**.

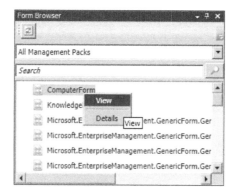

6. The Management Pack that includes the `ComputerForm` form will now be loaded by the Authoring Tool and displayed in the Management Pack Explorer. Also, the form will be shown in read-only mode in the Authoring Tool.

7. In the **Authoring** pane, click on **Customize**.

8. In the **Target Management Pack** pop-up window, make sure that the newly created management pack is selected, and click on **OK**.

9. You will now see that the form has been added to your management pack, and the form will also be displayed in the **Authoring** pane and can now be edited.

10. Click on the **ComputerForm (Customized)** form in the **Management Pack Explorer**, and then, in the **Details** pane, change the **Name** property to **Custom Windows Computer Form Extension** and clear the **Description** property.

11. Aligning controls on forms can be a bit tricky. Start with dragging a label control from the **Form Customization Toolbox** to the form in the **Authoring** pane. Still holding the mouse button, move the cursor over the **Principal Name** until both the label and textbox are surrounded with a selection box. Drop the label control by releasing the mouse button. The label should appear right underneath the **Principal Name** textbox.

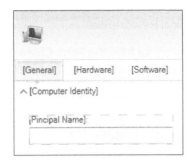

12. Select the newly added label control. In the **Details** pane, change the following properties:

    ❏ Width: Auto

    ❏ Horizontal Alignment: Stretch

    ❏ Top: 10

    ❏ Content: Special Reboot Instructions

13. Now, drag a Text Box control from the **Form Customization Toolbox** to the form in the **Authoring** pane. Still holding the mouse button, move the cursor over the **Principal Name** until the **Principal Name** label, the **Principal Name** textbox, and the newly added label are surrounded with a selection box. Drop the text box control by releasing the mouse button. The text box should appear right underneath the **Special Reboot Instructions** label.

14. Select the newly added Text Box control, and then, in the **Details** pane, change the following properties:

    ❏ Width: Auto

    ❏ Horizontal Alignment: Stretch

    ❏ Content: Special Reboot Instructions

15. In the **Details** pane, in the **Binding Path** property, click on the **...** button. Select the **Reboot Instructions** property from the **Binding Path** pop-up window, and click on **OK**.

16. Drag a Label control from the **Form Customization Toolbox** to the form in the **Authoring** pane. Still holding the mouse button, move the cursor over the Primary user until both the label and user picker are surrounded with a selection box. Drop the label control by releasing the mouse button. The label should appear right underneath the **Primary User** user picker control.

17. Select the newly added Label control, and then, in the **Details** pane, change the following properties:

    ❑ Width: Auto

    ❑ Horizontal Alignment: Stretch

    ❑ Top: 10

    ❑ Content: Technical Responsible

18. Now, drag a User Picker control from the **Form Customization Toolbox** to the form in the **Authoring** pane. Still holding the mouse button, move the cursor over the Primary user until the Primary user label, the Primary User user picker control, and the newly added label are surrounded with a selection box. Drop the User Picker control by releasing the mouse button. The **User Picker** should appear right underneath the **Technical Responsible** label.

19. Select the newly added User Picker control, and then, in the **Details** pane, change the following properties:

    ❑ Width: Auto

    ❑ Horizontal Alignment: Stretch

    ❑ Top: -9

20. In the **Details** pane, in the **Binding Path** property, click on the **...** button. Select the **Technical Responsible** property from the **Binding Path** pop-up window, and click on **Ok**.

21. Verify that the alignment of the controls match with the following screenshot:

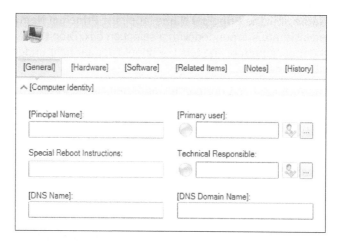

22. Save the management pack using the **Save All** option from the **File** menu.

23. Seal the management pack. For more information on how to seal a management pack, please refer to the recipe *Sealing Management Packs* earlier in this chapter.

24. Open the **Service Manager** console and navigate to the Management Packs view in the **Administration** section.

25. In the task pane, click on **Import**, and browse to the location where you stored your sealed management pack. On the lower-right, change **MP files(*.xml)** to **MP files(*.mp)**, click on the `Custom.ConfigurationItems.ComputerFormExtension.mp` file, click on **Open**, and then click on **Import**. When the import process is finished, click on **OK**.

26. Go to the **Configuration Items** section, open the **All Windows Computers** view, and double-click on any of the listed computers.

You will now see the newly added fields displayed on the computer form. If the fields do not show up, try closing and restarting the **Service Manager** console, as the view could be stored in your local cache.

How it works...

Service Manager forms are based on the Windows Presentation Foundation (WPF), which is part of the Microsoft .NET Framework. Each form is technically a WPF user control that is compiled into a DLL file. By extending a form, you are referencing the base form in your management pack. All the customizations are contained in the management pack XML code as tags that can be interpreted by WPF. When Service Manager loads the extended form, during the rendering process, it applies the customization tags to the base form before it is displayed to the end user.

There's more...

When you extend classes in Service Manager, you might notice a tab titled Extensions on the form of the extended class. The nature of this tab is explained on the following section.

The Extensions tab

When Service Manager loads a form, both the class of the object that is being displayed as well as the class to which the form that is being displayed is targeted are evaluated. If these classes differ, and if the form that is being displayed is not a generic form, an **Extensions** tab is added to the form. This tab displays all properties of any extension classes in the class hierarchy of the object. We learned about the **Extensions** tab when we originally created the Windows Computer class extensions in the recipe *Extending Service Manager classes*.

As we have now added the properties we want to the **General** tab of the computer form, we might want to remove the **Extensions** tab. This can be done by manually editing the management pack XML code. We will cover this scenario in recipe *Using an XML editor to modify Management Packs* later in this chapter.

See also

Refer to the following recipe for more information on how to create class extensions:

▶ *Extending Service Manager classes*

Creating your own forms

In the recipe *Creating new classes*, we have added a class to Service Manager to hold instances of peripheral devices in our CMDB. While the generic form that was used to manage the devices might be sufficient, you are still likely to come into the situation where you want to have control over what controls to display, and the layout of the form.

The Service Manager 2012 form infrastructure not only allows for the existing forms to be customized, but also offers the capability to add new forms.

In this recipe, we will walk you through the steps required to create your custom form using the Authoring Tool.

Getting ready

It is recommended that you follow the instructions in the recipe *Using the SCSM Authoring Tool* to get familiar with the user interface of the System Center 2012 Service Manager Authoring Tool. Also, you will need to be familiar with the process of sealing management packs, as explained in the recipe Sealing Management Packs earlier in this chapter.

You will need a basic understanding of the form infrastructure in Service Manager. It is therefore recommended that you read through the *Getting ready* section of the previous recipe *Customizing default forms*. Also, you will have to work through the recipe *Creating new classes* before continuing with this recipe.

How to do it...

We will now use the Authoring Tool to create a new form for the Peripheral Device class we defined in the *Creating new classes* recipe earlier in this chapter.

1. Open the Authoring Tool, go to **File | New** and create a new management pack named `Custom.ConfigurationItems.PeripheralDevice.Form.xml`.

2. Click on the management pack in **Management Pack Explorer**. In the **Details** pane, change the **Management Pack Name** property to **Custom Configuration Items Peripheral Device Form**.

3. Go to **File | Open**, and open the sealed version of the management pack that holds the Peripheral Device class (`Custom.ConfigurationItems.PeripheralDevice.Class.mp`).

4. Expand the **Custom Configuration Items Peripheral Device Form** management pack in **Management Pack Explorer**, right-click on **Forms**, and click on **Create**.

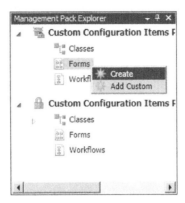

5. In the **Base** class pop-up window, select the **Custom Configuration Items Peripheral Device Class** management pack from the pull-down menu, and click on the **Peripheral Device** class, and click on **OK**.

6. In the **Create** form pop-up windows, enter **PeripheralDeviceForm** as the **Internal name**, then click on **OK**.

7. You will now see that the form has been added to your management pack, and the form will also be displayed in the **Authoring** pane and can now be edited.

8. Click on the **PeripheralDeviceForm** form in the **Management Pack Explorer**. In the **Details** pane, change the **Name** property to **Custom Peripheral Device Form**, and clear the **Description** property.

9. Drag and drop a Label control from the **Form Customization Toolbox** to the form in the **Authoring** pane.

10. Select the newly added Label control, and then, in the **Details** pane, change the **Content property to ID**:

11. Now, drag a Text Box control from the **Form Customization Toolbox** to the form in the **Authoring** pane, and drop it underneath the ID label.

12. Select the newly added Text Box control, and then, in the **Details** pane, in the **Binding Path** property, click on the **...** button. Select the **Reboot Instructions** property from the **Binding Path** pop-up window, and click on **OK**.

13. In the **Details** pane, change the **Is Enabled** property to **False**. We are disabling this control because the ID value is defined to be automatically assigned.

14. Repeat *steps 9-12* for the **Device Name**, **Description**, **Serial Number**, and **Asset Number** properties. Keep the **Is Enabled** property set to **True** for the text box controls of these properties.

15. For the **Type** property, add a Label control to the form as described in *steps 9-10*.

16. Now, drag a List Picker control from the **Form Customization Toolbox** to the form in the **Authoring** pane and drop it underneath the Type label.

17. Select the newly added List Picker control. In the **Details** pane, in the **Binding Path** property, click on the **...** button. Select the **Type** property from the **Binding Path** pop-up window, and click on **OK**.

18. If you want, you can also add a User Picker control for the **Owned By User** relationship property that is inherited from the `System.ConfigItem` class.

19. Now, ensure that proper layout of your controls using drag and drop or the properties in the **Details** pane. You might also want to add images and other labels to accommodate your layout and design requirements. The following screenshot illustrates a sample design of the form.

20. Save the management pack using the **Save All** option from the **File** menu.

21. Seal the management pack. For more information on how to seal a management pack, please refer to the recipe *Sealing Management Packs* earlier in this chapter.

22. Open the **Service Manager** console and navigate to the Management Packs view in the Administration section.

23. In the task pane, click on **Import**, and browse to the location where you stored your sealed management pack. On the lower-right, change **MP files(*.xml)** to **MP files(*.mp)**, click on the `Custom.ConfigurationItems.PeripheralDevice.Form.mp` file, click on **Open**, and then click on **Import**. When the import process is finished, click on **OK**.

24. Go to the **Configuration Items** section, open the **All Peripheral Devices** view created in recipe *Creating new classes* and double-click on any of the listed peripheral devices, or create a new one using the **Create Peripheral Device** task in the task pane.

From now on, Service Manager will use the newly added form when you work with instances of the Peripheral Device class.

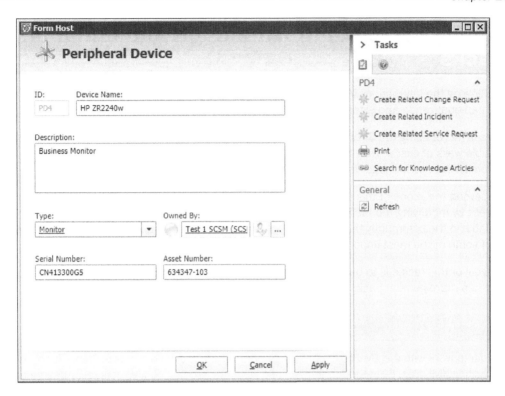

How it works...

With the creation of a custom form for the Peripheral Device class, Service Manager now no longer displays the generic form. By creating your custom form, you have total control over which properties are displayed on the form, over the layout of the controls, and also on the design of the form.

As Service Manager is using Windows Presentation Foundation (WPF) in the background, you can also use Microsoft Visual Studio to create your own WPF user controls that can be used in your custom forms. Using Visual Studio for advanced customization of Service Manager is out-of-scope for this book, but you will be able to find examples in some of the many blogs about Service Manager listed in *Appendix B*.

See also

Refer to the following recipe for more information on how to create a custom class for Service Manager:

▶ *Creating new classes*

Using an XML editor to modify management packs

By following the instructions in all recipes so far in this book you have gained an insight on the vast personalization and extensibility options available to Service Manager.

There is more! Using the **Service Manager** console and the Authoring Tool are only two possible ways of customizing Service Manager. There are much more options available to customize Service Manager by directly editing the XML code of your management packs.

It is beyond the scope of this book to cover all possible customization scenarios you can address by modifying the management pack XML. However, there are a lot of examples available in the community that you can apply to your environment. Refer to *Appendix B* for a list of some of the most important community websites to visit.

The goal of this recipe is to become familiar with the general process of modifying the XML code of a management pack.

Getting ready

In order to work with the XML code of management packs, you need to use software for opening and editing XML files. Even though you can use Notepad to edit XML files, it is recommended that you use a more advanced tool that offers color schemas and XML validation.

The first recommended choice would be to use the Visual Studio integrated development environment from Microsoft. Visual Studio is available in various commercial editions, and there is also a free edition named Visual Studio Express.

If you are not into developing software, Visual Studio is not the best choice, as the user interface might be too complex for simple XML editing. One of the many alternatives is the free tool Notepad++ that you can download and install from the following URL:

```
http://notepad-plus-plus.org/
```

How to do it...

In this example, we are going to create a new management pack that will hide the **Extensions** tab from the Windows Computer form. After we have extended the Windows Computer by following the instructions in the **Extending Service Manager classes** recipe, we have noticed that the **Extensions** tab, which displays the extended properties has been added to the form. As we have later customized the form to include the extended properties in the **General** tab, we would now like to hide the **Extensions** tab from the Windows Computer form.

Note that it is required that the sealed management packs that you created in the *Extending Service Manager classes* and *Customizing default forms* recipes are available and imported into Service Manager.

1. Open the Authoring Tool and go to **File** | **Open** and open the sealed management pack that includes the Windows Computer form extension from recipe *Customizing default forms* (`Custom.ConfigurationItems.ComputerFormExtension`).

2. Click on the management pack in Management Pack Explorer, and then, in the Details pane, write down the values of the following properties:

   - ❑ - Internal Name
   - ❑ - Key Token- Version (Major.Minor.Build.Revision)

3. In Management Pack Explorer, expand the **Forms** node, click on the **Custom Windows Computer Form Extension** form, and then, in the **Details** pane, write down the value of the **Internal Name** property.

4. Click on **Close Solution** from the **File** menu.

5. Go to **File** | **New**, and create a new management pack named `Custom.ConfigurationItems.ComputerFormExtension.HideExtensionsTab.xml`.

6. Click on the management pack in Management Pack Explorer. In the **Details** pane, change the **Management Pack Name** property to `Custom.ConfigurationItemsComputerFormExtensionHideExtensionsTab`.

7. Save the management pack using the **Save All** option from the **File** menu, and then close the Authoring Tool.

8. Use the XML editor of your choice, open the management pack XML file.

9. First, we will need to add a reference to the management pack that hosts the Windows Computer form extension. Add the following code to the **References** section just before the `</References>` tag:

```
<Reference Alias="ComputerFormExtension">
<ID>Custom.ConfigurationItems.ComputerFormExtension</ID>
<Version>1.0.0.1</Version>
<PublicKeyToken>249f95ca48020739</PublicKeyToken>
</Reference>
```

10. Replace the values for **ID**, **Version**, and **PublicKeyToken** with the corresponding values you wrote down in *step 2*.

11. Next, we will need to add a reference to the UI Administration management pack. Add the following code to the **References** section just before the `</References>` tag:

```
<Reference Alias="Admin">
<ID>Microsoft.EnterpriseManagement.ServiceManager.UI.
Administration</ID>
<Version>7.5.1561.0</Version>
<PublicKeyToken>31bf3856ad364e35</PublicKeyToken>
</Reference>
```

12. Replace the values for **ID**, **Version**, and **PublicKeyToken** with the corresponding values you wrote down in *step 2*.

13. Now, add the following code to the **Categories** section just before the `</Category>` tag:

```
<Category ID="HideComputerFormExtensionTab" Target="ComputerF
ormExtension!CustomForm_4045634b_48f3_4ec5_8c59_ff6e55f957eb"
Value="Admin!Microsoft.EnterpriseManagement.ServiceManager.
UI.Administration.Enumeration.HideExtensionTab" />
```

14. Replace the string **CustomForm_4045634b_48f3_4ec5_8c59_ff6e55f957eb** with the internal name of the form you wrote down in *step 3*.

15. Save the XML file and import it into Service Manager. When you now open the **Windows Computer** form, the **Extensions** tab will no longer be displayed. Please note that you might need to restart the **Service Manager** console for the changes to take effect.

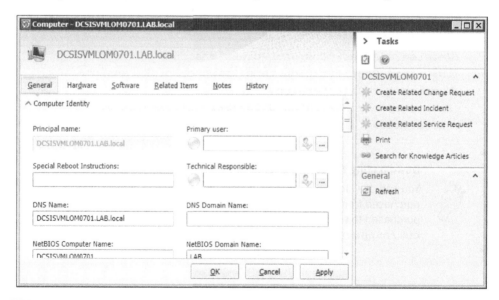

There's more...

The below section gives you information about where you can find the **XML Schema Definition** (**XSD**) for Service Manager Management Packs.

Management Pack Schema

Microsoft has released the XML Schema Definition (XSD) of the Management Pack XML structure used in Service Manager. The schema allows for better understanding of the content of the management pack XML code and enables schema validation when you work with management pack XML files.

The XSD file is part of the SCSM Job Aids that can be downloaded from the following URL:

```
http://go.microsoft.com/fwlink/p/?LinkID=232378
```

11
Automating Service Manager 2012

In this chapter, we will cover the following:

- ▶ Routing Incidents automatically using workflows
- ▶ Downloading and installing SMLets
- ▶ Using SMLets to delete a Work Item
- ▶ Exporting your unsealed Management Packs using the Service Manager cmdlets
- ▶ Creating a custom workflow in the Authoring Tool – Export your unsealed Management Packs
- ▶ Autoclose resolved Incidents with SMLets and a custom workflow
- ▶ Automating your Request Offerings with Orchestrator

Introduction

In this final chapter of the cookbook we will take a look at different scenarios for automating Service Manager. Besides working with the standard workflows within Service Manager, we will create custom workflows through the Authoring Tool and use SMLets to automate tasks. Also, we will take a look at how we can use System Center Orchestrator to automate our Work Items.

Routing Incidents automatically using workflows

We will start by taking a look at a simple workflow to route incidents to a certain user or a group. This functionality can be created using the built-in workflows within Service Manager.

Getting ready

Be sure that you have read and understood the creation of templates as described in the recipe *Creating an Incident Template* in *Chapter 6, Working with Incident and Problem Management*.

Make sure that Service Manager is up and running and that you have sufficient privileges to create workflows and templates (Administrator permissions are needed).

How to do it...

In this example we will create a workflow to route any incidents with the classification category **E-mail Problems** to the **Exchange** group.

1. Start the **Service Manager** console and go to the **Library** workspace.

2. Select **Templates** and create a new template based upon the **Incident** class. The only thing that you should define in this template is the **Assigned To** user.

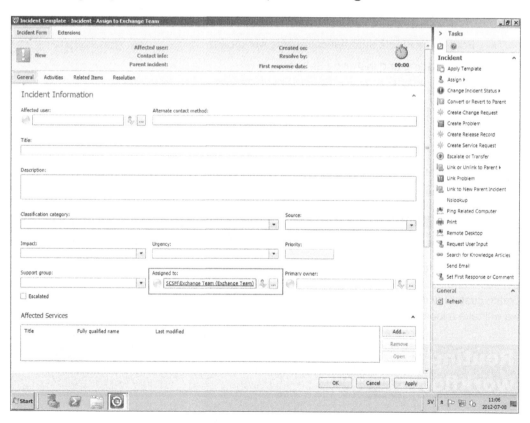

3. When you've created your template, go to the **Administration** workspace.

4. Expand **Workflows** and select **Configuration**.

5. Double-click on **Incident Event Workflow Configuration** to open the properties of it.

6. To create a new **Incident** workflow, click on the **Add** button.

7. Click on **Next** in the **Before You Begin** step of the wizard.

8. As the **Name** of the workflow, enter **Incident – Route E-mail incidents to Exchange group.** In the **Description** field, enter **This workflow will route all new incidents with the Classification Category set to E-mail Problems to the Exchange group.**

9. Make sure that **When an object is created** is chosen in the **Check for events** drop down and then create a new or select an existing Management Pack to store your workflow in. Then click on **Next**.

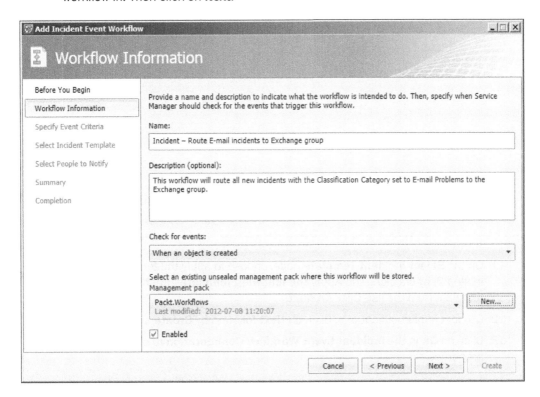

10. In the **Specify Event Criteria** page, locate the **Classification Category** in the **Available Properties**, select it, and click on **Add**. This will add the **Classification Category** to the **Criteria** section and all you have to do now is select **E-Mail problems** from the list. Click on **Next**.

> With this criteria specified, the workflow will now trigger on every new Incident where the **Classification Category** is set to **E-Mail Problems**.

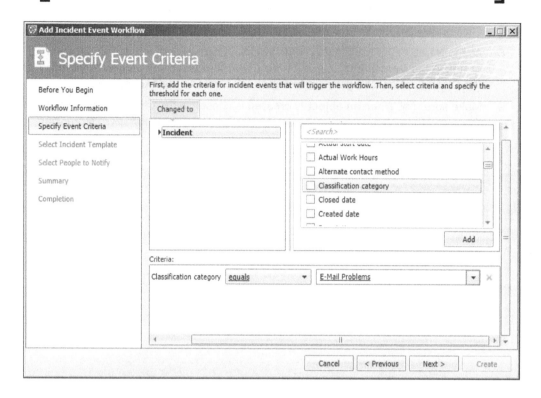

11. On the **Select Incident Template** page, choose to apply the template that you created in *step 2*, by checking the **Apply the following template** option and selecting your template from the list. Click on **Next**.

12. Do not enable notifications. Click on **Next** followed by **Create** and **Close**.

13. Click on **OK** in the **Incident Event Workflow Configuration** to close the workflow properties.

How it works...

When an Incident is created and the **Classification Category** is set to **E-Mail Problems**, the workflow will trigger and apply the template in which the **Assigned To** user is set to the **Exchange Group**. This will happen regardless of the Incident being created from the portal, by e-mail, or by an analyst in the console.

To test this workflow, create a new incident and make sure that the **Classification Category** is set to **E-Mail Problems**. Once you've created the Incident, give the workflow a minute to run. After that, open the **Incident** to confirm that the **Assigned To** user is set to the **Exchange Group**.

See also

For more information regarding templates, please see the *Creating an Incident template* recipe in *Chapter 6, Working with Incident and Problem Management*.

For more information regarding workflows, please see the *Creating a workflow* recipe in *Chapter 6, Working with Incident and Problem Management*, to notify the affected user upon the creation of an incident.

Downloading and installing SMLets

SMLets are a set of PowerShell cmdlets (pronounced as *command-lets*) to do administrative tasks and automate things in Service Manager. By using the different cmdlets in SMLets you can do things that you are unable to do from the console and create some very powerful scripts. This makes the SMLets a vital part of any Service Manager administrator's toolbox.

 Please note that SMLets is a community-driven project and is not supported by Microsoft.

Getting ready

Make sure that you have local administrator rights on the Service Manager management server in order to install the SMLets.

How to do it...

To download and install SMLets, follow these steps:

1. Open your favorite browser and go to `http://smlets.codeplex.com`.

2. Click on the large purple **Download** button on the right-hand side of the site and select a folder to save the file to.

3. Once the download is completed, locate the `SMLets.msi` file, right-click on it and select **Properties**. Now click on the **Unblock** button in the lower-right-hand side of the **Properties** dialog. Click on **OK**. This step might not apply to your environment depending on your current security settings.

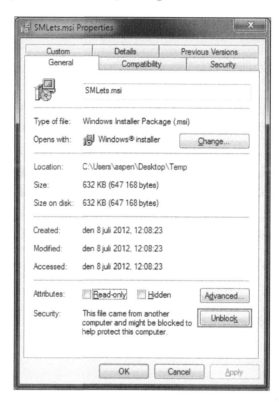

4. Log on to your Service Manager management server and copy the `SMLets.msi` file there.

5. Double-click on the `SMLets.msi` file to start the installation.

6. On the first page of the installation wizard, click on **Next**.

7. Check the checkbox to agree on the license agreement and click on **Next**, followed by **Next** and **Install**.

8. Once the installation is done, click on the **Finish** button.

How it works...

The SMLets should now be installed on your Service Manager management server and you are now ready to use the cmdlets.

In order to use the SMLets you might have to change your PowerShell Execution policy settings. To do so, start a PowerShell prompt with administrator rights and run this command:

`Set-ExecutionPolicy remotesigned`

To confirm the installation, follow these steps:

1. Open a PowerShell prompt and import the SMLets module by running this command:

   Import-Module C:\Program Files\Common Files\SMLets\SMLets.psd1

2. Once the SMLets module are imported, run this command to verify that it's working:

   Get-SMLetsVersion

   If everything is working correctly you should see some information regarding the SMLets version, as shown in the following screenshot:

```
Administrator: Windows PowerShell                                                    _|□|×|
PS C:\> Import-Module 'C:\Program Files\Common Files\SMLets\SMLets.psd1'
PS C:\> Get-SMLetsVersion

TargetProduct         : Microsoft System Center 2012 - Service Manager
WorkingCopyRootPath   : C:/Users/Administrator/Documents/WindowsPowerShell/CodePlex/smlets
URL                   : https://smlets.svn.codeplex.com/svn/Main/Source/SMLets/SMLets
RepositoryRoot        : https://smlets.svn.codeplex.com/svn
RepositoryUUID        : e17a0e51-4ae3-4d35-97c3-1a29b211df97
Revision              : 74609
LastChangedAuthor     : unknown
LastChangedRev        : 70086
LastChangedDate       : 2012-02-04 00:41:25 -0800 (Sat, 04 Feb 2012)
IsPrivate             : True
Changes               : <M         WiX/SMLets.X86.msi, M         WiX/SMLets.msi>
SMCompiledVersion     : 7.5.1561.0
SMInstalledVersion    : 7.5.1561.0
SM2012                : True

PS C:\>
```

There's more...

SMLets will be used in several of the next recipes in this chapter so we won't be giving any examples on how to use SMLets in this particular recipe.

See also

`http://smlets.codeplex.com`

Please see the recipes *Using SMLets to delete a Work Item* and *Autoclose resolved Incidents with SMLets and a custom workflow* in this chapter for examples of how to use SMLets.

Using SMLets to delete a Work Item

In this recipe we will take a look at how you can use SMLets to delete a Work Item. You cannot perform this action from the console or from the standard Service Manager cmdlets. Also, it's worth mentioning that this goes against all the rules of ITIL.

So why would someone need to delete a Work Item? Well, you might have created a couple of test Work Items to verify the production environment or to test a workflow, or something similar.

Getting ready

Make sure that you have downloaded and installed SMLets as described in the previous recipe *Downloading and installing SMLets*.

Make sure that you have installed the Windows PowerShell Integrated Scripting Environment through the **Add Feature** wizard in the Server Manager.

You also need Administrator rights within Service Manager to be able to delete a Work Item.

How to do it...

In this particular example we will take a look at how to delete an Incident. To do so, follow these steps:

1. Log on to the Service Manager management server and start **Windows PowerShell ISE (All programs |Accessories |System Tools | Windows Powershell)**.

2. In the upper part of the Windows PowerShell ISE, enter the following:

   ```
   Import-Module 'C:\Program Files\Common Files\SMLets\SMLets.psd1'
   ```

3. Now execute the script by pressing *F5* on your keyboard.

 The reason for executing this part of the script is to be able to use the PowerShell autocomplete function for SMLets. The autocomplete function allows you to press the *Tab* key on your keyboard to complete the command syntax. Try it out in the next step! Type Get-SCSMCl and press the *Tab* key; PowerShell should now autocomplete the command syntax.

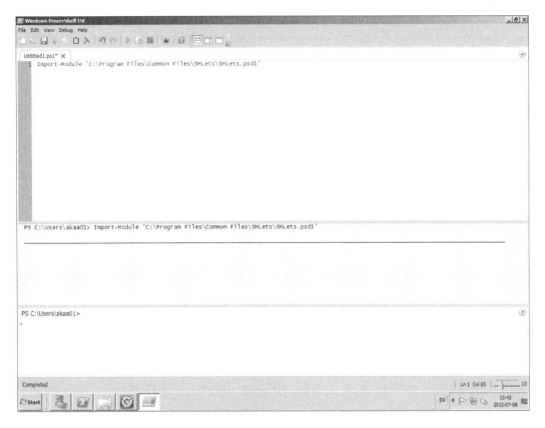

4. On a new line, type the following:

   ```
   $IncidentClass = Get-SCSMClass System.WorkItem.Incident$
   ```

5. The `Get-SCSMClass` cmdlets are used to retrieve a class from Service Manager and as we are going to remove an incident, we need to retrieve the `Incident` class.

6. On the next line, type the following:

   ```
   $Incident = Get-SCSMObject -Class $IncidentClass -filter "Id -eq
   IR401
   ```

7. We are now retrieving a particular Incident using the `Get-SCSMObject` cmdlets. The `Get-SCSMObject` cmdlets can retrieve any object in the Service Manager database. The `-Class` parameter tells `Get-SCSMObject` that we are looking for an object of the `Incident` class, and the `-filter` parameter is used to specify which object of the incident class we want to retrieve. In this example, we are looking for an Incident where the ID equals IR401.

8. Replace `IR401` with the ID of the Incident you want to delete. Then enter `$Incident` on a new line and press *F5* to execute the script.

9. The script will now run and display the Incident. Before proceeding to the next step, confirm that this is the particular Incident that you want to delete. There is no undo button if you accidentally delete the wrong Work Item!

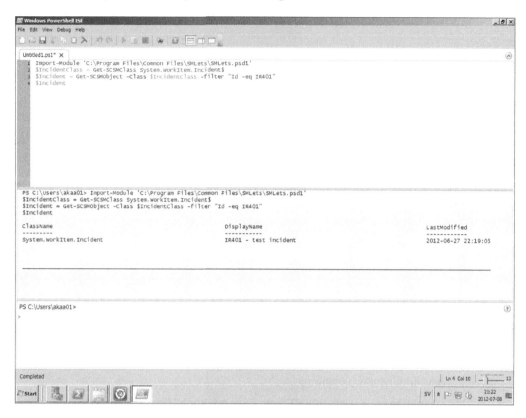

10. Right after $Incident on line 4, add the following (there's a space right before the pipe sign):

```
| Remove-SCSMObject -Force
```

11. This complete the script and it should now look like the following:

```
Import-Module 'C:\Program Files\Common Files\SMLets\SMLets.psd1'
$IncidentClass = Get-SCSMClass System.WorkItem.Incident$
$Incident = Get-SCSMObject -Class $IncidentClass -filter "Id -eq IR401"
$Incident
$Incident | Remove-SCSMObject -Force
```

12. Press *F5* to execute the script and delete the Incident.

How it works...

This script effectively removes the particular Work Item from the database. By defining another filter parameter you can remove several Incidents at once and if you skip the filter parameter, you may remove all your Incidents from the database. This is both good and bad so think twice before running your scripts in a production environment!

> Deleting all Work Items in an environment doesn't mean that the ID counter will get reset. It will still continue to count from the last known value.

There's more...

If you would like to delete other type of Work Items, all you have to do is pass another class to the Get-SCSMObject command. The name of each class can be tricky to figure out if you are new to Service Manager, and especially to the SMLets, so here is a quick list of the most common ones:

- Incident class = `System.WorkItem.Incident$`
- Problem class = `System.WorkItem.Problem$`
- Change Request class = `System.WorkItem.ChangeRequest$`
- Service Request class = `System.WorkItem.ServiceRequest$`
- Release Record class = `System.WorkItem.ReleaseRecord$`

If you want to list all the available classes in Service Manager, you could run `Get-SCSMClass` without any parameters.

> The dollar sign ($) at the end of each class name isn't actually a part of the class name itself. It's used as a stop sign telling SMLets to not retrieve anything that start with the class name. If you don't add the dollar sign, SMLets will actually retrieve subclasses of the class when running the `Get-SCSMClass` cmdlets. Try this by running `Get-SCSMClass System.WorkItem.Incident` and `Get-SCSMClass System.WorkItem.Incident$` and compare the results.

Export your unsealed Management Packs using the Service Manager cmdlets

As part of your backup routines for Service Manager you should always take a backup of your unsealed Management Packs. But in order to take backup of these, you will have to export them from Service Manager first and doing so manually from the Service Manager console every day isn't really an option. A better way to do this is using the Service Manager cmdlets.

How to do it...

The following is a pretty simple script that uses the Service Manager PowerShell cmdlets:

1. Log on to the Service Manager management server with an account that has Administrator privileges in Service Manager.

2. Open a PowerShell prompt and run this command to import the Service Manager PowerShell module:

   ```
   Import-Module 'C:\Program Files\Microsoft System Center 2012\
   Service Manager\Powershell\System.Center.Service.Manager.psd1'
   ```

3. Once the module has been imported, run the following command (make sure that the target directory exists prior to running the command):

   ```
   Get-SCSMManagementPack | where{$_.sealed -eq $False} | Export-
   SCSMManagementPack -Path C:\Temp
   ```

4. That's all you need to type in order to export all unsealed Management Packs.

If you try to run this command with both SMLets and the out of the box Service Manager PowerShell modules loaded, you will get an error saying A parameter cannot be found that matches parameter name 'Path'. This is because SMLets contains a similar cmdlet that wants other parameters. The solution to this is simply not to load SMLets in the same PowerShell session.

How it works...

So, all you have to do is run a single line of code to export all unsealed Management Packs. Let's take a close look at that line of code.

```
Get-SCSMManagementPack | where{$_.sealed -eq $False} | Export-
SCSMManagementPack -Path C:\Temp
```

The code consists of three different commands. The first one is `Get-SCSMManagementPack` which is used to list *all* the management packs within Service Manager. But as we only want the unsealed management packs, we are piping the results to a where statement such as the following: `where{$_.sealed -eq $False}`. This part of the command will make sure that only the Management Packs where the `Sealed` property is set to `False` is retrieved. Now we can pipe the results to our third command, `Export-SCSMManagementPack -Path C:\Temp` that simply exports the unsealed Management Packs to the directory we specified.

There's more...

You can also use the Service Manager PowerShell module to import Management Packs. This is especially useful when testing Management Packs that you are working with in other tools, such as the Authoring Tool.

The code to import a Management Pack is shown next:

```
Import-SCSMManagementPack C:\temp\Packt.Custom.Workflows.xml
```

Creating a custom workflow in the Authoring Tool – export your unsealed Management Packs

We have seen how we can use workflows to send notifications or apply templates in the other chapters and earlier in this, but now we are going to take it one step further and create our own custom workflow. So when do you need to create a custom workflow? Well, you might want to do something else than applying a template or sending a notification, or you might want to target another class than the ones you are able to target from the console.

Getting ready

Make sure that you have completed the previous recipe *Export your unsealed Management Packs using the Service Manager cmdlets* and that the Authoring Tool is installed and working properly.

How to do it...

In this example we are going to create a workflow that takes a backup of all our unsealed Management Packs every day. To do this we will use the PowerShell script we created in the previous recipe as a base.

1. Start the Authoring Tool.

2. Go to **File** and click on **New** to create a new Management Pack to store our custom workflow in.

3. Give the Management Pack a proper name and click on **Save**.

4. In the **Management Pack Explorer**, right-click on **Workflows** and select **Create**.

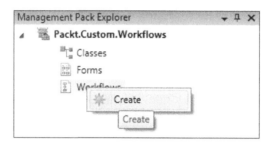

5. For the name of the workflow, enter **BackupOfUnsealedManagementPacks** (spaces are not allowed in the internal workflow name) and then click on **Next**.

6. In the **Trigger Condition** page, select **Run at a scheduled time or at scheduled intervals** and click on **Next**.

7. Specify whenever you want the workflow to run and click on **Next**, followed by **Create** and **Close**.

 Keep in mind that we want the unsealed Management Packs to be a part of our regular backup job, so make sure this workflow runs every day before the regular backup starts.

8. Now when we have defined the trigger to our workflow, we need to define what actually happens when it triggers.

   You should now have an empty workflow workspace in the Authoring Tool. Grab the **Windows PowerShell Script** activity from the **Activities toolbox** and drag it onto the workspace and release it on top of the text saying **Drop Activities to create a Sequential Workflow**.

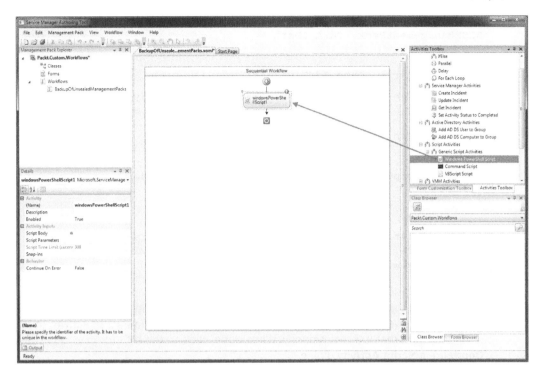

9. Make sure that the **WindowsPowerShellScript** activity is marked and go to the **details windows** and change the name to **RunBackupScript**. Then go to the **Script Body** field and click on the **...** button to launch the **Configure a Script Activity** dialog.

10. Click on the blue **View or Edit Script** bar and enter the following code:

```
Import-Module 'C:\Program Files\Microsoft System Center 2012\
Service Manager\Powershell\System.Center.Service.Manager.psd1'


$RootPath = C:\Service Manager MP Backup\

$Date = Get-Date

$Path = $RootPath + $Date.ToString(yyyy-MM-dd)


if ( ! (test-path $Path))
{
  $CreateOutput = New-Item -ItemType Directory $Path
}
```

```
Get-SCSMManagementPack | where{$_.sealed -eq $False} | Export-
SCSMManagementPack -Path $Path


$DeleteFolder = $Date.AddDays(-14)

$DeletePath = $RootPath + $DeleteFolder.ToString(yyyy-MM-dd)


if (test-path $DeletePath)
{
   $RemoveOutput = Remove-Item $DeletePath -Recurse
}


System.Center.Service.Manager, Microsoft.EnterpriseManagement.
Core.Cmdlets, Microsoft.EnterpriseManagement.ServiceManager.
Cmdlets | Remove-Module
```

11. The script is a refined version of the one we created in the previous recipe, we will go through all the code in the *How it works...* section later. It might be a good idea to run this in a PowerShell prompt before pasting it into the workflow script activity, in order to ensure that it works properly. When done, click on the **OK** button to close the **Configure a Script Activity** dialog.

12. That's all we need to do in the Authoring Tool. So let's save everything by going to **File** and selecting **Save All**.

13. We now need to copy the `BackupOfUnsealedManagementPacks.dll` file that the Authoring Tool has created for us to the installation directory of Service Manager on the management server (`C:\Program Files\Microsoft System Center 2012\Service Manager`). The DLL file is located in the same folder as your Management Pack that you created in *Step 2*.

14. When the DLL file is copied we need to import the Management Pack into Service Manager. So start the Service Manager console and go to **Administration** and select **Management Packs**.

15. Click on the **Import** task, locate your Management Pack, and click on **Import** followed by **OK**, when the import is done.

16. Now expand **Workflows** and select **Status**. Verify that our custom workflow is present by locating it in the list of workflows.

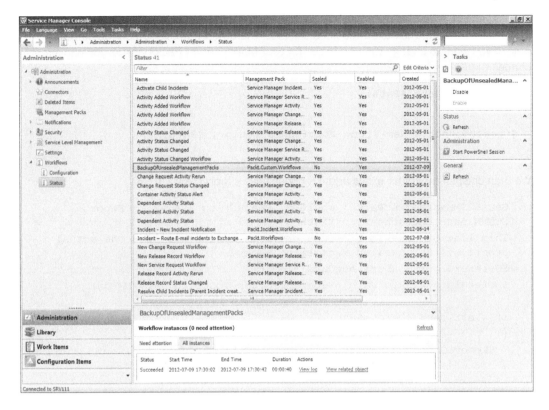

How it works...

So we created a custom workflow that triggers on a schedule and that runs a PowerShell script. The script itself exports all the unsealed Management Packs from Service Manager to a folder in a predefine path where the folder name matches the current date. If there's a folder in the same path with the name of the current date minus 14 days, it will also delete that folder to avoid filling up the disk.

The creation of the actual workflow is easy and pretty straight forward. Select a Management Pack to store the workflow in, define a trigger (schedule or database criteria) and create your actions (in our case, run a PowerShell script).

Let's go through the script:

```
Import-Module 'C:\Program Files\Microsoft System Center 2012\Service
Manager\Powershell\System.Center.Service.Manager.psd1'

$RootPath = C:\Service Manager MP Backup\

$Date = Get-Date

$Path = $RootPath + $Date.ToString(yyyy-MM-dd)
```

The first line of code loads the Service Manager PowerShell modules (as discussed in the previous recipe) and the next three lines calculate the target path, based on the current date. If you want to change the root folder for your Management Pack backup, you can simply change the `$RootPath` variable.

```
if ( ! (test-path $Path))
{
  $CreateOutput = New-Item -ItemType Directory $Path
}
```

We then check if the folder exists and if it doesn't, we simply create it.

```
Get-SCSMManagementPack | where{$_.sealed -eq $False} | Export-
SCSMManagementPack -Path $Path
This line of code is from the previous recipe and does the actual
export of the unsealed Management Packs.
$DeleteFolder = $Date.AddDays(-14)
$DeletePath = $RootPath + $DeleteFolder.ToString(yyyy-MM-dd)

if (test-path $DeletePath)
{
  $RemoveOutput = Remove-Item $DeletePath -Recurse
}

System.Center.Service.Manager, Microsoft.EnterpriseManagement.Core.
Cmdlets, Microsoft.EnterpriseManagement.ServiceManager.Cmdlets |
Remove-Module
```

Finally, we take the current date and subtract 14 days. We then calculate the path for the folder that were created 14 days ago and check if that folder exists. If it does, we simple delete it and all its content. The last line of code does simply unload the Service Manager PowerShell modules from the PowerShell session.

There's more...

The truth is that you might as well create a scheduled task within windows to achieve this, but when you are running the script as a workflow within Service Manager, you can use the console to check wherever it's executed or not. It also makes it easy to move this function between different environments—all you have to do is copy the DLL and import the Management Pack.

See also

Export your unsealed Management Packs using the Service Manager cmdlets earlier in this chapter.

Autoclose resolved Incidents with SMLets and a custom workflow

To automatically close Incidents that have been resolved for a number of days is a pretty common request among customers who's been working with Service Manager in production for a while. Even though this can be handled manually it's much more convenient to automate this process. The thought behind all of this is that when the Analysts change that status of the Incident to resolved, the Affected User has a number of days to contact IT before the Incident is closed. If the Affected User contacts IT before the Incident is closed the Incident gets re-activated, otherwise a new Incident has to be opened.

Getting ready

Make sure that SMLets and the Authoring Tool is installed and working properly and that you have read and understood these previous recipes in this chapter:

- *Downloading and installing SMLets*
- *Using SMLets to delete a Work Item*
- *Creating a custom workflow in the Authoring Tool – export your unsealed Management Packs*

How to do it...

In this recipe we will be using the SMLets to handle the actual automatic closure of resolved Incidents. We will then put the PowerShell script in a custom workflow and schedule it to run once a day—just as we did in the previous recipe.

 Keep in mind that we are creating a script/workflow to modify a large number of Incidents and if you mistype something you might end up closing every Incident in your system! I strongly suggest that you test this in a lab environment before implementing it into a production environment.

1. Start the Authoring Tool.
2. Open an existing or create a new Management Pack to store this workflow in.
3. Create a new workflow by right-clicking on **Workflows** in the **Management Pack Explorer** and selecting **Create**.
4. Give the workflow a proper name, such as **AutocloseResolvedIncidents**, and then click on **Next**.
5. Make sure that the **Run at a scheduled time or at scheduled intervals** is selected and click on **Next**.

6. Now specify when you want the workflow to run and click on **Next**.

 It might be a good idea to trigger this workflow outside your business hours since doing it during the day might be confusing to your Analysts. What if they actually are trying to re-activate the Incident when the script is executed?

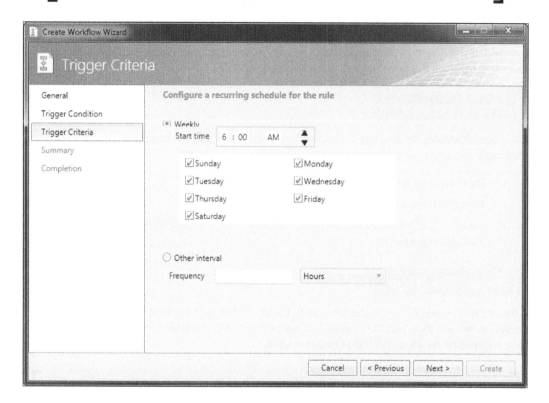

7. In the **Summary** step, make sure that everything looks okay, and then click on **Create**, followed by **Close**.

8. Now drag the **Windows PowerShell Script activity** onto the workspace.

9. With the **Windows PowerShell Script activity** selected, go to the **Details pane** and change the name to **AutocloseResolvedIncidentsPS**. Then go to **the Script Body** field and click on the **...** button.

10. Click the blue **View or Edit Script** bar and enter the following code:

```
Import-Module 'C:\Program Files\Common Files\SMLets\SMLets.psd1'

$NumberOfDaysResolved = 7

$Today = Get-Date
```

```
$ResolvedDate = $Today.AddDays(-$NumberOfDaysResolved)

$IncidentClass = Get-SCSMClass System.WorkItem.Incident$

$ResolvedStatus = (Get-SCSMEnumeration IncidentStatusEnum.
Resolved$).Id

$CriteriaType = Microsoft.EnterpriseManagement.Common.
EnterpriseManagementObjectCriteria

$CriteriaString = Status = '$ResolvedStatus' and ResolvedDate <=
'$ResolvedDate'

$Criteria = New-Object $CriteriaType
$CriteriaString,$IncidentClass

$ResolvedIncidents = Get-SCSMObject -Criteria $Criteria

if ($ResolvedIncidents -ne $null)

{

    $ResolvedIncidents | Set-SCSMIncident -Status Closed -Comment
Auto-closed after $NumberOfDaysResolved days in status Resolved

}


Remove-Module SMLets
```

11. Before proceeding to the next step, you should try this script in a lab environment to make sure it works as planned. If something is mistyped, you might end up modifying every Incident in your system! We will go through each line of code in the *How it works...* section later on.

12. Click on the **OK** button to close the **Configure a Script Activity** dialog.

13. Now save the Management Pack. Copy the `AutocloseResolvedIncidents.dll` to the installation folder of Service Manager on the management server. When that is done, import the Management Pack.

14. Verify that the workflow is listed under **Workflows | Status**.

How it works...

The steps outlined above are almost the exact same steps as in the previous recipe, what's interesting and new here is the actual script. So let's go through all the code.

```
Import-Module 'C:\Program Files\Common Files\SMLets\SMLets.psd1'

$NumberOfDaysResolved = 7
$Today = Get-Date
$ResolvedDate = $Today.AddDays(-$NumberOfDaysResolved)
```

First we import the SMLets PowerShell module then we have some logics to calculate the resolved date. This variable will be used in our criteria when we are searching for Incident to change the status of. If you want to change the number of days that an Incident should be resolved before autoclosing it, change the $NumberOfDaysResolved parameter.

```
$IncidentClass = Get-SCSMClass System.WorkItem.Incident$
$ResolvedStatus = (Get-SCSMEnumeration IncidentStatusEnum.Resolved$).
Id
```

Next we are using the Get-SCSMClass cmdlets to retrieve the Incident class and the other line of code is to retrieve the GUID of the Incident resolved status enumeration. To get the actual enumeration object you can use the Get-SCSMEnumeration cmdlets, but in this case we are only interested in the GUID and that's why we are just getting the ID.

```
$CriteriaType = Microsoft.EnterpriseManagement.Common.
EnterpriseManagementObjectCriteria
$CriteriaString = Status = '$ResolvedStatus' and ResolvedDate <=
'$ResolvedDate'
$Criteria = New-Object $CriteriaType $CriteriaString,$IncidentClass

$ResolvedIncidents = Get-SCSMObject -Criteria $Criteria
```

This part of code is pretty interesting. This is where we retrieve the Incidents with the Get-SCSMObject cmdlet. But instead of using the -Filter parameter, why are we using another one called -Criteria? The reason for that is because -Filter can only handle one argument. So we could either retrieve the Incidents with status Resolved or get the ones with a resolved date that is less than the one we calculated earlier. If you want to use several arguments when retrieving objects you will have to use the -Criteria parameter.

The criteria type should always be Microsoft.EnterpriseManagement.Common.EnterpriseManagementObjectCriteria but you will have to change the criteria string to fit your needs. Use these two together with a class to build your criteria such as this:

```
$Criteria = New-Object $CriteriaType $CriteriaString,$IncidentClass.
if ($ResolvedIncidents -ne $null)
{
   $ResolvedIncidents | Set-SCSMIncident -Status Closed -Comment Auto-
closed after $NumberOfDaysResolved days in status Resolved
}

Remove-Module SMLets
```

The final part of the script will check if the $ResolvedIncidents variable contains any objects. If it does it will change the status of these to Closed and add a comment to the action log. Finally we unload the SMLets module from the PowerShell session.

Automating your Request Offerings with Orchestrator

In *Chapter 5, Deploying Service Request Fulfillment,* we discussed how to create a Service Catalog and present your Service Offerings and Request Offerings on the self-service portal. This is great and allows the end-users to report Incidents and register Service Requests from the portal whenever they like. To make this even better we can automate the actual request by utilizing System Center Orchestrator.

> This recipe involves working in System Center Orchestrator and has some requirements within that product which we don't have to discuss in this book.
>
> For more information regarding System Center Orchestrator, see the official documentation on TechNet:
>
> `http://technet.microsoft.com/en-us/library/hh237242`

The whole process of creating automated Request Offerings can be summarized in these steps:

1. Create a Runbook in System Center Orchestrator.
2. Sync the Runbook to Service Manager through the Orchestrator connector.
3. Create a Runbook Automation Activity template-based on the Runbook created in *Step 1*.
4. Create a **Service Request** template—that includes the Runbook Automation Activity created in *Step 3*.
5. Create a **Request Offering** based upon the Service Request template created in *Step 4*.
6. Add the **Request Offering** to a **Service Offering**.
7. Test and verify.
8. Place into production.

This might seem like a lot of work to do, but the fact is that this is the easy job and once you get the hang of it you will be able to do it pretty quickly. The largest, most time consuming, and most important job is to get your idea documented and well thought through before starting these steps. Poor preparatory leads to a bad result.

It's also important to test your automated Request Offerings in a test environment before publishing them to your end users in a production environment to make sure they are working as planned.

Getting ready

Make sure you have System Center Orchestrator up and running, that you have sufficient privileges to create new runbooks and that you have the Integration Packs for Active Directory and System Center 2012 – Service Manager deployed.

In Service Manager you need to have the Self-service Portal installed and working properly as well as the System Center Orchestrator connector. You will also need Administrator permissions to perform the following recipe.

See the *Importing Orchestrator Runbooks* recipe in *Chapter 4, Building the Configuration Management Database (CMDB)*, on how to configure the Orchestrator connector and `http://technet.microsoft.com/en-us/library/hh667344` for instructions on how to deploy the self-service Portal.

How to do it...

In this recipe we will create a fully automated Request Offering to create new users in Active Directory. As stated earlier we will be working with Orchestrator but won't have the opportunity to discuss Orchestrator in too much detail here.

Here we go:

Part 1: Create the Runbook

1. Launch the **Orchestrator Runbook Designer**.
2. Expand **Runbooks** on the left-hand side and create a new Runbook in a suitable place.
3. **Check Out** the Runbook and change the name to **New AD User**.
4. Expand the **Runbook Control** Integration Pack on the right-hand side. Now drag the **Initialize Data** activity onto the workspace.

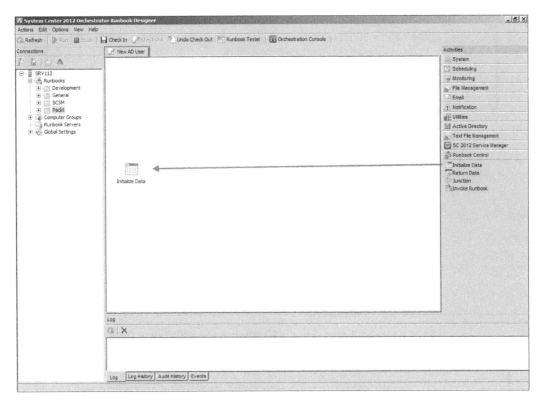

5. Double-click on the **Initialize Data** activity on the workspace to open the properties of it. Add two new parameters by clicking on the **Add** button. Rename one of the properties to **Firstname** and the other one to **Lastname**. Click on **Finish**.

6. Drag the **Create User** activity from the **Active Directory** Integration Pack onto the workspace. Connect **Initialize Data** to this activity by dragging the small arrow next to **Initialize Data** to **Create User**.

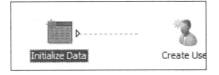

7. Double-click on **Create User** to open its properties and click on the **Browse** button marked with **...** to select your Active Directory connection and click on **OK**.

> The connection must be configured in Orchestrator for the Integration Pack otherwise this menu will be empty.
>
> For more information on how to do this, please see this link to TechNet: `http://technet.microsoft.com/en-us/library/hh553474.aspx`

8. Click on the **Optional Properties** button and add **Display Name**, **First name**, **Last name**, **Password**, and **SAM Account Name**.

9. Configure the properties like the following:

   ❑ **Common Name = <Firstname from Initialize Data><Lastname from Initialize Data>**

   ❑ **Display Name = <Firstname from Initialize Data> <Lastname from Initialize Data>**

   ❑ **First name = <Firstname from Initialize Data>**

   ❑ **Last name = <Lastname from Initialize Data>**

   ❑ **Password = P@ssw0rd**

   ❑ **SAM Account Name = usr_<Firstname from Initialize Data>**

> `<Firstname from Initialized Data>` means that you should grab the information from the databus by right-clicking on the field and select **Subscribe | Published Data**.

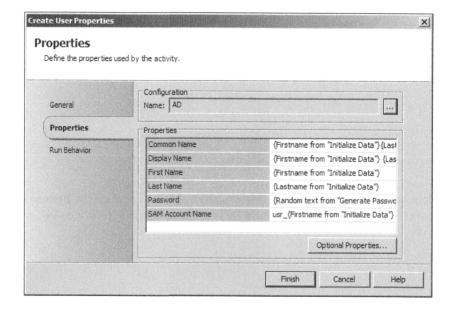

10. Add the **Enable User** activity from **the Active Directory** Integration Pack to the workspace. Connect **Create User** to this activity and double-click on it to open its properties.

11. Click on the **Browse** button marked with **...** select your **Active Directory** connection and click on **OK**.

12. In the field for **Distinguished Name**, add the **Distinguished Name** from the **Create User** activity by subscribing to the databus. Click on **Finish**.

13. Our simple Runbook is now complete and should look something like the following:

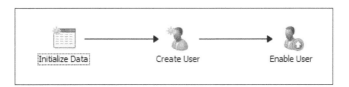

 This is a really simple Runbook and should only be used for testing purposes. In a production environment you should considering adding logging, error handling, password generation, and so on.

14. Verify that the Runbook is working properly in the **Runbook Tester**. Once this is verified remember to **Check In** your Runbook!

Part 2: Sync the Orchestrator connector

1. Start the **Service Manager** console and go to the **Administration** workspace.

2. Go to **Connectors**, select your **Orchestrator connector**, and click on the **Synchronize Now** task.

3. Give the connector a couple of minutes to run, then go to the **Library** workspace, and select **Runbooks**.

4. Confirm that the **New AD User** Runbook that we just created is listed.

Part 3: Create a Runbook Automation Activity template

1. Select the **New AD User** Runbook and click on the **Create Runbook Automation Activity Template** task.

2. Give the template a name, such as **New AD User (RAA)**, select an existing Management Pack or create a new one to store this template in. Click on **OK**.

3. As the title of our Runbook Automation Activity enter **New AD User** then make sure to check the checkbox that says **Is Ready For Automation**.

4. Go to the **Runbook** tab and take note of how the **Parameter mapping** is done. By default our properties should be mapped to **Text1** and **Text2** as seen in the following screenshot:

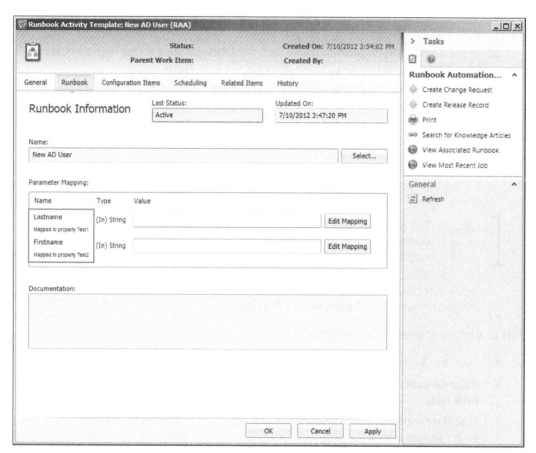

5. Click on **OK** to save the **Runbook Automation Activity Template**.

 You might of course specify more information in your template to make it more informative and seamless to your processes before saving it.

Part 4: Create a Service Request template

1. Next we need to create a Service Request template to use in our Request Offering. Go to **Templates** under the **Library** workspace.

2. Click on the **Create Template** task to create a new template.

3. Give it the name **New AD User**, select the **Service Request** class, and choose what Management Pack to store it in. Click on **OK**.

4. Enter the following information on the **General** tab:

   ❑ **Title = Request of new Active Directory user account**

   ❑ **Description = The Affected User has requested a new Active Directory user account. See User Input for details**

   ❑ **Urgency = Low**

   ❑ **Priority = Low**

   ❑ **Source = Portal**

   ❑ **Area = Directory\Account Management**

5. Go to the **Activities** tab and add our **Runbook Automation Activity** named **New AD User (RAA)**. Click on **OK** when the **Runbook Automation Activity** opens.

6. Click on **OK** to save our **Service Request template**.

Part 5: Create a Request Offering

1. Now we will have to create a **Request Offering** to use when the end user request a new AD user account.

2. In the **Library** workspace, expand **Service Catalog** and select **Request Offerings**.

3. Click on the task **Create Request Offering**.

4. Click on **Next** in the **Before You Begin** step.

5. Enter **Request a new user account** as the title of the **Request Offering**. As the **Description**, enter **Use this Request Offering to request a new Active Directory user account**.

6. Click on the **Select Template** button, select the template that we created earlier called **New AD User**, and click on **OK**.

7. Select a Management Pack to store this Request Offering in and click on **Next**.

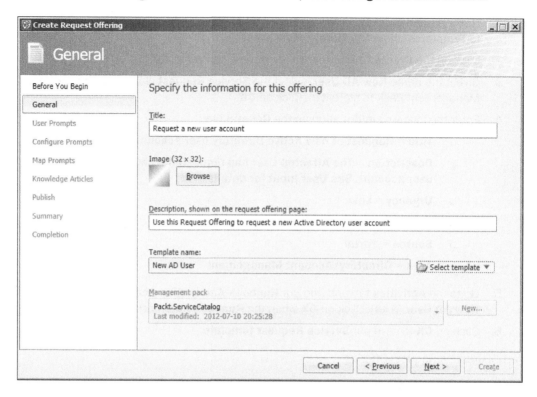

8. In the **User Prompts** step add two text prompts. One prompt called **Please enter the first name of the new user** and the other one called **Please enter the last name of the new user**. Click on **Next**.

9. On the **Configure Prompts** page, click on **Next**.

10. We will now get to an important step for the automated Request Offering scenario—**Map Prompts**. In order for Service Manager to pass the parameters to Orchestrator once calling the Runbook, we need to map our parameters to the same properties that we configured the Runbook Automation Activity to pass to the Runbook in *step 22*.

11. To do this, mark the **New AD User - (Runbook Automation Activity)** in the object picker and map **firstname** and **lastname** to **Text1** and **Text2**. Click on **Next**.

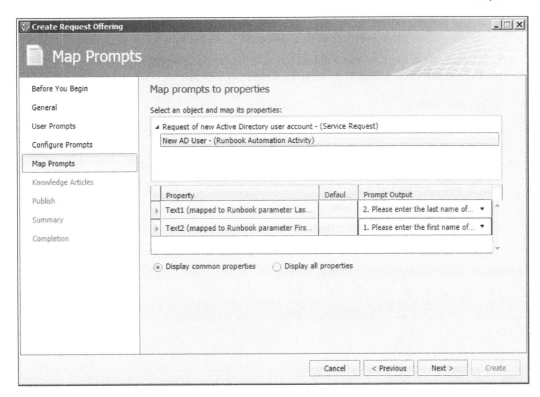

Again, if this mapping is done incorrectly the Runbook in Orchestrator won't get the necessary parameters to run the Runbook and the Runbook will fail. This will also cause the Runbook Automation Activity and the Service Request to fail.

12. On the **Knowledge Article** step, click on **Next**.

13. Set the **Offering Status** to **Published**. Click on **Next** followed by **Create** and **Close**.

Part 6: Create a Service Offering

1. Select **Service Offerings** underneath **Service Catalog** in the **Library** workspace.

2. Click on **Create Service Offering**. Click on **Next** on the **Before You Begin** page.

3. Give the Service Offering the name **Account and Access management**. As the **Overview** and **Description**, enter **Includes Request Offerings such as Request New User, Request Group Membership etc.**. Select a Management Pack to store the Service Offering in and click on **Next**.

4. Skip the **Detailed Information**, **Related Services**, and **Knowledge Articles** pages, by clicking on **Next** on each page.

5. In the **Request Offering** page, click on the **Add** button, locate and select our Request Offering called **Request a new user account**. Click on **Add** followed by **OK**.

6. Click on **Next** to get to the **Publish** page. Change the **Offering Status** to **Published**. Click on **Next**, followed by **Create** and **Close**.

Part 7: Test and verify

1. Open the self-service Portal and make sure that you can see our Service Offering called **Account and Access management**.

2. Click on **Account and Access management** and then click on the **Request Offering** called **Request a new user account**, which we also just created.

3. Click on **Go to request form**.

4. In the two prompts, enter a **first name** and a **last name**. Click on **Next**, followed by **Submit**.

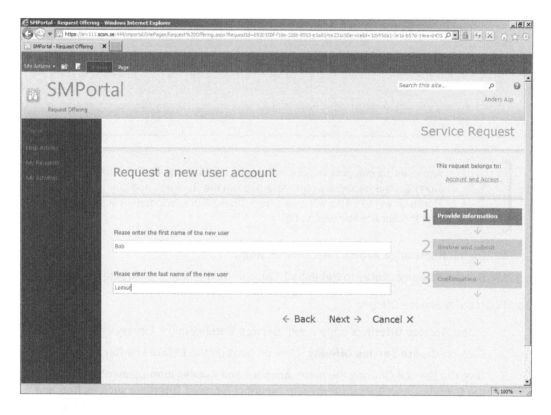

5. The Service Request will now be created and the Service Request ID will be shown. Take note of this ID.

6. Go to the **Work Items** workspace in the **Service Manager** console. Expand **Service Request Fulfillment** and select the **All Open Service Requests** view.

7. Locate and open the Service Request with the ID we noted in _step 53_.

8. Verify that the information in the **User Input** section is correct and that the **New AD User** activity is **In Progress**.

If you can't find the Service Request in the All Open Service Request view, it might already be completed or have failed. Look in the Completed Service Requests or Failed Service Request view to see if it's listed there instead.

9. Once you've verified that everything seems okay in Service Manager, open an **Active Directory Users and Computers** to see if the User account has been created.

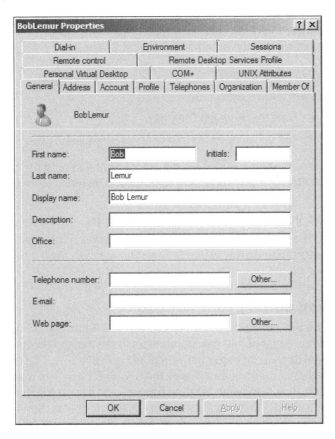

10. When the account is created the Runbook is finished and the Service Request should change status to **Completed**.

How it works...

When you've created your runbook in Orchestrator it can be synced to the Service Manager CMDB through the System Center Orchestrator connector in Service Manager. This runbook object in Service Manager contains information needed to trigger the runbook trough the Orchestrator web service, such as the Runbook GUID and required input parameters. From this runbook object you can create a Runbook Automation Activity template to use in your different Work Items. Whenever this activity is used and the status of it is set to **In Progress**, Service Manager will call the Orchestrator web service and trigger the related runbook together with the parameters mapped in the Runbook Automation Activity (as seen in *Step 22*).

There's more...

This was a very basic example of an automated Request Offering and as stated earlier you will need to plan and build all of this in more detail. There are many things to consider before you can create fully automated Request Offerings. Here are a few questions that might be good asking yourself when designing the automated Request Offerings:

- ▶ What do we want to achieve?
- ▶ How do we want it to be executed?
- ▶ Who is going to use this Request Offering?
- ▶ What kind of input do we need from the End User requesting this Request Offering?

When you got the answer to these questions the risk of having to redo the design of your automated Request Offering due to forgetting some details, is much more unlikely.

Make sure that your Runbook is Checked In

A runbook that isn't **Checked In** cannot be triggered from Service Manager. This means that the Runbook Automation Activity within Service Manager will fail if it tries to trigger the Runbook.

Be careful when editing your Runbook!

It's pretty common that you need to go back to improve your Runbook or add new features to it, but be careful! If you edit or add new parameters in the Initialize Data activity, the Runbook object within Service Manager will be marked as `Invalid`. This means that it won't be able to trigger the runbook ever again. The only fix for this is to delete the runbook object and re-import it. This also mean that you have to redo everything that is based upon this Runbook object, such as Runbook Automation Activity templates, Service Request templates that includes the Runbook Automation Activity, and Request Offering based upon that template!

See also

For more information regarding Request Offerings, Service Offerings, Service Request and the self-service Portal, please see entire *Chapter 5*, *Deploying Service Request Fulfillment*.

For more details on how to create automated Request Offerings, take a look at the following blog posts on the official blog for Service Manager:

- ▶ `http://blogs.technet.com/b/servicemanager/archive/2011/11/09/demo-automating-service-request-fulfillment-from-the-scsm-service-catalog-with-orchestrator.aspx`
- ▶ `http://blogs.technet.com/b/servicemanager/archive/2011/11/10/demo-automating-service-request-fulfillment-from-the-scsm-service-catalog-with-orchestrator-real-world-examples.aspx`

Community Extensions and Third-party Commercial SCSM Solutions

Introduction

Similar to the majority of technology solutions in the market, Service Manager does not address every organization's specific requirements. Microsoft solution provider partners create solutions, which complement and extend the product to address some of the common requested extensions to SCSM. This appendix will provide you with a list of some vendor extensions to Service Manager.

Provance® – IT Asset Management, Data Management, and Bar Code for Microsoft® System Center

Provance, a Microsoft integration and solutions partner, provides asset life cycle management extensions for SCSM.

Provance IT Asset Management Pack

The Provance IT Asset Management Pack provides extended functionality to manage the financial, contractual, and organizational information necessary to support additional IT Asset Management processes, including SAM, License Compliance, IT Asset Life Cycle Management, Contract Management, Vendor Management, and more cost-effective and efficient IT Service Management.

Asset information is maintained in the central System Center CMDB, where it is combined and shared in a single common repository with data from Active Directory®, Configuration Manager, Operations Manager, and Virtual Machine Manager. Powerful reporting and analysis using IT asset management information is delivered through the System Center Data Warehouse.

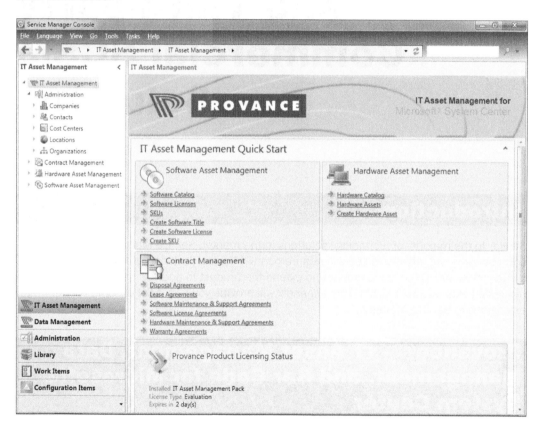

Provance Data Management Pack

The **Provance Data Management Pack (DMP)** simplifies, speeds, and automates the process of getting data into and out of the Service Manager CMDB, while simultaneously improving data consistency and accuracy. The DMP has an easy-to-use graphical interface, making it simple to automate data import from both files and databases, without coding or extensive knowledge of the CMDB structure. The DMP reduces the need for external manipulation and data cleansing, and also significantly improves the accuracy and consistency of the CIs in your System Center CMDB.

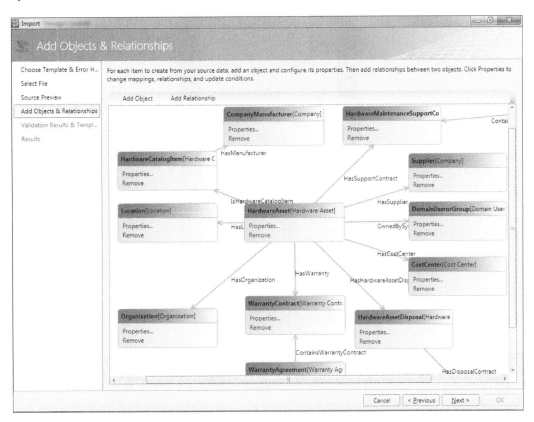

Provance Bar Code

Provance Bar Code is a solution built specifically to work with the Provance IT Asset Management Pack and Service Manager without any additional customization or integration. Unlike manual inventory, Provance Bar Code dramatically reduces the manual effort and human error associated with gathering and entering asset data.

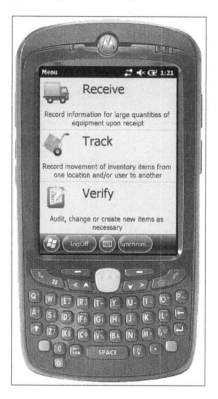

Derdack Enterprise Alert®

Enterprise Alert® adds a communication, closed-loop notification, and mobility framework to System Center Service Manager.

The range of notification channels goes far beyond basic e-mail communication, and covers all unified communication options including voice with text-to-speech, smartphone push, and SMS text. Analysts can acknowledge new incidents, escalate service requests, approve review activities, or even create new incidents on the smartphone.

IT users can be notified when incidents are assigned, modified, or closed. Inbound helpdesk communications can also be automated, for example, through automated IM-to-incident or voice-call-to-incident workflows.

The integration of Enterprise Alert® into System Center Service is based on the Service Manager SDK and specific management packs.

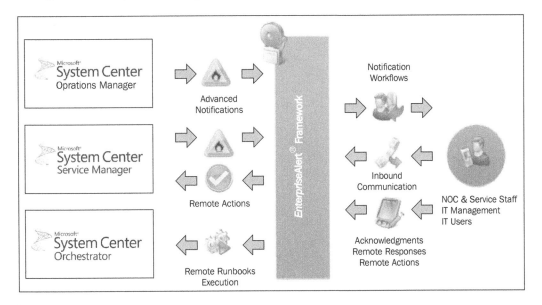

Seven-Winds Call Script Manager

Seven-Winds Call Script Manager is a solution focused on the Incident management process and aimed at improving the initial incident logging and resolution process. Some of the major benefits include but are not limited to the following:

► Reduce the time needed to register a call

► Reduce the time to resolve a call

► Reduce the skills required to operate call registration

► Significantly improves consistency in call registration

► Improves customer satisfaction

► Self-customizable to your situation, visually aided, Visio like, script design tooling

► Utilizes company knowledge base and makes real-time suggestions

The solution provides a custom form for the analyst to logically capture the initial call details as shown in the following screenshot:

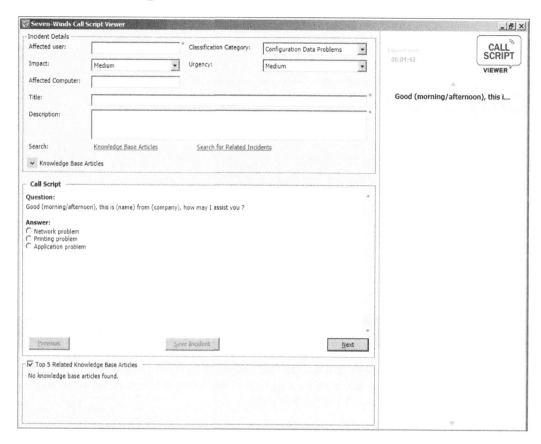

Call Script Manager – what it does and how it helps

Call Script Manager is a question based pre-incident form solution that is aligned with the natural incident logging process. The solution uses an agreed set of organization questions targeted at the initial diagnoses and logging of an incident. The solution is extended to the self-service portal for end users.

Call Script Builder

Call Script Builder is a component of the solution, which uses a Visio-like interface to create the call scripts.

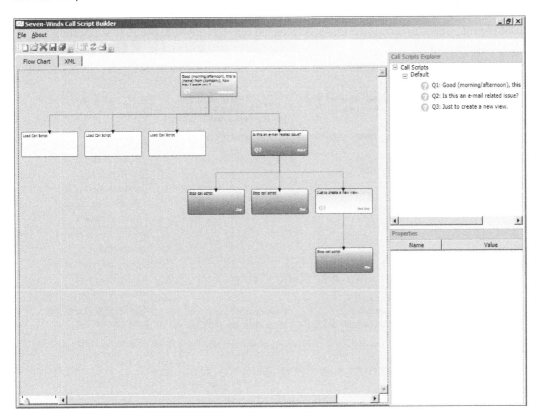

WebFront for Service Manager 2012

WebFront for Service Manager 2012 extends Service Manager by providing a web browser version of the Analyst console with reliable and scalable web technologies hosted on the Microsoft Windows® Server platform. WebFront mimics the standard console with familiar SCSM forms, views, and console tasks, accessible through any web browser supporting Microsoft Silverlight® 5.

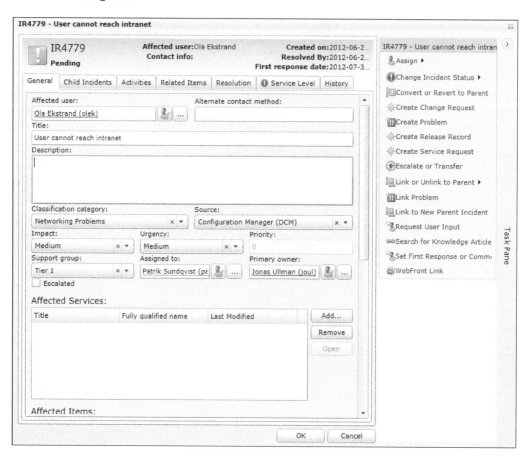

Useful Websites and Community Resources

Introduction

This appendix will list some helpful websites and communities for System Center service manager.

Useful community blogs

Anders Asp (MVP):

http://www.scsm.se/

Samuel Erskine (MCT):

http://www.frameworktorealwork.com/

Steve Beaumont:

http://systemscentre.blogspot.co.uk/

Dieter Gasser:

http://blog.dietergasser.com/

Andreas Baumgarten (MVP - German blog):

http://startblog.hud.de/category/mssc/service-manager/

System Center: Service Manager Engineering Blog:

http://blogs.technet.com/b/servicemanager/

Marcel Zehner (MVP):

```
http://blog.scsmfaq.ch/
```

Anton Gritsenko (MVP):

```
http://blog.scsmsolutions.com/
```

Patrik Sundqvist (MVP):

```
http://litware.se/
```

Maarten Goet (MVP):

```
http://blogs.inovativ.nl/auteur?u=maarten
```

Kurt Van Hoecke (MVP):

```
http://www.scug.be/scsm
http://www.authoringFriday.com
```

Nathan Lasnoski:

```
http://blog.concurrency.com/author/nlasnoski/
```

Steve Buchanan (MVP):

```
http://www.buchatech.com/category/microsoft/system-center/scsm/
```

Frameworks and processes

Official ITIL© website:

```
http://www.itil-officialsite.com/
```

Microsoft Operations Framework:

```
http://technet.microsoft.com/en-us/library/cc506049.aspx
```

ISO official website:

```
http://www.iso.org/iso/home.html
```

Valuable community forums and user groups

TechNet Forums – System Center Service Manager (EN):

```
http://social.technet.microsoft.com/Forums/en-US/category/
servicemanager
```

TechNet Forums – System Center (DE):

```
http://social.technet.microsoft.com/Forums/de-DE/systemcenterde/
threads
```

System Center Central – Service Manager:

```
http://www.systemcentercentral.com/tabid/60/tag/Forums+Service_
Manager/Default.aspx
```

MyITforums – System Center Service Manager:

```
http://www.myitforum.com/forums/System-Center-Service-Manager-f154.
aspx
```

SCSM.US:

```
http://scsm.us/
```

German System Center User Group:

```
http://scsmug.de/
```

Minnesota System Center User Group:

```
http://www.mnscug.org
```

Websites for SCSM solutions and extensions

CodePlex – SCSM PowerShell Cmdlets:

```
http://smlets.codeplex.com/
```

TechNet Library – System Center 2012 – Service Manager:

```
http://technet.microsoft.com/en-us/library/hh305220
```

TechNet Gallery – Resources for IT Professionals – Service Manager:

```
http://gallery.technet.microsoft.com/site/search?query=service%20
manager
```

TechNet Gallery - Resources for IT Professionals – SCSM:

```
http://gallery.technet.microsoft.com/site/search?query=SCSM
```

Provance Technologies Inc.:

```
http://www.provance.com/
```

Derdack GmbH:

```
http://www.derdack.com/
```

Gridpro:

```
http://www.gridpro.se/en/
```

Call Script Manager:

```
http://www.callscriptmanager.com
```

Online Wikis

Microsoft TechNet Wiki: Management Portal:

```
http://social.technet.microsoft.com/wiki/contents/articles/703.wiki-
management-portal.aspx#System_Center_Service_Manager
```

Microsoft TechNet Wiki: System Center 2012 Service Manager Survival Guide (en-US):

```
http://social.technet.microsoft.com/wiki/contents/articles/8113.
system-center-2012-service-manager-survival-guide-en-us.aspx
```

Microsoft TechNet Wiki: Service Manager Survival Guide:

```
http://social.technet.microsoft.com/wiki/contents/articles/service-
manager-survival-guide.aspx
```

Social network resources

System Center on Facebook:

```
https://www.facebook.com/pages/Microsoft-System-Center-
Support/111513322193410
```

System Center on Twitter:

```
https://twitter.com/system_center
```

Service Manager on Twitter:

```
https://twitter.com/ServiceManager
```

Index

Thank you for buying
Microsoft System Center 2012 Service
Manager Cookbook

About Packt Publishing

Packt, pronounced 'packed', published its first book *"Mastering phpMyAdmin for Effective MySQL Management"* in April 2004 and subsequently continued to specialize in publishing highly focused books on specific technologies and solutions.

Our books and publications share the experiences of your fellow IT professionals in adapting and customizing today's systems, applications, and frameworks. Our solution-based books give you the knowledge and power to customize the software and technologies you're using to get the job done. Packt books are more specific and less general than the IT books you have seen in the past. Our unique business model allows us to bring you more focused information, giving you more of what you need to know, and less of what you don't.

Packt is a modern, yet unique publishing company, which focuses on producing quality, cutting-edge books for communities of developers, administrators, and newbies alike. For more information, please visit our website: www.PacktPub.com.

About Packt Enterprise

In 2010, Packt launched two new brands, Packt Enterprise and Packt Open Source, in order to continue its focus on specialization. This book is part of the Packt Enterprise brand, home to books published on enterprise software – software created by major vendors, including (but not limited to) IBM, Microsoft and Oracle, often for use in other corporations. Its titles will offer information relevant to a range of users of this software, including administrators, developers, architects, and end users.

Writing for Packt

We welcome all inquiries from people who are interested in authoring. Book proposals should be sent to author@packtpub.com. If your book idea is still at an early stage and you would like to discuss it first before writing a formal book proposal, contact us; one of our commissioning editors will get in touch with you.

We're not just looking for published authors; if you have strong technical skills but no writing experience, our experienced editors can help you develop a writing career, or simply get some additional reward for your expertise.

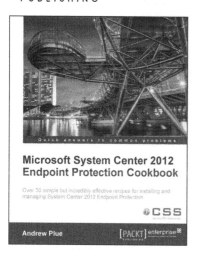

Microsoft System Center 2012 Endpoint Protection Cookbook

ISBN: 978-1-849683-90-6   Paperback: 208 pages

Over 30 simple but incredibly effective recipes for installing and managing System Center 2012 Endpoint Protection

1. Master the most crucial tasks you'll need to implement System Center 2012 Endpoint Protection

2. Provision SCEP administrators with just the right level of privileges, build the best possible SCEP policies for your workstations and servers, discover the hidden potential of command line utilities and much more in this practical book and eBook

3. Quick and easy recipes to ease the pain of migrating from a legacy AV solution to SCEP

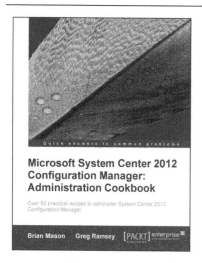

Microsoft System Center 2012 Configuration Manager: Administration Cookbook

ISBN: 978-1-849684-94-1   Paperback: 224 pages

Over 50 practical recipes to administer System Center 2012 Configuration Manager

1. Administer System Center 2012 Configuration Manager

2. Provides fast answers to questions commonly asked by new administrators

3. Gain administration tips from System Center 2012 Configuration Manager MVPs with years of experience in large corporations

Please check **www.PacktPub.com** for information on our titles

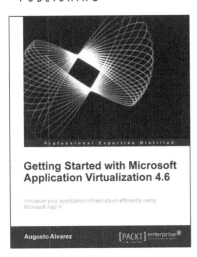

Getting Started with Microsoft Application Virtualization 4.6

Virtualize your application infrastructure efficiently using Microsoft App-V

Augusto Alvarez

Getting Started with Microsoft Application Virtualization 4.6

ISBN: 978-1-849681-26-1   Paperback: 308 pages

Virtualize your application infrastructure efficiently using Microsoft App-V

1. Publish, deploy, and manage your virtual applications with App-V

2. Understand how Microsoft App-V can fit into your company.

3. Guidelines for planning and designing an App-V environment.

4. Step-by-step explanations to plan and implement the virtualization of your application infrastructure

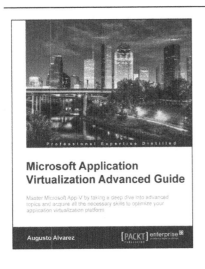

Microsoft Application Virtualization Advanced Guide

Master Microsoft App-V by taking a deep dive into advanced topics and acquire all the necessary skills to optimize your application virtualization platform

Augusto Alvarez

Microsoft Application Virtualization Advanced Guide

ISBN: 978-1-849684-48-4   Paperback: 474 pages

Master Microsoft App-V by taking a deep dive into advanced topics and acquire all the necessary skills to optimize your application virtualization platform

1. Understand advanced topics in App-V; identify some rarely known components and options available in the platform

2. Acquire advanced guidelines on how to troubleshoot App-V installations, sequencing, and application deployments

3. Virtualize server applications by using the upcoming platform Server App-V

Please check **www.PacktPub.com** for information on our titles

NVN. £30.99 9/15 ·

00079321 4/9/15 ML

NORTH WARWICKSHIRE COLLEGE